THE OUTSPOKEN DR MILLER

THE OUTSPOKEN DR MILLER

by

KENNETH MILLER

The Memoir Club

© Kenneth Miller 2006

First published in 2006 by
The Memoir Club
Stanhope Old Hall
Stanhope
Weardale
County Durham

British Library Cataloguing in
Publication Data.
A catalogue record for this book
is available from the
British Library

ISBN: 1-84104-159-9

Typeset by TW Typesetting, Plymouth, Devon
Printed by CPI Antony Rowe, Eastbourne

*To my wife, Betty, for her support and help both
as my personal assistant in The Engineering Council days
and since 1999 as my wife.*

Contents

List of Illustrations

Acknowledgements

I must thank The Memoir Club for suggesting to me some five years ago that perhaps I might care to write my memoirs. This was further reinforced at a party at Henley when we were idly talking about obituaries with Bill Harris, a retired master from Eton. He made the comment that in his experience obituaries rarely told the full story. Bill also pointed out that memoirs would be a record for my family. So here it is for my three sons Andrew, Ian and Allan to hear what the 'old man' was up to during his working life.

It is to my wife Betty that I dedicate these memoirs. Betty was my Personal Assistant during the six years of my time as Director General of The Engineering Council. It was during these years that Betty tactfully polished up my speeches, and improved my English with a change of a word here or a better construction of a sentence there. When it came to writing my memoirs, Betty's knowledge and understanding of the Engineering profession was of immense help. It was quite like old times!

I must also thank my sister Joan Baillie for producing some of the family photographs, and her good memory for names has been a great help.

I have kept in touch over the years with two of my colleagues from the exciting years of setting up The Engineering Council, Professor Jack Levy, Director – Engineering Profession and Ron Kirby, Director – Public Affairs, and they have given me their support and help. They both played an integral part in making a success of those early years.

It wasn't until some time after I retired that I read Charles Handy's book *The Empty Raincoat*, in particular, his chapters on The Federalist Idea. I found Charles' thinking on Federal Systems so compelling that it clarified to me the fundamental principles behind all federal systems and how it explains the necessary conditions to make a federal system operate successfully. The thinking is very pertinent to an understanding of the Engineering Profession. I am grateful to Charles for his agreement to my extensive quoting from *The Empty Raincoat*.

CHAPTER 1

Family Background and Early Schooldays

I WAS BORN IN GLASGOW IN 1926, but to understand the family I must take you back to the turn of the century. My mother's father, John Glen, was a successful Glasgow businessman. As a young man he had had an ambition to be a doctor, but he failed the preliminary Latin examination. His own father was of modest means and had a boot emporium in Dumbarton, and so it fell to John, the eldest son, to help his father in the business. In due course John took over and built up the business. He turned it into a successful thriving wholesale warehouse, John Glen & Company in Ingram Street in Glasgow, selling to small shops in the Glasgow area. While he himself never became a doctor, he encouraged and financially assisted three of his younger brothers, David, Alexander and Thomas, to become doctors.

In 1900 John Glen's wife, Margaret, died in childbirth at the age of 31. This was a devasting blow, particularly to my mother, Margaret Hutchinson Glen, who was only six at the time. Four years later John Glen remarried and his bride was Miss Margaret Miller, known as Peggy. She, too, came from a Scottish family whose leading members believed in education. Margaret Miller's mother, Christine, was a formidable lady. Although her husband, Ebenezer, was a modest ranking civil servant in Customs and Excise, Christine Miller urged her family of four sons and two daughters to improve their standing in society. Two of the sons, Norman and Allan, became doctors and the other two did well in Customs and Excise. Christine's other daughter, Agnes, also married a widower Jim Craig, who was a doctor in general practice in Glasgow.

The years passed, and the Glen family prospered. My mother went to Park School and her brothers to Glasgow Academy. They lived in a large granite built house, 'Hope House' in Sherbrook Avenue, Pollokshields, and had a summer home at Blairmore on Loch Long. In due course a second family came along of two sons, Jack and Norman, and two daughters, Muriel and Hilda. It was a well-respected Glasgow family. My mother went on to Glasgow University and to her father's great delight studied medicine, and graduated in 1917.

In 1923 my mother married her stepmother's younger brother, Allan Miller. He, too, was a medical doctor, and had been practising with his older brother, Norman, in Stafford. On his marriage to Margaret Glen he bought a practice in Glasgow and joined the large clan of Miller and Glen relatives.

My father was a charming and relatively easy-going man. From all accounts he was ideally suited to general practice. His bedside manner was much appreciated

1

Glen–Miller wedding, 1904

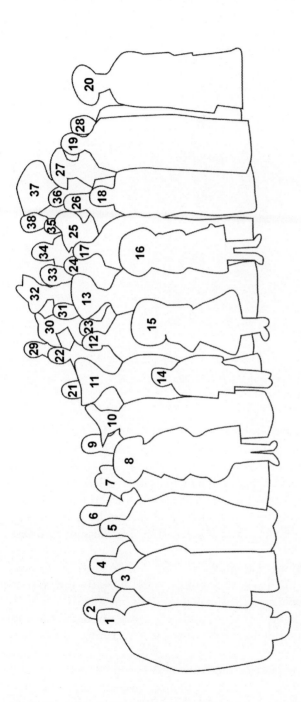

Key to guests in photograph

1. Rev. McLellan (Sherbrooke church).
2. Colonel Hall.
3. Dr Jim Craig (brother-in-law of bride).
4. Unknown.
5. Mr Miller – a relative.
6. Archibald Glen (father of bridegroom).
7. Mr Miller's sister.
8. Margaret Glen (daughter of bridegroom by first marriage).
9. Allan Miller (brother of bride).
10. Jessie Gilroy (cousin of bride).
11. The Bride – Margaret Miller (Peggy).
12. The Bridegroom – John Glen.
13. The Bridesmaid – Margaret Hall (cousin of bride).
14. Archie Glen (son of bridegroom by first marriage).
15. Pearl Craig (daughter of Dr Craig by first marriage).
16. Willis Glen (daughter of bridegroom by first marriage).
17. Dr David Glen (brother of bridegroom and Best Man).
18. Mrs Christine Miller (mother of bride).
19. Dr Norman Miller (brother of bride).
20. Mrs Montgomery (cousin of bride).
21. Arthur Miller (brother of bride).
22. Rev. Dr Macadam Muir (Glasgow Cathedral).
23. Mrs Georgie Gilroy (Jessie Gilroy's mother).
24. Mrs Rattray.
25. Miss Maggie Glen (sister of bridegroom).
26. Willie Miller (brother of bride).
27. Miss Jeanie Glen (sister of bridegroom).
28. Mr Montgomery.
29. Archibald Glen (brother of bridegroom).
30. Mrs Annie Robb (sister of bridegroom).
31. Russell (Jessie Gilroy's father).
32. Unknown.
33. Mrs Craig (Jim Craig's mother).
34. Nurse Smith.
35. Unknown.
36. Mrs Cissie Craig (sister of bride and and wife Dr Jim Craig).
37. Unknown.
38. Unknown.

3

My mother graduating with MBChB, Glasgow, 1917

by the patients, and he had a slightly roguish sense of humour. He referred to a hysterectomy operation as 'removing the nursery furniture'. My mother on the other hand was a very determined character. By the time she married Allan Miller, she had risen to be medical superintendent of Darnley Hospital. As was the social custom of those days she gave up medicine altogether on her marriage and settled down to be a housewife and mother. My parents bought a town house in Lansdowne Crescent off the Great Western Road in Glasgow. It was here I was born in 1926 and my sister Joyce, as she was then called, followed two years later. My first memory was going to stay on my own with my grandparents in 'Hope House' just prior to Joyce's arrival. It was a few weeks before Christmas and I was given my Christmas present in advance, a Tan-Sad peddle car. I was absolutely delighted with it, and as a result my nose was not put out of joint by all the attention my baby sister was receiving. I had my Tan-Sad!

After seven years in a Glasgow practice my father was becoming disenchanted with visiting patients in the Glasgow tenement buildings. My mother, too, was concerned about the many colds my sister and I were forever catching. So they decided to move south to England.

My father Dr Allan Miller around 1923

This proposed move south of the border really annoyed my grandfather. He was furious, not least because the family firm had done very well that year and a good dividend helped my parents to make this move. My grandfather in a last desperate attempt to persuade my parents, not to go south said to my mother 'and Kenneth will be brought up as an Englishman'. Looking back on this years later, I agree that my grandfather was absolutely right, but I would add 'So what'. It was however symptomatic of the attitude of Glasgow middle-class society.

So in 1931 the family moved south to live in Croxley Green in Hertfordshire. In this same year Grandpa Glen died and on his deathbed he asked my mother if she had another son would she christen him John in his memory. When a third member of the family arrived in 1933 and was a girl, my parents christened her Joan as the nearest they could get to John. It was decided that Joyce and Joan was too confusing, so Joyce's second christian name was used and henceforth she was known as Margaret.

In the thirties we enjoyed a comfortable middle class standard of living. Our father had the assured income of a general practitioner in the Home Counties. This was supplemented by our mother's private income. Our mother looked after the family finances. Being a very prudent and canny Scot, she was always

My mother and myself, November 1927

conscious that our father was fifty when my sister Joan was born and Joan would only be 15 when our father was expected to retire at 65. Thus it was that, as youngsters, a degree of prudence was fed into everything we did. In the end our father stayed in the practice until he was 75 and by then all three of us were through University.

The Scottish tradition of the importance of education was a top priority in the family thinking. As a graduate herself, our mother expected both her daughters to go to university. She tended, too, to make friends in the south with like-minded ladies. One such was Peggy Findlay, a Glasgow graduate, who was married to Jock Findlay, a tenant farmer. Jock was a fellow Scot, a truly rough diamond, and we all liked him. He was an extremely successful farmer and in due course bought the farm. The Findlays had three children: Margot five months younger than myself, John about Margaret's age and Elizabeth two years younger than Joan.

The two families became very friendly and it became a tradition to spend Christmas day together taking turns to host the party in alternate years. The Mums, too, helped each other in the choice of schools, and of course there was an element of friendly rivalry. The first occasion was when in the autumn of 1933 I caught measles and Margot Findlay wrote me a charming little letter 'Dear Kenneth, sorry you have measles. Hope you are better soon. Love Margot'. Now at this time I was aged seven and had been going to a little private school in Croxley Green. While I could do sums, the school was so lax that I could neither read nor write. Round one to the Findlays. My mother learned that Margot attended a little Dame's school in Rickmansworth run by Miss Miriam Dimsey. Thus it was in early 1934 I started at Miss Dimsey's. It was a very small school with individual attention and firm old-fashioned discipline. I stayed there for five terms and in my final school report Miss Dimsey said on English grammar, 'He failed to express himself clearly', while she added I should do well at mathematics. Overall she said 'Kenneth is industrious and has concentration'. Thus the balance of my academic talents, or lack of them, were clearly spotted by Miss Dimsey.

It was around this time that Peggy Findlay and my mother were looking for a good girls' school, and they hit on St Helens School in Northwood. My mother told me years later that she was determined that the two mums should go together to see Miss McKenzie the headmistress as my mother was fearful that the Findlay girls would be excluded because their father was a tenant farmer, and my mother was determined to work into the conversation that both she and Peggy Findlay were graduates of Glasgow University. Both the Findlay and Miller girls were accepted for St Helens. We would never know if my mother's fears were justified. It is true that the first offer for Margot Findlay was that she should start as a boarder, but in practice this qualification was never pressed home.

In September 1935 at the age of nine I went to my prep school, Shirley House School in Watford. Thanks to Miss Dimsey's firm guiding hand I was well up with my age group. You worked hard and played hard at Shirley House. Every two weeks we had form marks and places in the class. The forms were small, thirteen to seventeen boys in each form and only between six and eight in the top form. Furthermore you progressed up to a higher form when you were ready. Competitive games were taken seriously, too, and the school was very proud of the success against other prep schools in the district. I played for the school in all three sports, association football, rugby and cricket. My father took a great interest in the games I played at Shirley House and was a regular spectator.

Looking back on these early school days it was the emphasis on teamwork which left a lasting impression on me, helped and encouraged by my father. At the start of war in September 1939 half the school was evacuated to Akeley Wood in Buckinghamshire. This had been the country estate of the Price family, makers of candles. I went to Akeley Wood, and boarded in my last year. This was good way of being introduced to boarding. For about twenty four hours I felt homesick and told myself 'Don't be silly, you are a prefect and about to be captain of the school soccer XI'.

It was my mother who was determined that I should do well academically. There had been much uncertainty about which public school I should go to. Rugby, Glenalmond and Sedburgh were all considered, but because of the war, my mother's thoughts were to have us all near home and they decided to put me

Shirley House School 1st XI Soccer – Autumn 1937. Left to right: back row: *DJ Woolford, GAH Tassell, GIB Good, M Noakes, BS Crowther;* middle row: *PJB Pratt, FA Gutkind, Mr Hartley, JW Cornforth, DH Underhill;* front row: *KAG Miller, DP Ransom, EL Averill*

down for Merchants Taylors in Northwood. My school reports made it clear that though my maths was excellent, my English and French were only average and the headmaster didn't see me as a scholarship candidate. My strong-willed mother nevertheless entered me for the Merchants Taylors scholarship examination without consulting the new headmaster of Shirley House, Mr Stewart. Mr Stewart was not best pleased and told my mother I had not been prepared for the exam. My mother replied in her usual determined style that she wasn't expecting me to win a scholarship, only to enter a good form in the school. In due course I came home to take the exam at Merchants Taylors. While the Viva I had with the maths master was a pleasant chat, the French master started off talking in French and I was completely lost. I returned to Akeley Wood, not expecting any success. Out of the blue came the offer of a Scholarship. I wrote in my schoolboy diary 'I got the results of my exam today. I have pulled it off. Personally I think it is a fluke.' As it happened I got 95% in Maths III which was the highest they had had for several years. Just as well in view of my French!

By this time the fall of France was on us and my parents took the decision that my mother would take us three children out to Canada, where we had been invited by a second cousin of my father's, Helen Butler. In mid-July I left Akeley

Shirley House School 1st XV Rugby – Spring 1938. Left to right: back row: *KAG Miller, M Noakes, JDF Nichols, GIB Good, A Glendining, JP Hough, JN Smith;* middle row: *PJB Pratt, GLH Wise, Mr EMM Riley, JW Cornforth, DP Ransom;* front row: *FA Gutkind, DH Underhill, KGG Chambers, EL Averill, ACB Pratt*

Wood and the four of us sailed from Liverpool on the *Duchess of Atholl* for Montreal. Auntie Helen, as we soon called her, welcomed us into their home. Her husband, Everard Butler, was in Britain as a volunteer with the Canadian Army. He had clearly lied about his age, having sculled for Canada in the 1912 Olympic games. He and my father were soon bosom friends. Helen and Everard had one son, Billy, who willingly accepted this unusual influx into his home. Billy was my age, very musical and years later had his own dance band.

I started in September at the local high school in grade 12 of the Ontario education system. I was to take their junior matric, the equivalent of school certificate, at the end of that academic year. I would have expected to do this at an English public school, but the Canadians go at a slower speed in their primary schools. The result was that all the other pupils in my class were at least 2 years older that myself.

At this same time my mother was determined to obtain a job and not live off the Butlers. She had her medical degree, and although she had started to help my father in the practice on the outbreak of war, she said she was finding it difficult after a career break of sixteen years. Fortunately she was offered a post in the psychiatric hospital at Whitby Ontario, some forty miles east of Toronto, and she quickly re-established her medical career. Her first priority was not unexpectedly to send me and my two sisters to private schools where the brighter children were encouraged to progress at a faster rate than in the Ontario State schools. So it was that my sisters went to Ontario Ladies College in Whitby and I went to Upper Canada College in Toronto.

CHAPTER 2

Canada

I FOUND MY SCHOOL DAYS IN CANADA a very maturing experience. Though in many ways the influence of Britain was still very strong in Canada, the impact of the United States, so close and so financially and commercially dominant, was there for all to see. I found Canadians very conscious of this in so many ways and they were very sensitive of 'big brother' next door. I very soon learned not to say 'We do it differently back home' but rather 'So that's how we do it'.

I thoroughly enjoyed my time at Upper Canada College (UCC). It was, and still is, a quite outstanding School. Founded in 1829, it had some turbulent times in the second half of the 19th Century, but at the beginning of the 20th Century the college became truly independent. At the time of the 150th anniversary in 1979 Richard Howard, Headmaster of the Preparatory School, wrote a fascinating history of 'Upper Canada College 1829–1979'.[1] He completed his Epilogue by saying 'The author foresees a bright future for Upper Canada College. He believes that it will not only survive, it will prevail, because it has a core of compassion and endurance. This volume is about the courage, the honour, and the pride which have illuminated its past. It is not merely the record of Upper Canada College. It is intended as a pillar of hope for the future.'

As I entered the college as a new boy in 1940, I was unaware of this history, but I was soon very conscious of the pride we all took in the college. I found the expectations of working hard and playing hard were just the same as I had experienced at Shirley House and soon felt I was part of it. The games were slightly different, with Canadian rugby, ice hockey and basketball, though we did play cricket in the summer.

The masters, too, were dedicated to the college and the teaching was of a very high level. Lorne McKenzie, the mathematics teacher, known by the boys as 'Butch', was renowned throughout Ontario for the excellence of his UCC pupils' performance in the Provincial examinations. Jimmie Biggar inspired us with an understanding of Canadian history and the influence of Quebec. And then there was Freddie Mallett, who taught chemistry and supervised the cadet battalion. Mr Mallett was punctual in all things, and always most helpful. I remember an occasion in my third year when I was Regimental Sergeant Major in the cadet battalion and I had forgotten to carry out some task. Freddie Mallett's rebuke, if

---

[1] *Upper Canada College 1829–1979 Colborne's Legacy* by Richard B Howard. Published by Macmillan of Canada 1979.

you could call it that, was to suggest that in future I should keep a list on a piece of paper of all the tasks I had to do and cross them off when they have been done. I knew even then that I did not have a good memory, but I had the good sense to follow Freddie Mallett's advice, and I have kept such a list ever since.

'Big Mike' Bremner taught me physics and coached the first eleven cricket team. I found the physics easy and was inclined to take it easy. Mr Bremner knew this and on one occasion when I was not giving my full attention, he shied a piece of chalk at me. All I remember is that my reaction was fast enough and I got the desk lid up in time to intercept the chalk. No hard feelings, and we both smiled. Mr JJ Knights taught me English. I was told by others that he was very good, but it didn't seem to rub off on me. His comments on my school reports were not encouraging. 'Just enough. Must improve comp', then 'Critical faculty very undeveloped', and the one that really hurt 'too economical of effort'. On this latter occasion I had been working at my poor English as hard as I could. The situation was saved when on vacation an old friend of the family, Professor Roy, the Professor of English at Queen's University, Kingston, Ontario gave me the sound advice to write short sentences. It was almost as if he was giving away a state secret! Mr Knight's reports improved, too, with 'Developing splendidly' and 'Most encouraging progress'.

For the greater part of my time at Upper Canada College I was a boarder in Wedds House. Dr Bassett became the housemaster and at first we got the feeling he was a dry old stick, but this was not so. He had taken his PhD at Kings College, London University and he courted his wife with walks along the Grand Union Canal within a mile of my home in Croxley Green. He clearly had fond memories and I warmed to him. Much of my school life centred round Wedds House. We became fiercely loyal to our house teams.

In 1940 there was a strong contingent of English war guests (evacuees), several of whom were in my own form. David Pilkington, Robin Ibbs, and Jonathan Pritchard, who were later undergraduates with me at Cambridge, and all of them returned to distinguished careers in Britain. David Pilkington and I were in the same house, Wedds. We often went round together from form to form, and were sometimes mistaken for each other. The occasion I remember best was in 'Butch' McKenzie's maths class. Butch used to ask a question of the whole class and with an upward sweep of his cane he would motion us to rise – that is if we knew the answer. If you were uncertain of your answer and were at all hesitant as you rose he would point down at you and call out your name. On this occasion I wasn't at all sure of the answer and 'Butch' pointed down at me and called out 'Pilkington' and David, bless him, gave the correct answer from another place in the classroom. Butch wasn't the only person to make this mistake. The second occasion was when David and I had both gone up to Cambridge University. It was still war-time and we were expected to take part in the University Cadet Corps. David and I, not having done the Cert 'A' in the school battalion, found ourselves being marched round under the orders of Guards Sergeants who clearly took a certain pleasure in knocking some sense into these young men leading an easy life in Cambridge. We were only a small squad of nine and the platoon was three by three. David was on one corner and I on another. The Sergeant had one of us as his marker and much to the amusement of us undergraduates he mixed us up. He finally halted the platoon and in desperation moved me into the centre of the squad.

I thoroughly enjoyed playing Canadian rugby and ice hockey for Wedds. They were of course games I hadn't played before and I played in the Wedds Senior teams for both sports and the school magazine records that Wedds won both inter-house competitions. In cricket I had the advantage of having played it at my Prep school and was soon in the UCC 1st XI. We played three other boy's private schools: Ridley College, St Andrew's College and Trinity College School. We were known as the 'Little Big Four', a somewhat arrogant title but indicative of the view we took of ourselves. I had one moment of glory in my second year when we played Trinity College School. I came in first wicket down and carried my bat for the rest of the game scoring 24 and we just won by one wicket. It was

Upper Canada College 1st XI cricket 1942. Left to right: back row: *SP Burden, D Godefroy, Mr MWE Bremner, VV Spencer, JL Fichter, HR Lawson;* Middle row: *EFC Jeffs, MW Bremner, Mr TWL McDermott, SC Bebell, EDG Davies;* front row: *KAG Miller, RD Jeffs*

a lucky flash in the pan, and there was a write-up in the *Toronto Globe & Mail*, 'Miller shines as UCC wins'.

Even in those days I was very ambitious. Being made a house prefect or a school steward generally came to boys in their fourth year in the college and I was due to leave at the end of my third year. There was one possibility and that was the position of Head of House. This was the boarder who had achieved the highest school results the summer before. David Pilkingon and I were the two boarders who returned after taking our senior matric the previous June. Our results on the face of it were very similar and we were told we would have to wait until the school found out from the provincial examination authorities. After an agonizing couple of weeks the results came through and I was made Head of House and a House Prefect. David took it extremely well. I hope I would have taken it as well if the roles had been reversed. I relished the responsibility and authority.

I had as my opposite number as top day boy and 'Head of Town' Bunny McCulloch, who was also editor of the *College Times*. Bunny conceived the idea that we should jointly write a report on how the school might be improved. The main proposal was for the form representatives to be organized into a large committee under the joint chairmanship of the Heads of House and Town. We had high hopes. The board of stewards agreed to support it, but in the end the masters, quite rightly, quietly kicked our proposals into touch. It was my first experience of lobbying for changes in the social system.

Then there was the Curfew Club. Something like 20 senior boys were elected and met every second Sunday evening to discuss some controversial subject. Two members read papers and were encouraged to take up opposing views. The guest of the evening was then invited to lead the discussion. One of the masters hosted the meeting and gave us a good buffet supper afterwards, which was much appreciated. Jimmy Biggar was the leading light and he saw to it that we widened our interests to take in current affairs. The *College Times* reported on discussions on such widely differing subjects as 'The Far East', 'Conduct of the war', Co-education', 'Post-war reconstruction' and 'Communism or Capitalism'. The secretary of the Curfew Club was meant to write the minutes, and the first appointee was obviously failing in his duties. It was reported in the *College Times* of the Curfew Club that 'Probably the most startling change noticeable in the Curfew Club this term is the presence of minutes which are complete and correct. This striking change for the better is due to the sagacity of the members in electing Ken Miller as secretary.'

For the meeting on 'Communism and Capitalism' Bunny McCulloch and I are reported as presenting the papers, but for the life of me, I cannot recall whether I was in favour of communism or capitalism. I suspect the latter. We were reported to have taken up our position at the right on the sofa and the communists were forced to sit on harder seats on the left. The one meeting, however, which made a lasting impression on me was on the future of Canada, and our guest of the evening had told us that Canada's wealth was in the Tar Sands in the undeveloped north. I had visions of being part of this exciting new industry. For many years I wondered what had happened. I was well into my retirement when I heard that the Tar Sands were at last being exploited.

The time came round for us to leave UCC and there were many discussions we had amongst ourselves on what we would do in our future careers after the war was over. While we had been accepted most generously by our Canadian friends, there was a strong pull amongst the war guests that we should return to the UK.

I remember talking with David Pilkington and saying he had the family business of Pilkington Bros to walk into, while I had to make my own way. David came down on me like a ton of bricks. He made it very clear that he would have to get a respectable degree at university, and even then if accepted into the company he would be on probation for two years. In later years I appreciated how wise the Pilkington Directors were to take such a firm line with young sprigs of the family. David and I were hoping to go to Cambridge to take the Mechanical Sciences Tripos (engineering by any other name and now called the Engineering Tripos). This we did, but after Cambridge we went our separate ways. Our paths crossed some 25 years later when David had risen to be personnel director of Pilkington Bros and I was engineering director of the Heavy Organics Division of ICI. Our personnel director, Brian Jenkins, said at a Chairman's Monday morning meeting he was expecting a visit from David Pilkington to hear from ICI about unionization. Brian asked me to join the dinner party the evening David and a colleague arrived to see Brian. We had a delightful evening.

My parents had clearly been making inquiries not only about which university I should attend, but which subject I should read. My mother had been to a cocktail party at Queen's University at Kingston, Ontario and homed in on the Professor of Engineering saying she had a sixteen-year-old son who was thinking about engineering. I think the professor had had his full share of mothers lobbying for their offsprings. To my mother's inquiries he asked if I played with Meccano. My mother replied 'not at all, he just happens to be good at Maths'. At this the Professor brightened and said 'Now you are talking'. When my mother relayed this conversation to me, I as good as decided that engineering was for me.

Around Easter I received sample papers of the mechanical sciences qualifying examination which undergraduates were advised to pass before starting their first year. I took one look at the questions and realized I couldn't do a single one, so I took them along to 'Butch' McKenzie, who was now principal of the college. Butch took one look at the papers and said 'You get some tutoring over the summer holidays and you will sail through the exam'. I'm glad to say he was right.

While my mother and sisters remained in Canada for another year I came home in July 1943. I had expected to return in a troop ship with some pretty basic living standards. When we embarked at Halifax in Nova Scotia I found myself on the

The Banana Planter, a well-appointed boat which used to ply between New York and the West Indies. I shared a cabin with Martin Browne who, like myself, had just left Upper Canada College and was on his way home with his sister Barbara. There was quite a group of us young folk returning to the UK and we thoroughly enjoyed the sea journey. *The Banana Planter* was in a convoy and was a lead ship on the edge of the convoy. We had no fear of being torpedoed and indeed we had a smooth uneventful journey. It was years later that I learnt that it was only the previous month that the U-boats had finally been defeated.

I returned home to join my father. As he met me at Watford Junction I think my father was a little surprised by this young man whose voice had broken and who spoke with a Canadian accent. Dad had slipped back into a bachelor life with a housekeeper to look after the domestic side. It was hard not to get on with my Dad. After hearing about the stringent rationing in the UK, I remember being a little surprised next morning to find two eggs on my plate. When I inquired if this was the return of the prodigal son, Dad replied 'I have friends'. This turned out to be a grocer in nearby Sarratt who had a hypochondriac wife who, of course, needed a weekly visit from her doctor. In fact I learned to drive the car by chauffeuring Dad on his weekly visit to Sarratt.

It was soon arranged for me to go up to London twice a week to a cram school to prepare for the Mechanical Sciences Qualifying examination.

By this time my name had been put down for entry for Trinity Hall, and in early August my father drove me up to Cambridge for an interview with the senior tutor, Charles Crawley. By the time we arrived we discovered Charles Crawley had gone off on holiday to his cottage in Wales, but that the Vice Master, The Reverend Charles Angus, would see us. My recollection of the interview is that I hardly said a word and the time was taken up with my father and Charles Angus exchanging slightly risqué jokes. On that basis I found myself accepted, or so it struck me at the time. However, there was a little more to it. Charles Crawley knew the education adviser to the Canadian Army in Britain, and Charles had consulted him. The advice he received was that he should take any boy who came with a good report from the principal of Upper Canada College. Butch McKenzie had done me proud and the letter he sent to my parents, one copy to my father in the UK and another copy to my mother in Canada, tells it all (see Appendix I).

CHAPTER 3

Universities: Cambridge University and University College, Aberystwyth

S O IT WAS IN OCTOBER 1943 I went up to Cambridge. As Butch McKenzie had predicted I sailed through the qualifying examination, and started on a course in the engineering department to take the 1st Year preliminary examination the following June.

In the meantime my mother had done her research into Trinity Hall and had discovered that it was known for Law and Rowing. She was concerned about rowing because she had an old school and University friend, Lilias Maclay, whose younger brother, JS Maclay, had gone up to Cambridge, had rowed for Cambridge, but he only achieved a third in the Economics Tripos. The fact that he had become a leading Conservative politician and was later Secretary of State for Scotland was completely lost on my mother. I was duly instructed not to row, and even more surprisingly I obeyed, and for the first year I concentrated on my engineering course. In the 1st year preliminary examination I got a first and came top of the year. On the strength of this the college awarded me an exhibition.

In the summer long vacation we were expected to work in industry and get some practical training. My parents knew Mr Lawson who ran a small electrical company, Watford Electric, and they arranged for me to go and work there. I remember half-way through my first morning I was summoned to Mr Lawson's office for a chat with him. His leading question was 'What is the matter with your father's practice?' Rather lamely I replied that I didn't wish to be a doctor, but it did indicate the relative standing of a doctor and an industrialist, as seen in Britain at that time.

I soon realized that to be in the swim of college life I must take up rowing, and with my first year results behind me there was now no question of my mother objecting.

I was very fortunate to get first-class coaching from the day I first stepped into a tub. To my pleasant surprise I went straight into the college first boat. My college life revolved around a continuing concentration on my studies combined with time on the river. Very enjoyable but hard work and there was little time for other activities.

The second year academically led on to the second year preliminary examinations. I was joining the bright students of my own age who had just come up and had two years to cover the course to the Mechanical Sciences Tripos.

I was very determined to get a good degree, and I interpreted this as success in the examinations. To this end I would often shut myself in my room for three hours and do one of the old papers which Robin Hayes, my director of studies, would subsequently mark. In the preliminary examinations the students were told afterwards what marks they had gained in each paper.

During the period of the examinations in June 1945 I was rowing in the college First May Boat and the crew all dined together in Hall. The general conversation was about the ghastly exams they had been having and several members of the crew were very doubtful if they had passed. I endeavoured to keep quiet as I had had a mechanics paper that morning in which one was asked to attempt seven questions and to prove certain mathematical expressions. I had done seven questions and produced seven answers which fitted the examination requirements. I felt pretty confident that I had scored around 90%. When they pressed me I felt I should write it down a little and I foolishly expressed it in mathematical terms. Instead of saying that I thought it was all right, I said I thought I had scraped 80%. There were peals of laughter and I had my leg pulled unmercifully for the rest of the term about scraping 80%. When the results came out at the beginning of the next term I was again top of the year and in the mechanics examination, which I had written down to just scraping 80%, I actually achieved 100% and the college promoted me to a major scholarship. The Trinity Hall First May Boat bumped

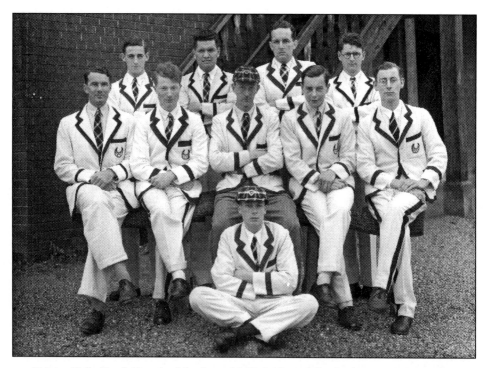

Trinity Hall, Cambridge, 1st May boat, 1945. Left to right: back row: *KAG Miller, OL Phipps, PLP MacDonnell, JH Neame;* middle row: *JG Gosse, EI Brentnall, GM Rushmore, PJ Bell, DCH Garrod;* front row: *AE Charlwood*

Clare I and we finished second on the river. We just failed to catch First and Third Trinity, who were Head of the River, and we were judged to be the fastest eight on the river.

Charles Crawley and my father applied on my behalf for me to be allowed another year of deferment of national service. As I had only had one year's deferment so far on account of coming up to Cambridge at 17, I wasn't surprised when my deferment came through, and I was allowed the full three years consecutively.

For my second Summer I did my vacation work at the Royal Aircraft Establishment at Farnborough. I had already decided to take aeronautics as a 'B' paper in my final year. It should have been an exciting time with a variety of Allied and German jets on the tarmac, but there was an almost lackadaisical attitude amongst the staff. It may have been exhaustion after the pressures of the war years, and at the end of my time there, I mentally ruled out a career in the scientific civil service.

It was during this second long vacation that I returned to Cambridge for part of the long vacation term, and met Launcelot Fleming. Launcelot had been appointed Dean and Chaplain of Trinity Hall in 1934. Although he was away as a naval chaplain for the war years, by the summer of 1945 Launcelot was in London working during the week on the selection of ordination candidates, and he came back to spend his week-ends at the Hall. Launcelot was one of the great characters whose influence has spread to many Trinity Hall graduates. His biography by Donald Lindsay is rightly entitled *Friends for Life*.[1] Indeed he was certainly that and he always made one feel his great interest in all one did. I was one of the many Hall oarsmen who was persuaded by Launcelot to go out in a pair with him, which was unusual for a don.

When I returned to the Hall in the autumn of 1945 there were five of us from the successful May Boat and we all found ourselves in the trial eights. Academically I took The Mechanical Sciences Tripos (Old Regulations). However, most of the undergraduates in the year went on to take the Mechanical Sciences Tripos Part I. The old Regulations included 'B' papers, which were essential for a first. There were only twelve students who took the Old Regulations and only two of us, JN Lowe and I, were taking the aeronautics 'B' paper. The day approached when the two trial eight crews were due to row their boats down to Ely where the trial's race was to be held. By chance this was the day of a lecture on aeronautics. With only two of us in the class, it wasn't a question of just missing the lecture, and furthermore the lecturer was an eminent engineer, Sir Melville Jones. When I spoke to Sir Melville to apologize, he accepted at once that I would miss his lecture and asked what was I doing on Saturday morning. Thus it was that Sir Melville gave the lecture once for JN Lowe

---

[1] *Friends for Life. A Portrait of Launcelot Fleming* by Donald Lindsay. Published by Lindel Publishing Co 1981.

and again for myself on the Saturday morning. Such was the respect for rowing in Cambridge.

I was in the losing crew in the trial eight race at Ely, and next term I returned to row in the College Lent boat. During the Lent term there was an outbreak of dysentery in the college. Like many others I caught it and hadn't fully recovered when the Lent races were on us. I foolishly struggled on and had to drop out after two days' racing. I spent quite a bit of the Easter holidays in bed at home and I still wasn't fit at the beginning of the next term, and now had sinusitis to contend with as well. My Director of Studies, Robin Hayes, was concerned that I would not be fit to take the Tripos and this would determine whether I obtained a degree at all. In the end Robin Hayes combined with Dr Bevan, the University Boat Club doctor, who had checked me over for the trial eights, and invalided me out of the College First May Boat so that I could concentrate on my Tripos exams. I found myself accompanying the Master, Professor Dean, following the college boats cycling along the tow path. On one of the key days of the May races, it was pouring with rain and knowing the Master was getting on in years, I said what a pity it was raining so hard. 'Not at all Miller,' he replied. 'It keeps the crowds

Cambridge University Trial Eights, 1945. Back row: *KAG Miller, H Symons, PT Pulman, RMTD Lindlar;* middle row: *DJD Perrins, PLP McDonnell, MJ Allman-Ward, MA Nicholson, GC Thomas;* seated: *RAR Dewar, TJ Sullivan, Q des Clayes, JS Paton Philips, DCH Garrod, JH Neame, JG Gosse, GJC Fisher, PRO Wood*

away.' The first boat caught First and Third Trinity and went head of the river for the first time since 1908.

In the meantime I continued my preparations for the Tripos examinations. The thing I most remember is going into the exams with a nose spray of a new drug called penicillin. In the end I got a First with distinction in aeronautics. John Davidson, the only other First in the Old Regulations, won the top Rex Moir prize and I contented myself with being second. John Davidson went on to a most distinguished academic career. He became Shell Professor of chemical engineering at Cambridge and Vice-Master of Trinity College, Fellow of the Royal Society (FRS) in 1974 and a Founder Fellow of the Royal Academy of Engineering (FREng) in 1976.

I had at least got my first and I learned an important lesson: that there are limits to one's achievements and to one's health. From then on I knew I had to pace myself. Robin Hayes was one of the few dons who devoted himself to the undergraduates. It wasn't until years later that I fully appreciated how Robin nursed me along for that final term.

One of my fondest recollections of Robin was when he invited me and another Trinity Hall engineer, ARM Reid, to a working week at his cottage in the Elan

Author after graduating at Cambridge University, July 1946

Valley in Mid Wales. Incidently Reid and I were contemporaries together at Shirley House School. I remembered Robin meeting us off the train at Rhayader. He was wearing a Sherlock Holmes deerstalker hat and a cape to match, and he drove us to his cottage in a wonderful bull-nosed Morris open tourer. As he drove us along, he confessed to us that everyone in Rhayader called him the professor. I was not surprised. He certainly looked the part. The task we had ahead of us was to replace a corroded pipe from the little dam Robin had built in a small stream above his cottage, which led down to his little generator house, the size of a small kennel, in which was housed a small pelton wheel and a generator. The pair of us sneaked a view of the generator house when Robin wasn't there and we couldn't resist bursting out laughing as we saw an ancient horseshoe magnet generator. We heard from Robin later that this museum piece had been thrown out of the engineering department many years earlier and Robin acquired it for his holiday home. The electricity generated was only enough to supply lighting in the cottage and when the lights were not on the energy was dissipated by a battery of electrical resistors filling one room of the Cottage. I was glad to say we completed the replacement job and before we left we saw Robin's generating Plant in action. Robin was one of those rare academics who put the teaching of students ahead of their own research and scholarship. I am glad to say that this was appreciated and a room in college has been named 'The Robin Hayes Room'.

I recall an occasion in the 1990s when I had been elected an Honorary Fellow. This was an accolade which I appreciated more than any other, and it allowed me to attend college Feasts. One in particular was the Dr Eden Supper. Dr Eden, the Master in the middle of the seventeenth century, left a bequest of certain sums of money to supply candles for the College Chapel and 'I doe appoint that the odd money of this later £28 p ann shall be imployed upon some prouison of Wine and Dyett to be spent yearely upon the Master, Fellowes and Scholars at Supp the night of that day on which the Comemoracon shall be made.' (*3. Extract from menu of Dr Eden's Supper 7.12.02*) Thus every year early in December there is a commemorative service in the College Chapel to the memory of Dr Eden and this is followed by the Supper when the Master, Fellows and Scholars enjoy a superb feast. When I first attended in my undergraduate days the oration to Dr Eden was in Latin and it was well above my head. When I came to attend the same feast as an Honorary Fellow, it was in English and I came to enjoy the oration, as the Fellow detailed to give the address was expected to talk about his or her work in the College and University. I was fascinated, too, to meet the current generation of scholars and I am always greatly heartened by their enthusiasm and bright conversation. I remember one recent Dr Eden Supper when one of the dons was waxing on about how poorly paid they all were. I was feeling particularly mischievious that evening and decided I would tweak them. So I started off by saying 'You academics have it all wrong when you allowed yourselves to become so dependent on the public purse.' I said that the voting public looked to the universities to educate their sons, daughters and grandchildren to a first degree. The politicians were only responding to this perceived need, while in reality the university staff put their research and scholarship as their first priority and the undergraduates were an unfortunate second. There was, of course, an immediate reaction to this point of view, and I was quickly backtracking and saying it clearly didn't apply to Cambridge. As was the custom at these suppers, we all retired to the Senior Combination Room after the main course for mineral water while the college staff reset the table with a different seating plan for the sweet. During this interval the scholars who had heard my exchange besieged me to say that I was absolutely right and a good deal of the lecturing in Cambridge was very poor. I quietly chuckled to myself, and thanked my lucky stars that Robin Hayes was around in my time.

At the end of my last term as an undergraduate, I was expecting to be called up to do my national service. I went before the recruitment board. I was asked which service I would like to join and when I said the Royal Navy, the reply was that there were no vacancies in the Navy. My second choice was the Royal Air Force. When I received the same reply that there were no places in the RAF, I was cheeky enough to say 'So it's Hobson's Choice'. Being in Cambridge I thought it was an appropriate comment. I was corrected. There was a choice between the Royal Engineers (RE) and the Royal Electrical and Mechanical Engineers (REME). I cannot remember which I chose, but other events took over.

Richard Morgan Davies who had been doing research in the Cambridge Engineering Department on the propagation of stress waves, was appointed to the chair of Physics at University College of Wales in Aberystwyth. He asked Professor John Baker, the head of the engineering department, for someone to become his Research Assistant to help him set up his laboratory in Aberystwyth. My name was put forward and after an interview with Professor Davies, the job was mine, and so it was that my national service turned out to be three very enjoyable years at Aberystwyth.

University College, Aberystwyth

Professor Davies was very keen to set up a stress laboratory with myself and the three newly graduated physicists from the physics department at Aberystwyth. They were Hugh Edwards, Eric Thomas and David Travena and we all got on very well together. Shortly after I arrived the Professor told me that I could take a PhD degree. This was a pleasant surprise and all four of us had this goal to aim at. The Professor also asked me to give one lecture a week to the first year students. This was my first experience of lecturing. It seemed to pass off satisfactorily. Many of the students were ex-service men and older than myself. When I got to know them, they admitted that when I first walked into the lecture room they expected me to sit down with them I looked so young.

Physics Department, University College Aberystwyth, June 1948.
The author is second on the right in the front row.

After the monastic life at Cambridge, Aberystwyth was distinctly co-education-al. I was only twenty at the time, so I entered into college life, and went to the college hops every Saturday in term time, and to more formal dances as well. There was a social life amongst the staff and I was invited to play bridge with Aneurin Richards and his wife, and had many a pleasant Sunday lunch with Mr LE Sulston, the manager of the physics department workshop, and his family.

The Professor was very Welsh, and he would speak Welsh whenever he could. I am afraid I was a real philistine and made no attempt to learn the language. There was one occasion when the Professor was about to take Hugh Edwards, David Travena and myself to a meeting at The Royal Society in London and he told the other two in Welsh that we would go in his car to a certain town and then take the train to London. He used the Welsh name for this town, and the other two didn't like to confess to the Professor they didn't understand which town it was, but they both realized that the Professor would have to tell me in English. So they both came round separately to ask me which town it was and I was able to tell them that it was Shrewsbury.

A lecture room at the end of the ground floor was converted into our laboratory. My project was a study of the propagation of flexural stress waves along a steel beam. The wave was set in motion by firing a 0.22 in bullet at right angles to the beam and the stress waves were measured by strain gauges at four points along the beam. The readings were amplified and shown vertically on a cathode ray oscillograph (CRO). At the same time the the reading on the CRO was swept from left to right to give a strain–time curve, which was recorded by a stationary plate camera. The whole recording took less than half of a thousandth of a second. The building, testing, and calibrating of the equipment took up much of the three years.

When it came to the interpretation of the result and how it should be presented there was a difference of opinion between the Professor and myself. There was a simplified theory used in most stress analysis which was fine for waves of long wavelength, but broke down for waves of short wavelength. The more accurate analysis by Timoshenko showed that even the waves of short wavelength had a maximum velocity. Unfortunately the differential equations required for the Timoshenko analysis did not lend themselves to a solution of the wave forms. I preferred to apply the simplified theory which gave a wave form which in qualitative terms showed a pattern which agreed with the experimental results. I was able to show where the simple theory deviated from the experimental results. For example the time it took the first wave to reach a distant point as recorded matched the Timoshenko theory, while according to the simplified theory they arrived sooner. This in many ways showed the difference in the thinking of a scientist and an engineer. I had no hesitation in using the simplified analysis to show where it matched the experimental results and where it broke down. The Professor, on the other hand, did not wish to consider the simple theory and give it credence, while I was perfectly happy to do so, but I included its limitations.

Fortunately for me the external examiner from University College, London fully supported the approach I had taken and my oral examination with him turned into a pleasant chat about judging the range within which simple solutions were applicable. After the interview I was pretty confident that I would get my PhD, and so I did. My parents came with me to Cardiff for the degree giving ceremony.

The problem came when I tried to get the Professor's agreement to publishing my thesis. I carried on a voluminous correspondence with Professor Davies from 1950 to 1953. There was always something else he would like to add to a joint paper. In the end I just gave up. My career with ICI was prospering, so it didn't seem to be worth the hassle.

There is no doubt that working in the University at Aberystwyth was very pleasant with congenial colleagues. This came home to me when in July 1958 while on holiday at nearby Borth I went along to the physics department at morning coffee time to find I knew everyone round the table. The only obvious omission was Professor Davies who had died the previous February.

It wasn't until May 1981 that I paid another visit to the University at Aberystwyth, when I was on a formal University Grants Committee visitation. At the formal dinner, I was sitting next to Sir Granville Beynon who was the professor of physics, and told him of my earlier visit to the physics department in 1958 and how Hugh Edwards and David Travena were still there. Sir Granville

Author after receiving his PhD, University of Wales, July 1949

said 'They are still here now. You must come and visit the department of physics, after the visitation is over.' This I was delighted to do and saw over their new department and renewed my acquaintance with Hugh and David.

Towards the end of my time at Aberystwyth I decided I must complete my training as an engineer. I was thinking of applying to a well-known engineering company like Metrovick for a student apprenticeship. To get some advice I called in on Mr Van Grutten of the Cambridge Appointments Board. To my surprise he recommended ICI. He said he would send me along to see an old friend of his, Sir Ewart Smith, who was technical director of ICI. He added that Sir Ewart sailed a large yacht, while he sailed a small one.

I saw Sir Ewart, and he was all for me starting the next Monday morning! I demurred and said I wished to complete my PhD thesis. He accepted this, but arranged that when I was ready I should go up to Billingham. I had no idea where Billingham was, but I wisely waited until I was in his outer office. Sir Ewart's PA explained that Billingham was on the river Tees on the border between Yorkshire and County Durham.

CHAPTER 4

ICI

IN DUE COURSE I VISITED Billingham Division of ICI and was interviewed by Philip Mayne, the engineering director, Rummy Sale his deputy and Sammie Saunders the production director. I was offered a post as a technical officer and Mr Mayne said they would send me for twelve months to gain experience on the shop floor at CA Parsons in Newcastle followed by a year in the drawing office at Billingham. I was assured by Mr Mayne that this would meet the requirements of the Institution of Mechanical Engineers for professional membership. I had no hesitation in accepting.

CA Parsons

I had only been at CA Parsons for a few weeks and was waiting at the bus stop to catch a bus to work, when out of the haze of a dark autumn morning who should arrive at the bus stop but Robin Ibbs. I soon discovered that he, too, was heading for CA Parsons as a student apprentice. Robin and I had been in the same form at UCC but he left a year before me to spend 2 years at the University of Toronto studying engineering. He then returned to the UK and we found ourselves in the same year doing the Mechanical Sciences Tripos in Cambridge. After that Robin did his national service in the Navy while I was at Aberystwyth and here we were together at Parsons. I was moved round the various workshops; Foundry, Welding Shop, Pattern Shop, Erecting Shop, Apprentice School, Tool room and Outside Erection and I was expected to write a monthly report to Mr Mayne on my activities on the shop floor. By far the most interesting month was February 1950 when the General Election was taking place. Robin Ibbs and I were working with Harry Learmouth, one of the fitters on Relay Valves. I wrote to Mr Mayne as follows:

> The most interesting part of the day's work is when Harry starts giving us his views. This is the first time I have spent such a long time with the same man, but the longer I remain with him the more communicative he has become. I purposely stayed on until the general election was over and as Harry is a staunch Trade Union man, we were able to have a rare dose of his political opinions. In fact it has called for a certain amount of tact not to put one's foot in it, when politics is being discussed, as the older men have very bitter memories of unemployment in the twenties and thirties. However we manage to avoid personal feelings as much as possible, and as a result I was able to hear just what Harry felt about the various political parties. What struck me most was the bitterness he has towards the Tories for the unemployment and lock-outs after the first world war, his unswerving loyalty to the trade unions, and

his implicit faith in the Labour Party's ability to maintain full employment. However, much as this latter faith may be subjected to disillusionment in the not too distant future, the conviction of it is very strong at the moment. On the subject of the trade unions, he has also been communicative and last week he lent me the February issue of the journal of the Amalgamated Engineering Union. This I found most interesting as it is a magazine intended for the internal consumption of the unions. As such it gave me an extremely good idea of the way in which the trade union leaders were thinking, and the way they presented such industrial problems as the stabilization of wages to their rank and file. This February issue also contained several political articles obviously intended to consolidate the Labour vote in the unions. One article in particular was very bitter towards any Trade Union man who was thinking of voting Conservative and struck me as coming very close to intimidation. Harry also took the same view, and he became most heated when he found any of the fitters in the shop who might be voting Conservative. Although he realized after a time that both I and Robin Ibbs were of right wing tendencies there was never any ill-will because of it, while he could be quite rude to one of the young fitters who might vote Conservative. The implication was that the fitter would be letting down his mates. I was also quite surprised to discover how many of the younger men were thinking of voting Conservative and the biggest surprise was to discover that one of the shop stewards also intended doing so.

Mr Mayne in his reply said he was very interested in the information I passed on about the political views of the fitters and he felt that if it hadn't been for Trade Union pressure on their members the Labour Party might have had quite a heavy defeat. He passed on my letter to the Labour Manager at Billingham.

Tube plates design

I started at Billingham in earnest in September 1950. I was posted to the Oil Design Office and was meant to be learning how to draw and find out how a drawing office functions. However I was getting bored with the tedium of detailed drawings, and I asked Peter Frost, the design engineer I was working for, if I could do some checking of his design calculations or any other technical problem he would like me to tackle. There was a problem. The new ethylene cracker which MW Kelloggs were designing and building for the division had a quench boiler. The design for the two tube plates at either end of the boiler were to be $1\frac{3}{8}$ inches thick while the Tubular Exchanger Manufacturers Association (TEMA) formula gave a thickness of 10.58 inches. I was asked to have a look at it.

An earlier paper by Karl A Gardner of the Griscom-Russell company suggested that the tubes connecting the two tube plates could give some support to the tube plates. I had been familar with the differential equation of a uniformly loaded thin plate, but the assumption I now wished to make was that there would be a further restraining force on the tube plate depending on the extent to which the tubes connecting the two tube plates had been stretched. This assumption gave me a more complicated differential equation, which, with my limited knowledge of mathematics, I was unable to tackle. Fortunately I was sharing digs with Guthrie

Petrie, a mathematician from Plastics Division. I asked Guthrie one evening how to find an answer. He took one look and said Bessel functions. Up to that point I had never heard of Bessel functions. Guthrie said that they could be expressed as a series, just like trigonometrical functions. He said there was sure to be a book on Bessel functions in the division's library.

Next morning I got a book on Bessel functions out of the library, and I was soon manipulating Ber and Bei functions as I would have done Sines and Cosines. I pressed on with this analysis and found the stresses in a $1\frac{3}{8}$ thick tube plate were within the allowed figure. There was another important point I spotted and that was that symbols in the Bessel function were all of dimensionless numbers. This meant that the complicated expressions could be read off a graph against a dimensionless number, which in our case ranged from 0 to 20. I could then devise a design procedure for a draughtsman in the drawing office to do the calculation.

I was busy putting all this into a paper, when I was called to Mr Mayne's office. Lord Fleck, the chairman of ICI, was about to visit CA Parsons and Mr Mayne wish to be certain the works chauffeur had the correct instructions on how to get there. Mr Mayne took the opportunity to ask me how I was getting on in oil design. Just as I was saying I was tackling an interesting problem and was having some discussion on it with George Lake of engineering research department, the telephone rang and I left Mr Mayne's office. Afterwards Mr Mayne wondered what on earth Miller was doing seeing George Lake. He called in JD Brown (JD as he was affectionately called) who was the senior design engineer in charge of oil design. Peter Frost hadn't told JD what I was up to. So JD stormed into the drawing office to ask me what I was doing. At the very moment JD arrived I had just completed a first draft of the note, all in my own ghastly handwriting. I told JD roughly what it was and gave him my manuscript. This manuscript he immediately took along to Mr Mayne and said this is what Miller has been doing. To my surprise Mr Mayne took my manuscript home with him, read it and completely understood the mathematics. When I was subsequently summoned to his office, he began by pointing out that I had three different ways of spelling 'periphery'. He said we must get the paper published as a Billingham Division central file report, and also submit it for publication in the *Proceedings of the Institution of Mechanical Engineers*.[1] He also thought we should do some experimental work on a heat exchanger with strain gauges to support my findings. Eventually he said he should really be annoyed with me for not doing the drawing office work, but he could hardly do that when I produced work of this quality.

The outcome of this was that we had the strain gauge test done on a heat exchanger on Oil works where I was posted as a trainee engineer, and the tests

---

[1] 'The Design of Tube Plates in Heat Exchangers' by KAG Miller, ICI Billingham Division Central File report No B.120788, and later published in *The Institution of Mechanical Engineers' Proceedings (B) 1952*, Vol. 1B, No. 6. Subsequently it was incorporated into British Standards BS1500.

supported my thesis remarkably well. The report on 'The Design of Tube Plates for Heat Exchangers' was published as a Billingham Division report in the summer of 1951. The report including the experimental work was accepted by the Institution of Mechanical Engineers and published with written communications in the Institution's *Proceedings* in 1952. At the same time George Lake was serving on the British Standards Institution's (BSI) panel which was reviewing BS 1500 covering amongst other things, Tube Plate Design. In due course my design method was incorporated into the British Standard.

At this point there might have been a risk that I would be labelled the 'tube plate expert' and expected to become a back room boffin. I needn't have worried as I continued as a plant engineer first as a trainee on oil works and later on gas and power works.

Works experience

From the spring 1951 to the summer of 1954 I was a plant engineer on the works. The plant engineer is responsible for the maintenance of the plant. He has a foreman and a squad of fitters and their mates. He works closely with and shares an office with the plant manager who is responsible for the operation of the plant. What follows is a resumé of a few of the more interesting incidents I was involved in.

There was one occasion on Oil works when a new distillation plant was starting up and a severe case of cavitation occurred in the bottoms pump pumping the hot liquid from the bottom of a distillation column. Mr Harris, the deputy works engineer, took myself and another young engineer, Bob Malpas, to see it. The bottoms pump should have been located right under the distillation column so that the pressure drop in the line from the column to the pump should be as low as possible. The pump was actually located at the other end of the pump house with a long suction line to the pump and several right angled bends. The pressure drop along the pipe takes the liquid from the liquid state to the gaseous state, and this sudden explosion does immense harm to the piping and is known as cavitation. As an expedient a new straight suction pipe was being installed and this line was also to be water jacketed. When I found myself as a design engineer on oil design, I went round the drawing office asking the draughtsman where had he situated the bottoms pump. I was soon getting the answer 'right under the column'.

It was some twelve years later when we made the same mistake again. I was by this time engineering director and Harry North, the production director, complained at a chairman's meeting about the cheap pumps we were putting into the new phenol plant. After the meeting I immediately telephoned the works engineer to be told they have the matter in hand, but it was the old story of cavitation.

There seemed to be a forgetting cycle. It takes some ten to twelve years for enough staff changes to take place for some of the good practical details to be forgotten.

In 1952 I was moved to Gas and Power works as plant engineer in the power station. I had as my foreman Albert Buckley, a wonderfully resourceful ex-seagoing chief engineer. Albert was right on top of the job. There was one occasion when Albert, in his enthusiasm, got carried away. There was a 'Good Housekeeping Competition' for the tidiest plant on the works. Albert was doing his best to see that the power station would win the competition. One day Albert came into work to find that someone on the generator floor had been smoking and had thrown their matches down the access well to the floor below. Albert to show his disgust had these matches swept into a pile and with chalk drew a circle round the matches and had written: 'Process matches'. There was the inevitable complaint which surfaced to the plant manager and I found myself smoothing down some ruffled feathers. On the other hand I felt sure Albert's outburst did some good because the power plant won the competition.

After a year on the smooth running power plant I was moved to be plant engineer on the boilers, looking after the Coal Handling equipment. It was a very grubby job and I was covered with coal dust a lot of the time.

I also inherited the post of treasurer of the Energy Group Sports Organization (EGSO). This organization ran a weekly raffle to raise money to take the children of those who work in the EGSO to a pantomime at Christmas and a summer outing to the beach at Redcar. Two collectors of the weekly raffle had spent the money and they each owed the sports organization £30.00 (Over £500 in today's money). I recorded in my diary that at the AGM my boss 'Mr Bradbeer was in the chair and I, as treasurer, faced a barrage over the arrears of the ticket collectors'. There was no doubt that feelings were running high amongst the men on the boilers. Taking money from children's treats was seen as a mortal sin. I was determined to do something about it.

I heard that the wife of one of offending collectors had recently received some money as a result of an industrial accident. I spoke to the husband and he produced the £30.00. The other man was a harder case. He had no nest egg to call upon. The question of him borrowing the money from ICI and agreeing to it being deducted from his wages was suggested but our labour department was particularly sensitive, because of some labour laws controlling deductions from wages. Fortunately the management in Gas and Power works were sympathetic for me to see the man concerned. When I saw him I stressed how strong the feelings were on the EGSO committee, and how they would like to prosecute him, however I had a way out for him to borrow the money from the company which he would agree to pay back over a number of weeks from his wage packet. This he accepted. The two transactions were kept quite separate. He collected the £30.00 in cash and I took no part in this transaction. I was, however, in the background ready to receive the £30.00 cash. At the time I thought it was just another job completed, but I hadn't appreciated just how strongly the workmen felt about the pantomime and summer outing for their children and how much they appreciated what I had done. When I left Gas and Power works six months later the members on the committee of the EGSO asked Mr Bradbeer to send me a letter of thanks on behalf of the committee. I was very touched.

Academia or industry?

It was on a bright May morning in 1954 as I sat in the office of the J. T. Boilers opening my morning mail that I received quite out of the blue a letter from Professor Dean, the Master of my old college Trinity Hall. In it he told me that Bernard Neal, the Trinity Hall Fellow who currently looked after the engineering undergraduates, was leaving to take up the chair of engineering at Swansea. Although they were still considering whether to appoint another engineer, he was writing to me to ask if I was interested. I wrote back that 'ever since Robin Hayes and Launcelot Fleming first suggested the idea to me in my undergraduate days it had always been at the back of my mind as a remote possibility'. I realized immediately that this would be a critical decision in the direction that my career might take. Only a visit to Cambridge and discussions with both the college and Professor Baker and the engineering department staff could give me a feel of what it would mean and critically whether I thought I would find the work and life in Cambridge satisfying.

So it was that a few weeks later I paid a visit to Trinity Hall and met the college committee of Professor Austin, Charles Crawley, Shaun Wylie and Trevor Thomas. I heard Gerald Ellison the Bishop of Willesden preach at evensong in the College Chapel and I then dined at High table. All very delightful and I have continued to enjoy the welcoming College's hospitality on many occasions since. Next day I saw Professor John Baker and his committee responsible for appointing demonstrators and lecturers, namely Professor Thornton, Mr Angus and Viscount Caldecote. I was pleasantly surprised to find that the combination of a demonstrators appointment in the engineering department with a College Fellowship would have given me a total income very similar to what I was enjoying as a young engineer with ICI. As seen at that time my decision boiled down to which sort of working life I would prefer. On the one hand I already had experience of university research at Aberystwyth and knew the friendly corporate life of Trinity Hall. On the other hand I knew the satisfaction I found in taking decisions and managing affairs. The final decision to stay in Industry was taken on a personal hunch.

My feelings at the time can be best expressed in the letter I wrote to Professor Dean on 15 June 1954.

Dear Professor Dean, Thank you very much for the very pleasant stay I had at the Hall last week-end and for all the trouble you took personally to make it so.

After leaving you on Monday morning I saw Mr Shire at the Cavendish, and then saw Professor Baker and several members of his staff. They were all very helpful, and I had a most useful and informative morning. Since then I have done some hard thinking, and I have definitely come to the conclusion that my temperament and outlook is more suited to an industrial career than an academic one, and I therefore ask you to withdraw my name from any election to a Fellowship.

It has not been easy to come to this decision, as I have always had the most delightful memories of my undergraduate days at the Hall, but knowing my own impatient nature, I do not feel suited to guide succeeding generations of undergraduates with that patient understanding which one expects from a Fellow, and I think I can find the best outlet for my energies in the hurly burly of competitive industry. I did think I could perhaps find some such satisfaction in research, but from my limited experience of it, I know that it's not in the solution of a particular problem, but in the application that I find most satisfaction.

I hope that this rather poor explanation may help to explain why I have come to this conclusion.

I really must apologize for all the trouble and bother I have given you. With kind regards.

Yours sincerely

Kenneth AG Miller

Professor Dean graciously replied that he was disappointed when he received my letter, but he had already formed the opinion or at any rate the expectation that I would think it wise to remain with ICI.

Professor Baker said he was sorry that I was not interested in a teaching post there, and, 'disappointing though your decision will be to many of us in Cambridge, we must abide by it.' He finishes his letter with the comment 'In any case I have no doubt that you will keep in touch with us on quite other matters'. On this last point he was oh so right.

Between the arrival of Professor Dean's original letter and my visit to Cambridge I was called in by Mr Malcolm Bone, the Gas and Power works manager, to sign the service agreement which I had been offered the previous Christmas and which would give me a bonus at the end of each year depending on how well the company had done. It was much valued as it gave you something like an additional 15% income. It also increased the notice period from one month to six months. As Mr Bone was reminding me of the details I mentally recalled that if I was going back to Cambridge the six month's notice from the end of May would take me to the end of November, and so I asked Mr Bone if I could delay signing for a week or two as I had been approached by the Master of my old college at Cambridge about the possibility of going back Cambridge at the beginning of the next academic year.

This was on a Friday at the end of May. By Monday morning Mr Bone saw me again and said he had spoken to Mr Mayne the engineering director and if I was returning to Cambridge they would give me a run round chief engineer's department first either on design or research. I said I appreciated this very much. Later in the afternoon Mr Bone phoned me to say my successor on the boilers would arrive next morning. While I protested that I hadn't yet decided to return to Cambridge, I was assured that I was due to be moved to design. So it came about that at the end of June I started as a design engineer in oil design working for Sam Salisbury.

Oil design

Sam Salisbury was a delightful person to have as a boss and he prided himself on how well his young men did in their subsequent careers in ICI. Jack Callard, later chairman of ICI, was one of them and other main board Directors such as Stan Lyon and Jack Lofthouse benefitted from Sam's guiding hand. In my case Sam shared with me many confidential pieces of information and I reciprocated.

Prospects and training of young engineers

As a follow-up to my visit to Cambridge, Viscount Caldecote, who was part of the engineering department team who interviewed me in June, was himself to move to English Electric to be a director and he was sufficiently impressed to put my name forward. I was approached by English Electric and after a visit to Rugby, they offered me a post as a senior design engineer in their atomic power department, at a salary some 50% above my current ICI salary. Somehow I didn't take to Dr Arms who would have been my boss, and as the prospects seemed so much improved with ICI, I turned down the English Electric offer. However, I took Sam Salisbury into my confidence on the matter, as I had a real worry that engineers in Billingham Division didn't have the same long term prospects as chemists. For years there had only been one engineer on the divisional board and half a dozen chemists. I aired my views to Sam and expressed the view strongly that if they wished to recruit first class engineers they really must do something about this imbalance. I had the opportunity a few days later to express the same views to Duncan Brown (affectionately known as 'JD') now deputy chief engineer and to Ray Pennock the staff manager.

Sam and 'JD' arranged for me to express the same views to Philip Mayne, the engineering director. He just couldn't believe the situation was as I described it. A few days later Sam confided in me that I had so impressed Ray Pennock and Duncan Brown that the pair of them had tried to convince Philip Mayne. I was also asked to see Dr Sammie Saunders, now a deputy chairman of the division. I had a long two hour talk with Sammie Saunders, who seemed to me to be much more appreciative of the true situation and the need for change. Finally back to Philip Mayne to be given my Christmas rise – a large rise of £200 nearly 20% up from £1,050 to £1,250 pa.

Then early in March 1955 a small panel of young engineers was set up to consider the training of young engineers and I found myself being asked to chair it. Our report finally came out in July 1955, and both Duncan Brown and Melvin

McKay were very pleased with it. At the same time I was asked to join another committee on the recruitment of engineers and draughtsmen. Duncan Brown chaired it, and Ray Pennock, the staff manager, and Eric Bowley, the division education and training manager, were on it. I was clearly being given the opportunity to express my views on personnel policy.

I should mention that once a year at Christmas there was a smoker put on at the senior staff club Norton Hall, and the smoker team did a series of sketches, often using Gilbert & Sullivan melodies to take off the directors and senior staff. The directors on the whole took it in good part. Main board directors came along too. I often thought it was an indication of the good morale of the division. Young sprigs like myself watched with interest who was at the receiving end. After all my outspoken comments, I should not have been surprised that in a quiz on the back of the Smoker programme in December 1955, there was one question: Who said 'God, this is an awful place' (a) Captain Scott (b) Dr KAG Miller (c) The gas plant manager. I was rather pleased and flattered.

The Butanols project and design models

When I arrived at the oil design, engineering department the case for the Butanols project was going up to London for approval and I was being lined up to look after the refinery section of this new project while an experienced design engineer, Tommy Dodds, was due to handle the high pressure end operating at 250 atmospheres (approximately 3,700 lbs per square inch). The project was sanctioned by the main board of ICI in November 1954. The sum authorized for the refinery was £250,000 (approaching £4 million in today's money). The new plant was due to be built in the middle of oil works. The refinery end was to incorporate two existing distillation columns with three new columns. The first problem we faced was an obvious lack of space around the two existing columns. To make room available we would need to remove a railway line encircling the two columns and leading in to a butane bottling plant right in the centre of oil works. Unbeknown to me the works manager Mr Gowing and his newly appointed works engineer, Jack Lofthouse, were both concerned about the fire hazard of this bottling plant where butane and other highly inflammable gases were pumped into rail tankers to be distributed to customers. When we suggested moving the bottling plant to a safer site, we now had two key supporters. Furthermore we made a simple preliminary model which showed the position in space of the main items of equipment. This tool was essential to convince higher management of the need to resite the bottling plant. This also helped the design team to get the views of the operating and maintenance staff.

Engineers are trained to describe three dimensional bodies on a two dimensional drawing. I must confess that it is often hard for us engineers to understand a two dimensional drawing and about the hardest example I can think

The Norton Hall Players

Present

"Festive Board"

A POT-POURRI OF CHRISTMAS FARE

to be devoured at the Norton Hall Club, Fri. 16th & Sat. 17th Dec. 1955

CHEF M. NORMAN HESS

PROVISION MERCHANTS & CORN CHANDLERS
MESSRS. JOHNNY DUNN AND STAN WARD

SERVING STAFF

NORMAN HESS	ANDY LORD	STEWART REID
GEORGE BRIDGER	MAURICE MALING	PERCY ROBERTS
MICK BROWNING	ERNEST MARCH	DICK SWAMBRICK
JOHNNY DUNN	GEOFFREY NORICKISS	JOE VERNON
FRED EGGINGTON	JOHN OWENS	STAN WARD
KEITH JONES	JIM PEACOCK	

*The serving staff are kept "on the lines" by
Frank Marshall (prompt) and made up (a look
presumable) by John Phillips assisted by Gordon Pitt*

KITCHEN STAFF under the direction of M. Maurice Maling

TOMMY ACKROYD	SAM ELLIS	JIM SEAWARD
MICK BORDGAN	JOE RICHARDSON	MIKE WHITTAKER

*During the meal music will be played by M. Harry Clough.
The musical arrangements are by M. Maurice Maling with
some assistance from M. Arthur Sullivan, and quite a lot
of help from Messieurs Sam Salisbury and Austin Wright*

The New Boys

By way of introducing the new members of the staff we give
the following biographical notes:—

NORCROSS, GEOFFREY
Education: Read Chemistry at Manchester. Spent a year at
either Princeton U.S.A. or Princetown Dartmoor—we're not sure
which. Served during the war—as a waiter at Claridges.
Interests — hardly anyone.

OWENS, JOHN
Education: Read Haberdashery at Merchant Taylors. Rowed at
Oxford. Read something but can't remember what. Interests—
shooting, following the beagles, hunting, etc.—the usual pursuits
of a Country Member.

REID, STEWART
Education: Read Motors at Oxford. Served for three years as a
regular in the WRNS—"the happiest years of my life". Interests—
beer.

WHITTAKER, MIKE
Education: Read Engineering at Sheffield. Didn't understand it
so read "Per Ever Amber". Didn't understand that either. Now
a design engineer. Interests—beer.

HOW GOOD ARE YOU?

The following quiz is designed to test your general knowledge.

1. A woman is a term applied to (a) A religious sect, (b) A Greek
   mythological creature, (c) A works manager.

2. "My secretary has a beautiful figure". Is this true or false?

3. In the sentence "They have just built a palatial entrance to 0.1
   building", what is the object?

4. Name my ten Commercial Directors.

5. What is the name of the Research Works Manager? Is he Childe
   with a plural "r" or is he just decidedly singular?

6. Who said "God, this is an artful place" (a) Capt. Scott,
   (b) Dr. K.A.G. Millar, (c) The Gas Plant Manager?

7. The "Laughing Cavalier" is (a) A portrait by Frans Hals, (b) A
   soubriquet for Dr. Rout?

8. Curie is (a) Her nuff, (b) Something highly active, (c) The
   cause of stomach trouble?

---

of is a piping general arrangement drawing. The mental effort to fully comprehend and understand what is being proposed is so exhausting that we seldom have enough mental energy left to make worthwhile suggestions to improve the design. This is where the piping design model comes in. On the Butanols Refinery we had the first piping design model in Billingham Division. At the same time Dyestuffs Division were using the same firm of model makers, Industrial Models Ltd, and we had several very useful discussions with Stan Lyon and Peter Adams of Dyestuffs Division on our respective projects. We also used this project to introduce girls from the tracing office to become part of the drawing office team to draw the isometric drawings of individual pipes. The drawing office shop stewards complained about the girls coming into the drawing office taking work which they considered was their members' work. I am glad to say that this was not supported by the men in the drawing office, and the girls were welcomed in, and we had no further adverse comments.

The Butanols Refinery started up at the end of February 1957 and within a week Ernie Wright, the plant engineer, telephoned me to say how well the refinery had started. This was the compliment I most valued. Ernie was one of

Piping Design Model for Butanols Plant, 1956/57

Butanols Plant as built

those characters whom I describe as 'the salt of the earth'. He started at Billingham as a fitter and worked his way up to be the plant engineer, and when I was on Oil works as a trainee engineer I found Ernie so helpful and modest. When ICI commissioned Mr Wheatley to paint portraits of some fifty ICI staff, Ernie Wright was one of them. Looking back on this early experience of leading the Butanols team brings home to me the excitement and thrill of pulling together all the bright ideas. It wasn't all plain sailing though. There was one occasion when I was truly grateful to Sam Salisbury's guiding hand. There was a design section which was responsible for all the piping on the pipe bridges and supplied the important services of steam, water and chemicals. The design engineers didn't enjoy the commitment which those of us with a specific plant to build enjoyed. It was very routine, and design engineers were pushed from pillar to post with conflicting demands. Nor did they attract and keep the same high quality of staff in the drawing office which we on project design could attract. The design and ordering of the pipework on the pipe bridges for us was slipping badly from the programme. Bob Syres, my section leader in the Drawing Office, tried hard to impress his opposite number, but with little effect. I tried the design engineer, but with no more success. The completion date of the whole project was now in jeopardy, and in desperation I took the problem to Sam. As soon as I described the situation, Sam said 'Come with me'. So we went round to see George Taylor, who was in charge of this service design section. We entered George Taylor's office and after the usual friendly greetings Sam said: 'George, we are in the shit'. George was soon asking what he could do to help. When we left, George had agreed to do all I had asked for, and as promised he subsequently carried it out. I do not know to this day which other projects suffered, but Sam had used some of his good will with George for the benefit of my project.

The preliminary and piping design models played an important part in improving the flow of experience and ideas to be incorporated into the design. In the end I wrote an ICI central file report on the 'Use of models in design and construction'.[2] It came out almost six years to the day after my earlier effort on 'The design of tube plates for heat exchangers'. Compliments flew around and it was around this time that I was promoted from plant level status to section status, as it was known.

The planning of design work and functional design

1957 was in many ways a follow-up to the success of the Butanols Refinery, with the new design tool of the Piping design model. We had a string of visitors from other parts of ICI, and Sam Salisbury and I found ourselves giving talks on piping design models.

The experience of the Butanols project gave me the opportunity to develop my thoughts on the planning of design work, and in particular the staff requirements of draughtsmen at the various stages of the design sequence. I was supported in doing the collecting together and editing of the planning of the drawing office staff load on the Butanols Refinery by Sam Salisbury. By the end of August Sam was dropping hints to me of the possibility of a major re-organization of the whole of the Billingham Division.

On 30 October we heard that the old Billingham was to be split. Billingham Division was to keep the ammonia and fertilizer business, while the new division, to be called Heavy Organic Chemicals (HOC) is to have all the petrochemical products on oil works and olefine works. We were told the names of the divisional directors. Melville McKay was to be the engineering director of Billingham, and Duncan Brown was to be the engineering director of HOC Division. Sam Salisbury told me in confidence that he was to be Melville McKay's No. 2, and dropped hints to me that I would not be disappointed.

By 22 October Duncan Brown had seen the draft of my note on planning and was keen that it should come out as an official report. When I next saw Duncan

---

[2] 'The Use of Models in Design and Construction' by KAG Miller, ICI Billingham Division Central File report No. B.17,134 issued 7 June 1957.

Brown on 4 November he chatted about functional design in the new division. I should explain that we already had functional design for civil engineering covering the design and ordering for the drains, foundations, structures and buildings. Naturally the design engineers here were qualified civil engineers. We also had specialist sections for electric motors and an instrument section for the sophisticated instruments and control systems which were developing fast. Up until this point in time the design and ordering for the mechanical equipment of pumps, vessels and piping were undertaken by the project section who were responsible for the overall layout of the plant, the cost control and the completion on time.

There are clear advantages in having separate design sections as the design engineers build up their knowledge of the engineering companies with whom we place orders for equipment such as pumps and vessels and for contracts such as piping fabrication and erection. Duncan Brown had come across functional engineering in the offices of major engineering contractors such as MW Kelloggs who designed complete ethylene crackers for ICI which had been built on Olefine Works at Wilton. Duncan Brown was keen that the new HOC engineering department should have functional design sections to carry out the design and ordering of the mechanical equipment. I was soon asked to let him have the breakdown of the time spent in mechanical design, which I quickly produced and I naturally incorporated them into my report on planning which was published on 13 January 1958.

Jack Lofthouse, then Oil works engineer, had commented on my draft planning report in November and I wrote in my diary that 'he was most complimentary'. By the end of December it was announced that Jack Lofthouse was to be Duncan Brown's No. 2.

Engineering Department, Heavy Organic Chemicals Division

Early in January 1958 I was told by Duncan Brown that I would be project group engineer in the new HOC engineering department in charge of all the project engineers. I wrote in my diary on 7 January – 'I knew Sam had hinted at this, but when I was told officially I could hardly credit it. It is a pretty colossal step up. Bob Malpas is also to get the same status and will be in charge of mechanical design.'

Two other group engineers were appointed: Lewis Jenkins in charge of the civil design group and Guy Shute the instrument and electrical group engineer. I had worked closely with Lewis Jenkins on the Butanols refinery when his draughtsmen did the civil engineering, and I had already found him a first class man to work with. I was delighted when I heard of Lewis's appointment. Guy Shute I had not worked so closely with in the past, but he very soon became a valued member of Jack Lofthouse's team. The final member of the team in charge of administration group was Ken Leigh-Winter, who had recently retired from the Army with the rank of Brigadier. Ken was a little put out as he was not allowed to use his Army title at work. To his military mind 'Mr' was for non-commissioned officers, but this was industry. Jack Lofthouse was a first class engineer and like Duncan Brown and myself was a Cambridge man. Some people found him domineering, but this never worried me. We might disagree, and would state our opinions openly, but we always respected the other's point of view and there were never any hard feelings.

Bob Malpas began to build up his Group of three sections of (i) machine design (ii) vessel design and (iii) piping design. I took over the immediate running of the oil and olefine sections which had been doing both the project engineering as well as the mechanical design, and Bob Malpas would do the mechanical design of all new projects as they became live. By this means we ensured that there were no unfortunate hiccups of trying to pass over the mechanical design half way through the design sequence. I was only too delighted for Bob's staff to become operational, but both of us and Jack Lofthouse wished to ensure a smooth transfer to the new functional design. I was gratified to find that my report on the planning of design work[3] was the basis by which we would estimate the drawing office requirements for staffing, and the new piping design section took my report as the starting point for their methods of working.

Duncan Brown was very keen on the functional mechanical design, having seen how MW Kelloggs operated in designing the early olefine plants, and as engineering director of the new division he was keen for an early implementation. I recorded in my diary on 13 November 1958 'JD Brown had a meeting of the group engineers to see how we are getting along with the reorganization. JD was pressing hard for us to swing over quickly. We had an interesting discussion on the handling of small projects. JD is coming round to the view that the load on the project Group is pretty great and will continue to be so.'

I was clearly getting on well with Jack Lofthouse (JAL) and on 22 September I recorded in my diary 'JAL was quite chatty and started to talk aloud re our future drawing office loading. It is a gratifying sign of his confidence.' Then at the end of the year there is an entry for 19 December when I wrote 'I had a long chat with Jack Lofthouse. He became very chatty and told me about the recent meeting Saunders (the division chairman) had had with the management. It was on this occasion when they were instructed to pass more work down the line that Jack said how fortunate he was in his henchmen. It is quite clear that Jack will continue to delegate the work, and as in the last year, I will continue to have a large say in the running of the department.' It was indeed an indication on how well the new department's senior staff were working as a team.

1959 showed the signs that I was now part of the senior staff. I had already been invited to join the senior management luncheon room, and in March I had my

---

[3] 'The Planning of Design Work' by KAG Miller, ICI Billingham Division Central File report B.123,172 issued December 1957.

first experience of interviewing candidates for joining the company as technical officers. There was a well established system whereby three or four senior staff took part. Each in turn interviewed the candidate on a one to one interview. Each interviewer then wrote a brief report and rated the candidate from $\alpha+$ to $\beta-$. The interviewers then met up with the personnel manager for an interview conference. The personnel manager read out the three reports. The conference then decided whether or not to offer a job and at what salary. The most senior interviewer would then see the candidate and tell the individual the result of the conference. It was interesting to see how one's subjective judgement compared with that of one's colleagues. Later in March I had my second experience of technical officer interviews, and on 12 March I wrote in my diary 'More interviews. This time three candidates. This time we turned them all down. I thought one of them should have been offered a job, but Charles Tanner (Ammonia Works engineer) marked him right down. Quite incredibly Mayne (Billingham engineering director) gave him $\alpha-$. Harry North (HOC production director) $\alpha-$. I gave him $\beta+$ and Tanner gave him $\beta-$.

Jack Lofthouse spent a great deal of time during 1958 in developing a scheme for new offices for HOC division at Wilton, but early in 1959 the ICI main board turned the proposal down. The question of offices for the new division was a recurring theme and I will refer to the position as it was much debated over the next decade.

At the beginning of September I started a secondment with British Rail, and Bob Malpas took over from me as project group engineer. Before leaving I went into print with a series of notes to Jack Lofthouse on (i) drawing office loading, (ii) principles for a new project system, (iii) some thoughts on estimating of capital works, and (iv) basis for design manning forecast curves. This was me putting down a marker on how I thought the department should continue to develop.

On Friday 14 August I said my farewells to Jack Lofthouse and I recorded in my diary 'He was most appreciative of how I had backed him up. I could honestly reciprocate it and said how much I enjoyed working in the HOC engineering department.'

CHAPTER 5

Secondment to British Rail

O NE DAY TOWARDS THE END OF March 1959 Mr Banks, the ICI personnel director, was visiting the division, and quite out of the blue I was interviewed by him and Sammie Saunders the HOC division chairman and his deputy, Jim Palmer. It was suggested to me that I might be put forward for a one to two year secondment to the British Transport Commission (BTC). A few days later I was told that Paul Chambers had asked Sammie Saunders for a sample of my written work, and next day I wrote in my diary 'Dr Saunders told me I had made a good impression on Mr Banks. Sammie was quite impressed how I had conducted myself at the interview. I left "Sammie" with copies of my reports on "Models" and "Planning of design Work" to send to Banks as examples of my work.'

From then on the top people both in my division and at Millbank were doing everything they could to safeguard my position and ensure that I had a return ticket to my division. I was interviewed by Mr Dunbar the manpower adviser, and Mr Hollingworth the traffic adviser, both at BTC. It was suggested that I should be PA to Mr Hollingworth, but they only had the vaguest idea of what I would actually do. Nevertheless it was agreed that my secondment should go ahead.

John Gough of ICI's central personnel department was to be my main contact with ICI during my secondment, and on a visit with John to BTC on 24 July we were introduced to Sir Brian Robertson, the Chairman of BTC, and I had a twenty minute interview with him. I remember that he asked what position I had in ICI and I explained that I was in charge of all the project engineers carrying out the capital programme in HOC Division. Sir Brian was sufficiently impressed and as he was concerned about the British Rail Modernization Programme he decided at the last moment to send me along to the London Midland Region to be the PA to Mr Arthur Pearson, the assistant general manager who was responsible for the electrification of the London–Manchester–Liverpool line. While this was a bit of a shock, as I only heard about it a few days before I was due to start with BTC, in reality it was an absolute blessing and made the whole secondment a wonderful experience for me.

Electrification of Euston–Manchester–Liverpool line

On 1 September after a few words with Mr Dunbar, the manpower adviser, I was taken over to Euston and met Mr Pearson the assistant general manager. In my diary for this first day I wrote of him 'Outspoken, but honest. I think I will like working with him'. This comment of mine was fully justified by our subsequent working relationship.

I was in attendance at the regular Monday morning meeting which Mr Blee, the general manager, held with the chief officers on the electrification project. The Railway's engineering organization was traditionally divided into three departments. The chief civil engineer's department was responsible for the design and construction of all the rail tracks, the bridges, stations and other buildings. The chief mechanical and electrical engineer's department was responsible for all locomotives, coaches and freight wagons. The signals engineer's department was the tail end charlie who was responsible for the signals and internals of signal boxes. He didn't even have the title of chief engineer, and this meant a lot in railway circles.

The civil engineer's department controlled the site of the railway. The mechanical and electrical engineers came along to supply the locomotives, coaches and wagons. With electrification a new complication arose with the mechanical and electrical engineers coming along for the first time with overhead gantries to carry the high voltage cables from which the electric locomotives draw their power. It was now important, too, that the signal engineers' coloured light signals were not obscured by the overhead gantries of the power cables. It was obvious from this new situation that there had to be detailed co-ordination in the design and building of the new equipment for the electrification. Engineers would spend the whole of their career within their own department and there was no cross-fertilization of staff. Departmentalism was rampant.

By the time I arrived at Euston it had been agreed in principle that a chief electrification project officer was needed, but no one had yet been appointed. A planning department was in being to co-ordinate the pre-authorization stage of capital proposals and to write up the financial case and the planning officer, Bill Reynolds, was already in post. I was familar with the equivalent situation in HOC Division. I was very soon involved with Bill Reynolds drafting a note on the relationship between the two departments. A few days later we saw Arthur Pearson on the two remits and he agreed with our general proposals.

In mid October FL Lambert was appointed chief project officer, but before he could take up the post I found myself chairing the first ever progress meeting of the electrification project on Friday 23 October. Sure enough the civil engineers' representative raised the problem of water troughs on the lines to be electrified. Once overhead cables were installed and became operational the water troughs could no longer be used because of electicity shorting to earth. I asked how many water troughs we had on the lines to be electrifed and was told 126. I immediately said we couldn't sort this out that afternoon, and I asked Mr Kirby of traffic services department to chair a working party. This was pretty straightforward, but to my astonishment Mr Butland, the chief civil engineer, raised the matter of water troughs at the general manager's meeting the following Monday. I immediately intervened and explained that the question of water troughs came up at the progress meeting the previous Friday and a working party has been set up to examine the problem and make recommendations. Mr Blee was clearly delighted and thanked me profusely. Both Bill Reynolds and Arthur Pearson were also delighted and as Arthur Pearson said to me afterwards 'We are launched'. Mr Butland was not pleased. I had already clashed with him because at a meeting for the replanning of electrification I had the nerve to ask about the cost of raising bridges to allow for the electrified cables, and horror of horrors a civil engineer from the Commission gave the answer. According to Mr Butland, only his officers from his department should give an opinion on civil engineering costs. On this earlier occasion I had done my best to pacify him without giving ground and leaving myself room to manoeuvre in the future. As I wrote in my diary 'it is a ridiculous business of professional pride and departmentalism'.

I decided very early in my secondment that as soon as a railwayman was available I would hand over any executive work I had been doing and retire gracefully. This I did with the progress meetings and immediately handed over to Mr Lambert. This made a great difference to my relations with Pearson, Lambert and Reynolds. I continued to sit in on many of their meetings. It was at their specific invitation, and it was clearly in a supportive role. I had been instrumental in urging the use of 'bar charts' to progress both drawing office work and site construction, and had chaired two meetings on 12 and 25 November to agree the boundaries of the 44 areas or items as we called them. By the end of February 1960 for the first time we had bar charts before us and in my diary of 26 February I wrote 'They did the job well. The technical departments will need watching and keeping up to the mark.' By the end of March I wrote 'It is well under way with Mr Lambert so well in charge that I could easily disappear completely.'

Both Mr Lambert and Bill Reynolds were first class executives and I felt that the management of London Midland Electrification was going ahead well. They both wished to recruit a strong team in their departments. Mr Lambert was looking for his assistant project officer. From the applications which he had received there was a bright Cambridge civil engineer, MCB Johns, whom Mr Lambert was keen to interview. As I said in my diary of 27 January 1960 'Butland, the chief civil engineer, tried to delay approving his list, and then recommended a much older candidate of 57 and not Johns. Pearson however agreed that they should see Johns.' Next day Lambert took his interviews for his assistant and I wrote in my diary 'Lambert told me later that they are choosing Johns for the job, but that Butland is objecting – incredible'. On Friday 29 January I wrote 'Lambert told me that at lunch both Arkle and Cox thought he was wrong to take Johns. It might prevent him becoming a chief officer by taking him out of his department. It just shows how narrow some people are in their outlook.' Then on 3 February I wrote in my diary 'I gather that Butland may get his way over

Johns. Blee and Pearson are afraid that he (Butland) may have a nervous breakdown.' In the end Butland won, and he kept Johns in his Department. This showed up very clearly how deeply ingrained is the idea of a career wholly within one department.

Bill Reynolds had his problems too and on 30 March 1960 I wrote 'I sat in on the interviewing of the candidates for Reynolds' young men in the planning office. We chose two good young men, Peel & Holdroyd. Both graduates and traffic apprentices. They were the only two graduates and were No's 96 and 97 on the list of 105 candidates.' At least Bill Reynolds' persistence has paid off.

Personnel policy

Arthur Pearson had been chairing a committee of assistant general managers to report to the railway general managers on 'Entry into the Railway Service and training of persons for senior posts in the future'. I had already had discussions with Arthur Pearson on personnel policy. In mid December Arthur showed me an early draft of their report, and invited me to comment.

I thought the report itself was very good, and they were facing up to some of the deterrents to recruit good staff and in my comments I agreed with them that the most important points are (i) the poor financial position of the railways, (ii) the impact of politics on the organization and (iii) the relatively poor prospects of remuneration in the middle period.

I elaborated on these points in turn, calling on my ICI experience. I emphasized the trend of a larger percentage of young men now going to university and the importance of looking more to the universities for the high quality recruits.

Arthur Pearson appreciated my relating the railway recruiting problem to my ICI experience, and while I could speak with some knowledge of the recruitment of engineers I offered to go back to ICI central personnel department to check the position of other streams of entry for chemists, physicists and arts graduates. This offer was followed up and I was able to give Arthur Pearson an informative note on ICI's recruitment of the other disciplines.

Clearly my comments on recruitment met with the agreement of both Arthur Pearson and also of David Blee, the general manager, so in February 1960 I decided to put down in print my thoughts not just on recruitment, but a wider report on the Management of British Railways.

This covered not only the calibre of present staff, recruitment, but also training, experience and promotion policy. I went on to comment on the organization including the 'line and staff' policy, and in my view the need to emphasise the line function. Finally I commented on the modernization plan and the need for a degree of inter-departmental co-ordination not experienced before.

On 10 March I received useful comments on my first draft of my report on the Management of British Railways in a long discussion with Blee and Pearson, largely agreeing with the points I was making. My report was finally typed by 12 April and that same evening David Blee and Arthur Pearson entertained me to dinner at the Athenaeum Club.

My report on 'Some comments on the Management of British Railways' has until now been a private communication. What follows is a brief precis of what strikes me in retrospect as the key features. For those who wish to see the full report it appears in Appendix II.

In the Introduction I emphasized that these comments were 'my personal opinions and are not necessarily the official views of the British Transport Commission, the London Midland Region or Imperial Chemical Industries Ltd'. I said 'I shall always be indebted to Mr Blee and Mr Pearson for the way they launched me in the Region. The arrangement they made for me to join in meetings of the chief officers gave me a rare opportunity to see the senior management at work.' My comments on recruitment and training of staff largely echo the views expressed in the report of Arthur Pearson's committee.

On the quality of staff I said 'The importance of having first-class men in all ranks of management has not been fully appreciated. Despite this there are still some outstanding men in the railway service. The regret is that there are so few of them.' I went on to say 'The immediate post war loss of young staff now aged 35 to 50, due no doubt to the uncertainty of nationalization and the unsettling effect of war service, has left an unfortunate gap. The opinion has been expressed to me that those who left included some of the best men of that age group. The full impact of this loss will be more heavily felt when the present 'over 50s' have retired. These older men were too far committed in pension schemes to leave the service in 1946–1950, and are now carrying the bulk of the load of middle and top management. It must be remembered, too, that these older men grew up in the inter-war years when the railways were on little more than a care and maintenance basis. These same men have in the last six years set in motion the virtual re-building of the railways, at a pace which would stretch the capacity of the most progressive industrial firm. It is not surprising, therefore, that there is a shortage of men of imagination and foresight, who can grasp the essentials of any problem and not get lost in a welter of detail.'

I went on to say 'There is a regrettable tendency for staff to be limited in their outlook by the confines of their department. Far too often, I have heard chief officers express a narrow, parochial view. The fact that the departments are so large and that chief officers arrive at the head of their department towards the end of a long career spent entirely within this one department no doubt contributes greatly to this extreme departmentalism.' I went on to say 'In formulating this criticism of the calibre of the present staff, I have been greatly helped by the willingness of the staff themselves to be forthcoming in their views'.

I finished the chapter on the 'Calibre of Present staff' by saying 'The railways are such a highly technical and specialized industry, that I do not think the importing of first-class men with experience in other industries will offer any effective solution. I am convinced the long-term salvation must rest on the recruitment of young men of ability, for a career in the railway service. They must be given the right training and experience to develop the necessary qualities, so that in 20 years time there will be enough of them in all ranks to ensure a strong, lively management.'

On 'Recruitment' I was in agreement with the Pearson Report that the three deterrents to recruitment were (i) The poor financial position of the railways, (ii) The impact of politics on the organization and (iii) The relatively poor prospects of remuneration in the middle period of service. From what I was able to assess, the salary prospects were only about 50% – i.e only half the salaries available in private industry, and this is the heart of the problem. I pointed out that 'the static or contracting position of the railways has a bearing on the relative prospects in the middle period. Young men are well aware that an organization which is expanding creates middle management jobs in the process and can have a big effect in giving early promotion to some. I know at first hand how the rapid expansion of ICI on Teesside since the war has given early promotion to a considerable number of young men.' I went on to say that 'The dead hand of promotion by seniority can have a disastrous effect on the prospects in the middle period, and this will scare off ambitious, able young men more quickly than anything else. I have formed the opinion that the effect of advertising vacant positions, combined with the alacrity with which the staff union is prepared to take up the case of the unsuccessful, but senior candidate, does produce a tendency for the selection board to take the easy way out and promote the senior man.'

I go on to assess the source of future talent and refer to more and more young men of ability going on to university. I suggested that since the war the quality of the traffic apprentices has dropped. The quality of the internal candidates has declined due to the educational trends mentioned above and the prospects offered certainly do not attract outstanding graduates. I was convinced 'that the railways have some radical re-thinking to do in their staff policy, and that if they wish to get their fair share of the future talent for top management they must look more and more to the universities.'

On training, experience and promotion policy, I said 'The organization must be adjusted so that in the first five to seven years after the apprenticeship, the young men are moved round to a series of jobs in different departments giving them wide experience and at the same time giving them some real responsibility'. I would recommend 'a deliberate policy of moving the ex-traffic apprentices round the operating department, commercial department and motive power department in a variety of jobs in their first five to seven years after the apprenticeship.'

The railways lost some good men after the war. I suggested trying to attract some of the good ex-traffic apprentices back, but they are up against an agreement with the unions that they would have to start again on the bottom rung. I suggested it would be worthwhile pressing the unions to rescind this particular agreement.

On the organization I again referred to 'the emphasis placed on their profession by chief officers and their career history of experience only within their own department tends to make them oblivious of the points of view and requirements of other departments. I have not observed any sense of corporate responsibility amongst the chief officers.'

I said that 'I am certain that "line and staff" policy must be accepted as the basis of the organization'. I quoted Kelf-Cohen's definition in his book on nationalization. ' "Line" is the chain of administrators responsible for deciding on policy and its execution; "staff" are the technical advisers to each level in the "line"; they advise on the best technical means of carrying out the policy decided by the "line" '.

I said that 'Regrettably, there is evidence of British Transport Commission's Railways central staff using the functional channels to the Regions for executive control'.

I was convinced that 'greater decentralization of functional responsibility and authority to the Regions must take place'. I also pressed for a more industrial type of Board in the Regions. In summarizing this section I said 'I am certain that "line and staff" policy must be accepted as the basis of the organization. One and only one line of executive authority should be clearly defined. At a time when there is a bias for the senior staff to place so much emphasis on functional matters, the supremacy of "line" over "staff" should be exaggerated.'

Stedeford Committee

On 6 April the government announced the setting up of a new planning board to look into the affairs of the Railways. As I wrote in my diary 'Planning board announced: Sir Ivan Stedeford, chairman of Tube Investments, as chairman, other members Mr CF Kearton, managing director of Courtaulds, Dr R Beeching, technical director of ICI and Mr HA Benson, partner in Cooper Bros chartered accountants. I was truly delighted. As well as Beeching being ICI, Kearton is ex Billingham.'

'Thursday 7 April: Pearson saw me first thing about the planning board.' I wrote in my diary 'Labour are up in arms about no TUC rep on it and editorials not very favourable. Pearson's greatest fear is that the present commission will prevent the planning board finding out the facts. He as good as invited me to get my highly critical report on the management of British Railways into Dr Beeching's hands.'

On Friday 8 April I wrote: 'I went over to Millbank and saw John Gough. I told him about relations between LM Region and the commission re planning board (now to be called BTC advisory group). I also said the region have as good as invited me to get my highly critical report back to the buildings. I will let John have my report as soon as it is typed and he will offer it to CM Wright (ICI personnel director) who is sure to see the point and pass it on.'

I posted my report to John Gough on Wednesday 13 April. By Tuesday 26 John Gough told me over the phone that Mr Wright had said that my magnum opus was splendid. Then next day John telephoned me in the evening, asking me to lunch the following Monday. As I wrote in my diary, 'Beeching & Wright are to be there! Well well, the plot thickens. I only wish Pearson would return so that I can keep him informed. (Mr Pearson's wife had sadly died over the previous week-end).'

On Monday 2 May I went over to Millbank for lunch. As I wrote in my extended diary for that day 'I had lunch with Mr Wright, Dr Beeching and Ray Pennock (John Gough was down with flu). Beeching was quizzing me about my views on the railway management. The planning board have been sent off to the eastern region to see their wonderful decentralization – Beeching and company doubt the wisdom of bringing commercial and operating departments together. He has clearly discovered the trouble of the commercial areas cutting across the line operation. When Beeching first said they had been sent to the eastern, I said "Oh I might have known that!" Ray Pennock laughed with great glee and Beeching smiled.

'I told Beeching what Russell Currie has said "Struggling with a self adjusting soggy sponge" and I told him the tale of the signal engineering department. He was amused at our antics, but I think he saw the point that they were stalling. In the same connection Mr Wright asked me what the management thought about the planning board. I said that the general manager and assistant general manager levels were clearly concerned and had to go easy as they had their careers to think of. Dr Beeching said they appreciated this. I said the lower levels didn't really think they would be affected.

'Beeching asked me about capital proposals and were they economically examined. I told him the story of the electrification and gave him the low-down re electrics and diesels. He said he had already asked for the report. I mentioned the original Mertz and McLellan report. He agreed that they were too far committed, though I did hint that it might be stopped south of Crewe, but quite a lot would have to be written off.

'We discussed the prima donna chief engineers. Beeching was quite certain there should only be one head of all technical departments in a Region. I fully agreed. He also agreed that the present area board set-up was an oddity for middle management.

'We talked about the unions' influence in staff matters. I told the tale of the organization changes having to be told to the junior staff by the unions. Beeching agreed that this was the surrender of management function. I stressed this was since nationalization and hinted at Sir John Benstead. I explained that many railwaymen agreed, but Roberts said "they have their lords and masters".

'They were all most interested in the parochial attitude as a result of spending their whole career within their own departments and also the professionalism of technical officers. Beeching said that "we have some of that in our company".

'I had the impression that Beeching and his colleagues are starting from square one and questioning the need for a railway. He has not received a convincing answer yet. He is not impressed by the argument that the railways exist, if we have to spend a further £1,600 million – this is virtually rebuilding it.

'Beeching on leaving said he hoped to see me again soon – I wonder if I will be called! Mr Wright said jokingly that HOC would get a shock when I came back. I stressed finally the unofficial nature of my comments and Beeching said he appreciated this.'

Two days later on Wednesday 4 May I wrote in my diary 'Mr Pearson came in for a short time. He told me from what Mr Blee had told him of Mr Blee's talk with Sir Ivan, it was clear Sir Ivan was quoting from my report. So it has reached Sir Ivan! Mr Pearson told me that he and Blee are going to stall on putting in the commercial/operating set up of Sir Reginald Wilson. I think they feel they are getting the ear of the planning board and it is worth fighting. Pearson also said that Sir Ivan has latched onto my suggestion of a regional board with full time executives.'

Early in February it had struck me that the planning system and the use of bar charts to progress the work on the electrification project was well launched. The planning department was also fully operational and I had made my main contribution, so I told Mr Pearson I could do with something more to occupy myself. Shortly afterwards he invited me to comment on the Martech Consultants report on General Merchandise Freight Traffic. This was another story that I will come to later.

Then when it became clear that the Stedeford Committee were looking critically at the electrification project Arthur Pearson agreed I should effectively retire from the work of helping Lambert and Reynolds on the electrification Project. Nevertheless both Lambert and Reynolds were so concerned at how their re-appraisal of the electrification project was proceeding, that they both were seeking my opinion on the draft notes which they were preparing to submit to the Stedeford Committee.

Thus it was I continued to know unofficially how they were presenting the case and they often consulted me on how I thought it would be received by Dr Beeching. The whole concept of the electrification project was correctly based on a comparision between diesels and electric locomotives, bearing in mind that electrification required the additional cost of the overhead electric cable system, which is an additional cost that has to be debited against the scheme. On the other hand the capital and operating costs of electric locomotives were considerably cheaper than the equivalent diesels. As the traffic density increases the case for electrification improves, and there is a cross-over point, when electrification is financially justified. In the very early assessments done on the London to Manchester railway the total traffic was above this cross-over point and the fundamental decision was taken to proceed with the project. However, when they came to develop the scheme in detail, they discovered that a considerable amount of the traffic was cross traffic which started on other lines and had a short distance on the electrified line before going off on another line. The railwaymen judged that a train would need to be on the electrified line for at least 50 miles to justify changing the engine to an electrical locomotive, and for less than 50 miles it was operationally preferred to keep the same diesel locomotive on the train and run it under the electrified line. There was so much of this cross traffic that they reckoned at the final count they needed 236 electric locomotives and 271 diesels to run under the electrified lines. This put them below the break even point, and diesels had a better financial case. Instead of coming clean and admitting the position, the railwaymen struggled on trying to prove the impossible. The original proposals had taken 1957 as the base line and assumed a steady growth. They now projected forward to 1970, but completely ignored the serious drop in receipts between 1957 and 1959. In these critical two years London Midland had a drop of 18.1% in freight train traffic, though the passenger train receipts only dropped by 0.4%. Overall the London Midland Region receipts had dropped from £145 million in 1957 to £127.9 million in 1959. The interest rate they had assumed for the extra capital was only 4%, while in reality the money has to be borrowed at a rate which varied between 5 and 6%. They also assumed £2.0 million additional receipts from passenger traffic due to electric traction and that the passengers will be put off by the diesel fumes.

On Tuesday 17 May I wrote in my diary 'I gathered from Bill Reynolds that the commission are producing a note on electrification for the planning board. Reynolds discussed it with Wansborough-Jones yesterday and said it was a good case. When I pressed the use of 4% interest rates when we really paid 5½ to 6%, and the effect this had on the comparison between diesels and electrics, he looked a little sick. I mustn't press it too hard.'

On Thursday 26 May 'I saw Pearson. He was wanting my view of Beeching and the planning board. Pearson showed me the note on electrification that the planning board was to be sent. Pearson has advised them not to send it, as he reckons it would be suicide both for the commission and electrification.'

On Wednesday 20 July the Select Committee of the House of Commons report on the Railways was published. I wrote in my diary 'Part of it whitewashes Sir Brian and the commission, but other parts of it rightly castigated them, particularly on the development of capital schemes. Here they spent four pages on the LM Region Electrification.' I felt then they had been too kind to Sir Brian and the British Transport Commission. They had yet to feel the full brunt of the three industrialists and a leading accountant on the Stedeford committee.

Pearson invited me to come to the conference meeting on the reappraisal of electrification. Next day 21 July I wrote in my diary 'I read the re-appraisal of electrification and it is a poor case; future receipts are grossly overstated and the electric v diesel comparison is biased horribly towards electrics by the extra £2 million passenger receipts – no real reason: also the type of diesels put in for comparison. I told Blee and Pearson what I thought of it and said they should give the ungarnished facts. Pearson said they would be sacked if they did. Pretty appalling.'

On Friday 22 July I attended the reappraisal meeting. Pearson had altered the text on the receipts a little, by giving a range and then saying they were choosing the top end of it. I told them it would be open to criticism.

Four days later at lunch in the Euston officer's mess I threw out the jocular comment that what we needed were men in high places who could afford to resign and retire to their estates in a huff. There was one of those unexpected silences and my jocular comment was heard by all present. The president of the mess turned round to me and said 'Dr Miller, You do not know how right you are'.

On Wednesday 17 August I wrote in my diary: 'I gathered from Bill Reynolds that the electrification report is back from being printed and is to go on to the government and no doubt the planning board. I told Bill Reynolds that from my knowledge of the way businessmen think, it will be shot down in flames.

Liner trains and Martech Report

The London Midland Region had called in Martech Consultants Ltd to examine the general merchant business between London and Manchester. They discovered that the road competition were offering and giving an overnight service while the traditional railway service with marshalling yards gave a variable delivery of between 1 and 13 days. This of course was quite unacceptable and it was not surprising that the railways were only carrying 1.0% of the general merchant business between London and Manchester. Martech Consultants pointed out that what the railways could do best was the transport from railhead to railhead. Their real problem was the collection and delivery of goods at either end of the journey. Here flexibility of road transport was dominant. What Martech were recommending was to use road transport at either end of the journey and develop a simple transfer system at the railhead by the simple device of an overhead gantry crane. This called for a standardized size of container with railtrucks and lorries to match.

I recorded on Monday 18 July 1960 that 'Pearson told me they are going to set up a domestic working party on containers and would I go on it. They are also going to invite Everard Taylor of Martech.' I was only able to attend one meeting of this working party before I returned to ICI. It was reported in the minutes of the meeting on 9 August 'Dr Miller emphasized the urgency of adopting new methods of freight handling to help to take the place of the private

Presentation of 'Long Service Watch' by David Blee, September 1960

siding and to give the speed and reliability traders demanded. He felt that the suggested method involving large containers handled by gantry cranes was right, but emphasized the need for proper assessment of the costs involved.'

Arthur Pearson would have liked me to continue on this working party after I returned to ICI. Perhaps I should have, but I was keen that I should have a clean break, and this came about. I have a postcript to both electrification and liner trains, but with great relief I made my departure from the London Midland Region in good order.

At the end of my secondment I wrote a carefully worded personnel report on my secondment which, with the blessing of Blee and Pearson, went up to Sir Brian Robertson (see Appendix III). Pearson clearly wished my personal report to get to Sir Brian before I saw him. On Wednesday 31 August I wrote in my diary 'I saw Sir Brian Robertson and the short interview passed off very smoothly. We exchanged platitudes on the professionalism of Engineers. Sir Brian is going to write to Mr Chambers and thank ICI for seconding me.' The week before key staff on electrification project including Blee and Pearson presented me with a signed miniature 'bar chart' of 'LMR Euston Main Line Electrification' with an overprinted inscription 'With good wishes for your future planning and progress'. Then on the same day that I saw Sir Brian I was entertained to lunch by the general manager and his chief officers. They presented me with a 'long service' gold watch with the inscription 'Dr K.A.G. Miller London Midland Region British Railways 1959–1960'. As I said in my diary 'Blee was far too complimentary in his remarks about me. I replied as best I could.'

Friday 2 September. This was my last day at Euston. As I wrote in my diary 'At lunch the Euston mess presented me with a beautiful silver ashtray. After lunch I said good-bye to Mr Blee and Mr Pearson. Mr Blee gave me a signed photograph of my presentation.

Postscript to secondment to British Rail

I understood that in September a moratorium was placed on the electrification project and work was halted, while a fresh study was done on the project. Any new comparison at this stage between diesels and electric locomotives would have to assume that a good deal of the money already spent on electrification would have to be written off if they decided to go for diesels. This study showed that the region was so far down the electrification route that it was better to continue. Mr Marples, Minister of Transport, announced on 30 January 1961 that the London to Manchester electrification would go ahead.

It is quite possible that with further extension of electrification schemes more of the core locomotives will become electric drives and edge the ratio of electrics/diesels towards the break-even point in favour of electrics.

On 13 March 1961 it was reported that Dr Richard Beeching was to be chairman of the new railway board at his present salary of £24,000 a year. The government had made it clear when they set up the Stedeford Committee that they had given no undertaking to publish the subsequent report and they held to this.

Then on 20 July 1961 when Mr CM Wright, the ICI personnel director, along with Mr Paine, another ICI main board director, were visiting Teesside, I was present at the lunch party. I wrote in my diary that 'Mr Wright told me that Dr Beeching had submitted an independent report to the rest of the Stedeford Committee. His report was the one accepted by the government and both the Minister and the Prime Minister pressed him to take on the chairmanship. Mr Wright added that Beeching is asking Shell and Unilever for directors for the railway board.' Forty odd years on, I have every reason to believe what Mr Wright had told me is a correct version. Years later I awaited with interest the release of documents to the Public Records Office of the papers associated with the Stedeford Committee.

I discovered when I visited the Public Records Office (PRO) at Kew in January 2006 that no formal report of the Special Advisory Group (SAG), the name used for the Stedeford committee, was ever published. However the supporting papers in the Public Records Office do show that SAG recommended a writing off of some of BTC's debts and a tighter control of capital expenditure. Such minutes of the SAG which are available (27 of the 61 meetings of the SAG are available in the PRO) show that there was disagreement on the type of organization they would recommend, with Stedeford and Kearton's with one version and Beeching and Benson with another. The SAG had their last meeting on 3 October 1960 and there is no further reference to the organization problem, between the end of September 1960 and Dr Beeching's appointment in March 1961. There is nothing in the papers on the SAG that contradicts the view which Mr CM Wright, the ICI Personnel Director, expressed to me in July 1961 that Dr Beeching had submitted a separate report on the organization. The fact that less than half the minutes of the SAG are available suggests there has been a certain amount of vetting of what should be published. Another telling omission was in Mr Blee's personal papers now in the PRO. His papers go from 1946 to 1958. To my certain knowledge David Blee was still general manager at the Midland Region up to 1961 and his papers for 1959 and 1960 do not appear in the Public Records Office. I would have found these papers very pertinent to the modernization and organizational changes.

The other follow up was the work on containers and liner trains. When I left Euston, Martech were working for the London Midland Region, and there was no support at the British Transport Commission. However with the appointment of Dr Beeching the situation changed. Henry Novy wrote an excellent letter to Dr Beeching dated 9 October 1962 outlining the case for liner trains and mentioned I had worked with Martech. Then two weeks later on 31 October Dr Beeching spoke at the Institute of Directors annual conference and quoted liner trains as a feature of their freight business.

CHAPTER 6

Technical Department, Heavy Organic Chemicals Division

O N MY RETURN TO ICI, my old Division Heavy Organic Chemicals were pleased that I should rejoin them and they proposed that I should take up a new post of assistant technical manager in technical department and be the deputy to Dr Denis Huebner, the technical manager. It was understood from the beginning that I would lead an examination of the organization of technical department. I knew Denis Huebner from my days as project group engineer, and I was confident that I would get on well with him. There would be support for Denis and my efforts to improve the working of the technical department team from the deputy chairman, Jim Palmer. There was a question mark in my mind over Denis' immediate superior Dr James Woolcock, the technical director. James was the old style of 'Imperial chemist'. Often chemists had the view that you just employed chemists who got a first at Oxford and if you threw them in at the deep end they would swim! I realized that there might be problems trying to cope with this approach, but I also knew that I would have the full support of both Duncan Brown, the engineering director, and the engineering manager, Jack Lofthouse. They both expressed to me their delight that I was taking up this post.

Department re-organization

Technical department was responsible for preparing the economic case for all major capital investments in the division. They were also responsible for the chemical engineering design and the flow sheets. The engineering design and capital cost estimates were the responsibility of the engineering department. The preparation of the proposal document and liaising with sales on market information, with research department on new research information and accounts department on finance were all part of technical department's co-ordinating work.

Traditionally technical department was staffed by chemists who generally started in the company as research chemists in the research department where they spend four to five years followed by a spell on the works as a plant manager. Some of them would then move to technical department to do the economic assessments of future capital investments. By this time they were probably over 30. They were also expected to do the flowsheeting for the technical side of their projects. To many of them this was just an irritating chore, and the quality of this work often left a lot to be desired. The engineering department had the task of trying to pick up the details of the project, often with considerable difficulty.

In mid October 1960, we carried out a random observation survey to determine how much time our staff spent on economic assessments and how much on process design and flowsheeting. I wrote in my diary on 10 November, 'I had a long chat with Denis on how my job was planning out. We clearly saw eye to eye on how the re-organization of the department might go. If we can have a free hand without James Woolcock putting his spoke in our wheels we will get things in order.' At the turn of the year James was moved sideways and Charles Cockram became technical director. This was a vital improvement for Denis and myself.

The concept we developed was to create a process design group within the technical department which would do all the process design including flowsheeting. We also thought it should be staffed by chemical engineers recruited direct from university. An important part of this policy would be that after two to three years in process design, the chemical engineers would be transferred to the works to be plant managers. I was able to convince Edward Challis, the Oil works manager, to take some of these young chemical engineers. Edward was himself a chemical engineer so it was really a matter of talking to the other works manager. Within a year Frank Wrigley, the Olefine works manager, was also prepared to take these young men as plant managers. They were around the age of 25 when they got to the works, while the chemists they were replacing generally had a PhD and had spent five years in the research department which put them around 30 when they went onto the works. It was quite a cultural shock after six years in a university chemistry department followed by about five years in Billingham research department to come onto the works to deal with a labour situation of strongly entrenched unions. Many of them did make the transition, but engineers as undergraduates were more familar with uncertainty, and had not been brought up in the tradition of chasing after absolute knowledge.

For our new policy to succeed it was important to get first class young chemical engineering graduates. At that time I had formed the view that Cambridge University and Imperial College, London were producing some of the best chemical engineering graduates in the country. I was able to arrange that I involved myself with the visits to the chemical engineering departments of these two universities to do the initial interviewing. The arrangement was that the interviewing was to be done jointly with the old Billingham Division.

On 22 February 1961 I went along with Dr Clayton and Dr Harding of Billingham Division to the Cambridge chemical engineering department. In my diary of that date I wrote 'we interviewed four good candidates for jobs – too few I fear. I was able to put over our proposal for using young chemical engineers on process design. Denys Armstrong and John Davidson (both lecturers) were very enthusiastic – Dr Clayton fears I will pinch their good men!'.

I was delighted, too, that Ron Silsby was appointed to run the process design group and promoted immediately to Group Manager. I had already formed a high opinion of Ron's managerial capability, and I had been pressing for his appointment. This coupled with attracting good chemical engineers ensured the success of the group.

The new organization started on 1 May 1961, and very soon established a good reputation. A year later I wrote in my diary 'Charles Cockram told me that he had told the chairman that the process design group had fully justified itself by the tubular reactor'.

Years later when I was on the divisional board and we were having a staff movements meeting Harry North, the production director, said it was young chemical engineers that he wanted for plant managers. Praise indeed coming from Harry.

When I was Engineering Director, I had another comment about our chemical engineers and this came from an unlikely quarter. As part of the broader development of ICI as an international company, I undertook to take two young engineers from ICI Europa in Rotterdam to spend two years with HOC Division on Teesside. When Crawford Petrie, now engineering manager of ICI Europa, first discussed this with me, Crawford told me he would send over two bright Dutch engineers in their late 20s, who were Delft graduates. They were very bright, but tended to be a bit arrogant and Crawford said we really must give them work which would stretch them. I said fine and told Crawford we would put them in the start-up team for the new olefine plant. In due course their two year spell was up and they were due to return to Rotterdam. I was told that they had fitted in well, and made a useful contribution, but they had been making noises about wishing to stay with HOC on Teesside. I had to make clear to them that this was not on, and they had an important contribution to make to ICI in Rotterdam. Then I had a final chat with the pair of them to hear what they thought of their time here. One of them started off by saying he had completely changed his opinion of British engineers. He mentioned two of the chemical engineers who were on the start-up team, and said they were as good as the best Delft graduates who would be a good three to four years older. They were of course two of our best young chemical engineers or they wouldn't have been on such an important start-up team.

The two Dutchmen had clearly enjoyed their social life with other young ICI staff. They appreciated that young staff were able to buy their own home (generally a modern semi-detached) which young graduates in Holland were not able to do. I could understand this with the scarcity of land in Holland. What surprised me was the next comment, that there was more culture in Middles-brough than Rotterdam. 'Yes,' they said, 'there was a very good string quartet in Middlesbrough.' This was news to me!

Discounted cash flow

The capital cost of continous chemical plants do not increase linearly with output. It was more like a Square Root Law. Doubling the plant output will often only require about a 40% increase in the capital cost. The HOC technical department was in the lead in examining the sensitivity on actual projects. Key questions were asked of the Sales Department if greater sales could be achieved at may be lower realizations per ton of output.

The case for the cash flow approach was justified by the case of the para-xylene project. Para-xylene being one of the raw materials for terylene. The initial thinking was to compare the existing 25,000 tons per year (t/yr) plant augmented to a total capacity of 40,000 t/yr with scrapping of the existing plant and building a new plant of 40,000 t/yr. The additional capital cost of the new 40,000 t/yr plant over extending the existing plant was £740,000. Due to the reduced operating cost of the new plant, an additional net cash flow would be generated over the operating life of the new plant of £3.5 million, and this gave a discounted cash flow (DCF) rate of return of 43%. This made the case for scrapping the existing plant. The attraction of a larger scale of operation was such that the sales department launched a vigorous sales campaign and by reducing prices secured a large share of the European market. The European dimension raised the question of siting the plant at Wilton or at the factory in Rotterdam. Cash flows and DCF rates of return were called for and the most advantageous case was for a 60,000 t/yr plant at Wilton followed by 60,000 t/yr at Rotterdam. Supported by this assessment a 60,000 t/yr plant at Wilton was proposed and subsequently sanctioned by the ICI main board.

The main board were clearly impressed with our approach and on 1 August 1961 I wrote in my diary 'We had a visit from General Chemicals Division who came over to hear about cash flow. The para-xylene Form 'A' has been sent round to all and sundry as a model!'

HOC division then used DCF on a variety of projects. In May 1962 Frank Stewart, the deputy chief accountant, and I wrote a confidential report on 'Some Experience in the use of discounted cash flow'.[1]

Crude oil with Shell Mex and BP

ICI bought a fraction of crude oil (naphtha) from Shell Mex and British Petroleum (SM and BP), a joint marketing company. Naphtha was a crucial raw material for our petrochemical activities. Tom Clark, HOC Division chairman, wishing to strengthen our commercial position, persuaded SM and BP to give us the know-how for a crude oil plant taking the crude from them.

---

[1] 'Some Experience in the Use of Discounted Cash Flow' by KAG Miller and FE Stewart, ICI Heavy Organic Chemicals Division report O.20,455 issued 11 May 1962.

ICI and SM and BP set up a technical committee for the handing over of this know-how and I found myself leading the ICI team from the technical and engineering departments. By this time, in April 1961, our two departments were working well together and the situation and flow of information on our part was well defined.

SM and BP were a marketing outfit and they had to call on their parent companies for the technical specification, and it varied between the two main companies. I described the first meeting on 14 April 1961 as decidedly sticky at first, but it warmed up later. For the second meeting I was able to say in my diary 'It went much better than the first one', though at the meeting on 22 September 'As usual it started off with one of their key men being bloody awkward. It finished much better and we were fortunately in agreement on the preferred contractor. When we met on 5 October they came up to Teesside, and I chaired the meeting. I wrote in my diary that day 'We covered a lot of detail and it seemed to go very well'. Overall the relationships were very good. I had a certain amount of wry amusement as I prodded them for advice. I remember one key question. Do we install a desalter to remove salt from the crude? BP recommended we have one, but Shell said it wasn't necessary. I prodded them to give us a firm answer. It came down to Shell's opinion winning out, since SM and BP were owned 60% by Shell and 40% by BP. So on the face of it we accepted Shell's view, but eventually we put in a desalter. The crude oil unit was authorized by the ICI main board on 29 September 1961.

Effective use of young technical officers

In February 1962 Harry North, the personnel director, persuaded his fellow directors that he should appoint a study group to discuss ways in which the energy and originality of technical officer staff may be stimulated. I was asked to chair this study group. We were a strong team of bright middle managers. As well as chairing the group, I covered for the staff in technical department. The other six members were Andrew Duncanson from research, John Hopkins from engineering, Bruce Neale from personnel, Michael Robinson from sales control, Felix Schwarz from technical services and development, and Rab Telfer from Olefine works.

We decided to discover, as a starting point, the views and opinions of technical officers on matters affecting them in their work. As a guide to our enquiries we formulated a list of questions under the following broad headings. (i) selection, (ii) placement and induction, (iii) training, (iv) functions and responsibilities, (v) delegation of authority and acceptance of responsibility, (vi) recognition and development of abilities. There were some 300 technical officers in the division, and we interviewed 60 of them. They co-operated readily in answering our questions and volunteered information on other matters as well. This was our starting point. In the summary of the report we concluded:

(i)   Although the methods and practices connected with recruitment and selection have worked reasonably well, they are capable of substantial improvement. For example, individuals promoted to jobs in which they will be required to undertake selection interviews should be trained, and established interviewers should also be given the opportunity of this training.

(ii)   The present arrangements for induction are thoroughly unsatisfactory, largely because of a lack of planning and guidance by immediate supervisors.

(iii)   There is a need for more systematic training. For example each department should prepare its own list of topics and where these occur in common in a number of departments the training should be undertaken by divisional courses and seminars.

(iv)   There is a need to re-examine the division's assessment forms and procedures for technical officers. We recommended that the division appoints a small working party to devise a revised assessment form and procedures suitable for all technical officers.

(v)   Inadequate systematic arrangments exist for technical officers to make known to heads of departments their own views about the way in which they hope their careers may develop. For example more publicity to the policy of transfers between departments of technical officers.

(vi)   Technical staff are not sufficiently confident that specialists are properly rewarded. There is a strong feeling that to achieve success in the company, individuals must turn themselves into general purpose managers at an early age. We recommend that the structure of the research department should be reorganized to permit more readily the development of a progressive career for people devoting themselves full-time to research. There should be opportunities for research scientists who remain entirely without administrative duties, to be promoted to group level. Such promotions should carry appropiate titles and all the privileges and status of managerial posts with similar salaries.

(vii)   A greater degree of delegation should be practised throughout the division. We believe managers should control by exception, leaving it to their staff to report the unusual. Delegation of authority is never helped by long lines of command, although they must be long enough to ensure that the span of control of any individual is not too wide. However within the Division there are a number of situations in which a manager has responsible to him only one person of the level immediately below. We believe there is prima facie evidence that the lines of command can be shortened so that substantial savings in middle management positions can be achieved. We strongly recommend a close examination of the lines of command.

(viii) Technical officers carry out a considerable amount of routine work which could be done by less qualified staff. We recommended that each department examines the activities of technical officers using random observation survey techniques.

(ix)   There is a degree of ignorance and misunderstanding about the functions and responsibilities both within and between departments. We recommend that the main responsibilities of all departments are examined, defined and published.

(x)   Communications to technical officers on policy matters and background information could be improved. We recommended a wider circulation of the minutes of the formal committees, or at least selected extracts from them, are circulated to the technical officers concerned.

Our report was formally submitted to Harry North on 18 July 1962. He enjoyed reading it and didn't suggest any changes. The study group felt quite rightly that the division's organization and committee system were outside the remit of the study group, but encouraged by Harry North I quickly put my thoughts down on paper with a strictly confidential note on 'Some thoughts on the division's organization and committee system'. I was very rude about 'one over one' relationships and pressed that each executive had a span of between three to six subordinates. I was particularly critical of the development management committee and the operating management committee and suggested they were replaced by five product committees. I had been influenced by the highly successful carbonylation study group. This was a shot in the dark, but Harry North was very sympathetic and before I knew it, Harry, with the chairman's agreement, circulated my note on the organization and committee systems to all the directors and to be discussed alongside the report on 'The effective use of staff of technical officer level' at the chairman's meeting on 30 July.

In the intervening days I was receiving unsolicited support. On Thursday 26 July I wrote in my diary 'Alex McLean, sales director, was most complimentary about the study group report. So was David Jones, research director. He described it as a "Do it yourself" kit for HODs. Denis Huebner has just read my report on the organization and thoroughly approved.'

On Friday 27 July I wrote in my diary 'Peter Robinson, finance director, agrees completely with my note on the organization. He said at lunch that we should save 50% of the admin staff in ICI. I put it at 30%, but JD (Duncan Brown) would only allow 10%. I suspect he is scared stiff he would be retired early. I suspect there will be some directors who are extremely lukewarm about it.'

Then on Monday 30 July I wrote 'Harry North told me that the study group's report was well received by the chairman's meeting, as was my note on the organization. There was little criticism. The directors will discuss it again. In the meantime Grange Moore, Wilton personnel director, is to call the study group together to get our views on the implementation of the recommendations. Harry North told me Sammie Saunders nearly telephoned me up last week to congratulate me on the report. This is better than we had dared to hope.'

On Friday 10 August the study group met up with Grange Moore and I wrote in my diary 'In the afternoon the study group met with Grange Moore. I had the impression that he is the old type of director wanting only brilliant people who had to be thrown in at the deep end. I hope he takes the point of specifying responsibilities and jobs.'

After our talk with Grange Moore, I was pleasantly surprised to hear from Bruce Neale that Grange Moore reported favourably to the chairman's meeting on his meeting with the study group. I can't believe why?! Bruce also saw Harry North and heard that WG Davies is being asked to look at the lines of command with the study group report beside him.

I would like to have thought that something really worthwhile came out of the the study group on the use of technical officers, but the middle management continued in their old ways. My quickly written comments on the committee system and the desirability of product committees had most influence when a year later a new area committee system was inaugurated. I will come to this in a later chapter.

By the end of 1962 I had completed the major task of examining the organization of the department, which I had been given on my appointment in 1960, and at Christmas Charles Cockram gave me a good rise, and as I wrote in my diary on 18 December 'Charles told me they are trying to find a suitable job for me. He thought I had been long enough in technical department and he felt the one ATM remaining should be a chemist. I mentioned I was afraid I might fall between the two stools of chemists and engineers.' When I had a long chat with Denis Huebner in the New Year, he was much more encouraging and considered my experience suited me for higher management. He also thought there were good prospects for me.

Sure enough, I didn't have to wait long. On 18 March I wrote in my diary 'Charles Cockram walked into my office to tell me that Bob Malpas is going to Alcudia in Spain as general manager and I will be offered the job of engineering manager of HOC. I was delighted and told Charles so. I had a few words with Bob. He goes at Easter.' I wrote in my diary on 21 March 'Maurice Hodgson congratulated me on my appointment and made the remark "next step the board"'.

CHAPTER 7

Engineering Manager, and later Engineering Director Heavy Organic Chemicals Division

I N FEBRUARY 1962 SAMMIE SAUNDERS, the HOC Division chairman, told the senior staff that HOC Division would be taking over control of the Wilton site and in due course the headquarters of the division would move to Wilton.

Merging the two engineering departments

On 1 April 1963 I started to take over from Bob Malpas and by mid April I was fully in charge of the old HOC engineering department. Bob had already been having discussions with David Reed, the Wilton engineering manager, on the merging of the two departments. On Bob's departure to Spain I immediately continued these talks. David was a real gentleman. He accepted without any reservations that I would take over the Wilton engineering department from him, and David would become PA to the division chairman for the remaining time until he reached retirement age in the following year. This change was now set for mid August.

David's opinion of the characters I was now dealing with was invaluable. Derek Portus, the construction manager at Wilton, I found difficult to deal with, but as a new boy at Wilton I didn't wish to be seen as being heavy handed. On Thursday 26 September I wrote in my diary 'JDB had a meeting with Portus and myself on construction matters. JDB fell over backwards to be considerate to Portus who personalized everything. I didn't help matters by inferring he was pressing it to the limit. JDB quietly pointed this out to me afterwards.' On 14 October I wrote in my diary 'I asked David Reed's advice about how to handle Derek Portus. I was pleased to hear that his approach was to see very little of him and get our subordinates to co-operate. I was coming round to the same view.' The following day I wrote 'Derek Portus agreed my note on the relationship between our departments.'

So it was that by mid August I was in charge of two engineering departments each having about 200 staff: HOC on the north side of the river Tees and the Wilton organization on the south side some ten miles distant. The HOC engineering department did the engineering and project work for all HOC's new capital plants. The Wilton organization did all the services, steam and electricity for all divisions operating at Wilton, and some 40% of their work was sub-contracted design work from other divisional plants at Wilton.

It was quite a task, but there was a lot going for us. I knew the HOC staff pretty well. I had been part of the original team five years ago. Lewis Jenkins in charge of civil design group, and Guy Shute in charge of instrument and electrical design were two colleagues I could trust implicitly. Their judgements on technical matters were outstanding and I could delegate activities to them with great confidence. Maurice Pool was in charge of mechanical design with the three sections of vessels, pumps and piping. I had shared digs with Maurice some ten years before. I knew him well as a sound reliable engineer. John Hopkins, the project group engineer was also out of the old HOC stable and clearly the old HOC Division senior staff were fitting in naturally to the key positions in the new organization.

On top of this I sensed from my discussions with David Reed and his colleagues that the morale at Wilton was none too good. In fact I wrote as much in my diary on 19 August. There was further confirmation of this when on 31 October I interviewed two trainee technical officers and I wrote in my diary 'I got ample confirmation that the middle ranks of the drawing office are frustrated'.

Perhaps a key decision was the appointment of the administration group manager. The choice was between Ken Leigh-Winter, a retired army brigadier who had been the HOC adminstration group manager since the division was formed in 1958 and Jim Ross, the Wilton administration manager. Jim started as a clerk at Wilton and had worked his way up. He was indeed the salt of the earth, and Duncan Brown had already decided that Jim was the man for the job. This was a key appointment. Word went round the Wilton engineering department that Jim had made it. On 18 September I wrote in my diary 'I had a session with Jim and his organization is taking shape'. There was one other area of potential friction in the functional design of vessels, pumps and piping in the equipment group. As early as 20 June I wrote in my diary 'I went over to Wilton and saw David Reed and his colleague David Simpson. They had a hundred and one reasons for going easy on the functional design. Duncan Brown and I were so convinced of the advantages, as experienced over the last five years, that this wasn't negotiable. It was up to me to convince my Wilton colleagues.'

On 24 September I wrote in my diary 'I had a lively group engineers' meeting and we are really getting underway as a department'. At the end of October the new organization chart for the joint engineering department came out. Then on 14 November I went over to Wilton for a meeting with all the technical officers in the new joint department. It was quite a gathering. I put over my views on how I wished the department run. As I wrote in my diary 'I think it went off pretty well'.

On 13 December I held a mass meeting of the whole department and as I wrote afterwards 'It was quite a crowd. It seemed to go down reasonably well. The questions were such I was able to give constructive answers.' There were in fact questions from both sides of the two previous departments which reflected the fears each group had about the attitude of the other group and concern that their old loyalties wouldn't be valued. I was determined to show that it was the new department that mattered, and we must build up our new support for and our belief in it. I told them the story from my British Railway experience. I said one senior railwayman told me proudly, did I realize that the chap who brought the morning coffee was wearing on his frock coat the buttons of the London & North Western Railway (LNWR). Now the old London & North Western became part of the London Midland & Scottish Railway in 1924. This was said to me in 1960 some 36 years after the merger. Somehow the old loyalties had been kept alive for these many years. Now I believed our job was to build our loyalties to our new department.

The following April on the 8th, I found myself entertaining a Mr Carr and Mr Wells from Hopkinson Valves. They asked how the merger was progressing. Ron Johnson, a colleague who had come from the Wilton side, said 'At first we called it a "merger". Later it became a "takeover" and now we call it a "walkover".' By this I knew I was home and dry with the merger.

My management philosophy

My arrival as the Manager of HOC division's engineering design department gave me the chance to consolidate and hone my style of management. I was greatly influenced by the scope I had been given by Sam Salisbury when I worked for him between 1954 and the end of 1957, and this confirmed my intention to apply the delegation of authority to the engineering staff in the department as much as possible. I was greatly helped in this by the high quality of my immediate staff. Lewis Jenkins in charge of civil engineering, and Guy Shute of instruments and electrical engineering, were both technically outstanding in their knowledge and understanding of their subject, and their judgement of people and situations was first class. John Hopkins was very loyal and hard working and Jim Ross could be relied upon to see that the administration ran smoothly.

As well as applying as much delegation as possible, there was an even greater imperative to create a climate so that staff at all levels would be prepared to speak up and express views that may differ from the accepted norms. This was particularly important as we went through the period of overstretched resources during the 1960s. For capital projects, I believe it was vitally important that staff pass up the line information on any shortcomings which would affect the capital costs or completion dates. Sometimes the engineering industry supplying equipment was overloaded, and sometimes the labour situation on construction became out of hand with wildcat strikes. It was, to my mind, vital that all news of overspending and lateness on completion should be passed up the line. As engineeering director these would come up to my desk. For the six years I held this post I had many such cases to deal with, and it was up to me to justify and make an adequate case.

This philosophy was not just to retrieve situations of over-expenditure, but the preparedness to listen to ideas coming up from staff was essential in all high-tech companies. Listening to thoughts against the perceived wisdom of the time is to my mind an essential requirement of all good managers and directors. There was an unfortunate tendency developing in ICI not to rock the boat and only tell your bosses what you thought they would like to hear.

An indication of this happened when the main board chose Sir Peter Allan to succeed Sir Paul Chambers as chairman and not Lord Beeching. On Wednesday 1 November 1967 Lord Beeching visited us to make the presentation at the HOC's Long Service dinner. I wrote in my diary that day 'We had lunch with Lord Beeching and then had a heart to heart discussion afterwards. He sounded us out on the future organization of ICI. He has clearly been out of line with the other directors and he feels that the present set-up needs a drastic change to make it more international – also we must shape the long term strategy and not just let it drift. Oh so true, but I fear the traditionalists at Millbank.' Two days later Jack Lofthouse our division chairman and I discussed the appointment of Sir Peter Allan. I wrote in my diary 'Jack said he had heard from both Tom Clark and Sir Paul that Beeching was too dictatorial with the directors and in particular his attitude in his plan to reorganize ICI. It was like it or leave it. We just hope that some of the ideas will come through. We fear Sir Peter Allan will not change anything or do anything about the ICI (Europa) set-up'.

During my first year as engineering manager, Duncan Brown as engineering director of the new HOC division continued to give me his full support. Duncan retired at the end of May 1964 and was succeeded by Charles Cockram who had been technical director during my time in technical department, and I had always got on well with Charles. He, too, was now within a year of retirement. It was quite a trial for him to slot in as engineering director for this his last year with the company. I made it my business to see that Charles always received a good briefing on all engineering matters. This often meant briefing Charles for a luncheon with an equipment manufacturer. I remember one occasion when the luncheon passed off very well. As our guest left, Charles turned round to me and said 'I rather enjoyed that'. Charles retired at the end of April 1965 and I became engineering director.

I received some unexpected compliments on the performance of the HOC division engineering design department. We had been doing some of the design of Nylon V at Wilton and Lewis Marsden their engineering director said in January 1966 that HOC's part was very good. Then in June that year, Jack Callard, then technical director of ICI Ltd and later chairman of the company, told Jack Lofthouse after a visit to the division that 'they were a salty crew of engineers at Wilton'. John Hopkins, who succeeded me as engineering manager, wrote a note on the size of the engineering department for the division board at a time when all departments in the division had to justify their size and activities. As I recorded

Heavy Organic Chemicals Board, 1968, in Wilton News Supplement. Left to right: back row: DJ Allen, JH Harvey-Jones, RP Robinson, HE North, KW Gee, LW Norfolk, KAG Miller; front row: AB Patrick, AW Taylor, JA Lofthouse, DG Jones, DW Huebner, AD McLean.
Inset: EJ Challis

in my diary 'John Hopkins' note on the size of the engineering department came up at the chairman's meeting. It was an excellent note and was well received and accepted. Jack Lofthouse (now chairman of the division) described it as well documented and presented – an unanswerable case.'

Despite the quality of the staff, we were up against an overload of work, and we were faced with a labour situation on construction which was far from easy. Any complacency I might have had was rudely shattered when one of our project engineers, Tom Hay, returned from secondment assisting a Japanese company to whom we had licensed our know-how for a para-xylene plant in Japan. It had taken us 26 months from authorization to start-up of our para-xylene plant in the UK. The Japanese built a similar plant in 18 months. This brought home to me that we were not meeting the best international standards on completions. From then on our chaotic labour situation in the UK haunted me. It took Margaret Thatcher and Ian MacGregor to right the balance of power between the unions and management.

There was one other self-imposed restraint on the speedy completion of chemical plants, and this was late design changes. A typical example was on the design on a new phenol. On 8 March 1965, I wrote in my diary 'I had a session with Pool, Shute and Watson and I got the feel of the extent of the design changes on phenol. They are considerable.' Next day I wrote 'I brought Charles (Cockram) up to date on phenol. He says Tom Clark (chairman) is being very reasonable. I gave him the gist of the design change story. It is very considerable. Later I saw Maurice Hodgson (then deputy chairman). He is being more reasonable about phenol now and took my point about the design changes.'

Shortly after I became engineering director, I spoke to the chairman's meeting of senior staff and said some hard things about late design changes. The essence of the problem was that late design changes beyond the point in time when the design should have been decided has a delaying effect on the final completion of the plant. I then instituted a system by which all late design changes had to be referred to me as engineering director. I had no idea how many I would be faced with, but in reality they were almost none at all. Some six months later on 6 December 1965 I wrote in my diary 'Peter Gibson (project engineer on olefines IV) told me that my authorization of design changes on olefines has had the desired effect'.

With extensive delegation, I relied heavily on my staff reporting to me the unusual and unexpected, and in particular not to be afraid of passing bad news on to me. I am as convinced as ever that this is an essential part of the managerial climate one must set for the staff to give of their best, often way beyond the normal call of duty. There was one other action I took to assist me in keeping an eye on what was happening on the division's engineering. In my early days as engineering design manager and again when I became engineering director, I arranged to spend an afternoon every two weeks to go round and have a meeting with some three or four engineers at the technical officer level. I made it a firm rule that it was a listening experience for me and no way would I give any instructions direct. By this means I was able to sense the morale of that part of the organization, and it was an encouragement to the engineers that I was prepared to spend an afternoon listening to their account of the work they were doing.

I had one 'hair shirt' working for me whose judgement I just did not trust. All my best endeavours to guide him were of no avail. He was not listening. Slowly other directors came to the same view and he finally left the company, but not before a great deal of time had been spent trying to guide him. I look back on the whole incidence as a failure of my management, but I consoled myself that other senior managers had the same experience of this character. In a more authoritarian company he would have been sacked.

Location of Engineering Department and Division HQ

Dr Saunders, the division chairman, had a special meeting of heads of department and group managers on 14 February 1962 to tell us that HOC division would take over the control of the Wilton site and we shall be moving to Wilton on the south side of the River.

By the time I became engineering manager in April 1963, the new offices were put back in time, and we faced the prospect of making do with existing offices with only minor modifications. Duncan Brown, my boss, was certain that we should combine the two engineering departments and locate them at Wilton in the Castle huts. I was already having serious doubt about the new engineering department being located in Wilton Castle huts as all the other departments working on the development of new business were located at Billingham ten miles away. At the division executive on 28 May, I had the chance to put over the view that we should have our second line of defence ready to consider the split. I pressed for the development of new business being on the north side of the river. Duncan Brown had been on holiday when I expressed these views. When he returned on 30 May I wrote in my diary 'He was well pleased with how everything had gone, except my views on the move to Wilton. He said he was determined we should move to Wilton at any price.' By early July he was pressing me for an expenditure proposal for modifying the Wilton Castle huts. As I wrote in my diary on 8 July 'I again dropped my hint about bringing the engineering department to Billingham. JD said they would welcome suggestions and if I had any I should put them up quickly, but I would have to get the other HODs to agree. I set to with gusto.'

Thus we reached the novel situation that the engineering director was preparing a note for the engineering department to be located at Wilton while I, as engineering manager, was preparing a note to say we should be located at Billingham. It was a clear sign of Duncan Brown's magnanimous approach that he let it get as far as this. It did give me the chance to prepare a draft note and to circulate it to the other heads of departments. It soon became clear that the heads of departments were supporting my view and copies of my draft note had reached some of the directors. By the end of July the division chairman, Dr Saunders, decreed that the engineering department was to move to Wilton. He wouldn't even discuss my note. I wisely kept quiet at the executive. The idea of a move back to Billingham was not completely dead. At the operating management committee at the end of August when we were discussing the transfer of staff from Billingham to Wilton, Tom Clark from the chair turned to me and said I may have to move them back again. I wrote in my diary 'another key man who agrees'. Towards the end of September we heard that Tom Clark was to succeed Sammie as the Divisional Chairman. Then at the operating management committee on 15 October Tom Clark referred to the new office Form 'A' and said that if we didn't get agreement in principle for the whole scheme at Wilton, we would rather stay at Billingham and spend £300,000. The physical move of the old HOC engineering department to Wilton took place in late November and early December. It wasn't long before I was complaining about the isolation of the engineering department. I wrote in my diary for 23 December 'I was annoyed to hear that JD and company had held the meeting to decide the olefine IV contract at Billingham last Friday without either John Hopkins or myself being there. Typical of the trouble we are going to run into with being over at Wilton.'

At the beginning of 1964 Tom Clark became the division chairman and before January was out he was asking me for an order of cost estimate for permanent HOC offices at Billingham. Tom Clark had his first meeting with senior staff on 4 March 1964 and he broke the news to them about the offices and that a move back to Billingham was being seriously considered. On Thursday 5 March 1964 I had my quarterly meeting with all the design engineers and I wrote in my diary 'I told them that serious consideration was being given to a return to Billingham. It was pretty well received. I think I am now well enough in command of the department to carry this through. I had earlier agreed with JDB that Lewis Jenkins would be the project engineer on the Billingham offices'. I had the staff committee meeting on 16 March and I wrote in my diary 'I spent considerable time getting myself briefed for the staff committee. Just as well. The move back to Billingham came up and I said my piece. My hardest question was from one of the Billingham lads who asked why the financial point hadn't been checked last summer. How right he was. One of the Wilton boys started to mumble about a staff referendum on the move, but I sat on that one hard.' By June Lewis Jenkins and Mike Thornley, our division architect, had developed the scheme and I recorded that 'It looks a reasonable project'. The Scheme encroached slightly onto the Billingham Division's playing fields and on 19 June we had a meeting with Stan Lyon who gave us Agricultural Division's comments. They were surprisingly restrained. The project was approved before the autumn was out.

When the project was complete I went round the new organic house extension with Lewis Jenkins and I wrote in my diary of 12 May 1966 'They are really very fine indeed. I gave the chaps full marks'. The actual move back to Billingham took place in mid September 1966.

In December 1966, Tom Clark was promoted to the main board and Jack Lofthouse who returned to HOC division at the beginning of 1966 as a deputy chairman succeeded Tom Clark as chairman. Jack was clearly keen that the division should apply for the full scheme of a new complex of offices at Wilton, and by early 1969 he had obtained sufficient support from the main board for the engineering department to be asked to prepare a scheme. Lewis Jenkins, who had been the project engineer for the move to Billingham, now became the project engineer for the full scheme at Wilton, and he was soon recommending the Building Design Partnership (BDP) as the architects.

I liked the sound of them. They weren't a group of prima donna architects with named individuals, but a business partnership whose partners included not only architects, but also civil, structural and heating and ventilating engineers. This combination appealed to me, so they were invited up to Wilton for a dinner party at Wilton Castle. Their senior partner, Mr Bain, was, like Jack Lofthouse, a strong willed individual. The pair of them spent the dinner party talking at each other and not really listening. Despite this, Lewis Jenkins and I persuaded Jack Lofthouse that we should appoint BDP as our architects.

From the very beginning I was impressed with their approach. They wished to assess where each department would be located on the basis of the extent of the contact between the various departments. BDP wished to interview each head of department to ask each in turn which other departments they wished their department to be near. I had no trouble in getting the directors to agree. Neither I nor the other directors were surprised when BDP came back to say we had a complicated management where there was a great deal of interchange of ideas and contact between all departments, and this influenced their choice of office layout. They recommended a layout on only three levels and a horizontal layout around four courtyards. When I came to selling this idea to Jack Lofthouse, I feared there might have been an emotional reaction to Mr Bain, but I only had to say to Jack as we walked over to lunch one day that it was like a college at Oxford or Cambridge. Jack nodded and I knew we were home and dry.

It was a scheme that appealed to the directors and an expenditure proposal was submitted to the main board and sanction given at the end of February 1970. It was after I moved to Millbank that the offices were completed, but I heard later that BDP gained a prestigous award for the Office Complex at Wilton.

Product Area Manager

At Harry North's instigation in July 1962 I produced a note 'Some thoughts on the Division's Organization' and suggested that the development management committee and the operating management be replaced by five product committees chaired by directors. Little did I appreciate that the concept of product committee would be followed up.

At the end of December 1963 we were told that we were to have twelve product areas with a director or head of department to lead each product area. Six of the product area managers would be on the chemical products committee and report to Maurice Hodgson, the deputy chairman and chairman of the chemical products committee. Similarly Jim Palmer, the other deputy chairman will be chairman of the hydrocarbons committee.

I had been head of the engineering department for less than a year. I was surprised and delighted to hear that I was to be the product area manager for oxides and glycols. Then Maurice Hodgson phoned me on 21 January 1964 and asked me as oxides and glycols product area manager to present the first review of my product area to the chemical products committee the following Monday. I felt honoured that Maurice invited me to be the first product area manager to present a review. I had my first meeting of the product area on 24 January and I wrote in my diary 'Over to Billingham to have my first meeting of the oxides and glycols product area. I was well satisfied at how it has started. I kept Maurice Hodgson informed.' On 10 February I wrote in my diary 'I had my second meeting of the oxides and glycol product area committee. It went down very well and I think we are going to get some worthwhile target figures.' On 19 February I presented the review note on the oxides and glycol targets to the business area committee and I wrote in my diary 'it seemed to go down well'.

On 21 April I attended the hydrocarbons business area committee, standing in for Duncan Brown and the following day the chemical products business area. In my diary of 22 April I wrote 'It is interesting to compare the two business areas. Maurice Hodgson with the chemical products is run much more on the product areas, while Jim Palmer still harps back to functional departments.' I was much more on Maurice's wavelength. By August I wrote in my diary about my product area meeting on the 18th that 'it is certainly humming now'.

In November I ran into my first problem on oxides and glycol with an over-expenditure on Di Proplyene Oxide (DPO) at the chemical products committee on 19 November and I wrote in my diary 'I ran into a little trouble on the ethylene oxides air compressor, but even more so on DPO overexpenditure. I am not at all happy about the cost monitoring particularly with weaker project engineers.' By the following Monday 23 November I wrote 'I had a most useful meeting on DPO over-expenditure. I have at least got a reasonable story now.'

By the turn of the year things were on a sounder basis. I wrote in my diary on 4 January 1965 'I saw Maurice Hodgson and we see eye to eye about the long term approach to ethylene oxide. He holds similar views to mine on central research.' Three days later I had a useful few words with Maurice and wrote in my diary on 8 January 'The oxides business seems to be reasonably well on the rails'. A month later I wrote in my diary on 10 February 'I saw Maurice Hodgson and he was complimentary about how the oxides and glycol product area is doing'. It continued to prosper.

There was one amusing incident which occurred in May 1966. I was now engineering director of HOC Division and I attended the six monthly meetings of the Engineering Conference, when the division engineering directors met under the chairmanship of the main board technical director. At the summer meeting we were at Paints Division headquarters in Slough. In the afternoon we were all expected to take part in a golf competition which on this occasion was at the prestigious golf course at Stoke Poges. My golf was down to once a year at the Engineering Conference and on this occasion I was going round with another golfing rabbit, Jim Hamilton of Imperial Metals Industries. At one tee we found an impressive foursome accompanied by four caddies on a nearby green. We both instinctively waited until this party moved off before we drove. Then to my surprise a member of this foursome gave us a cheery wave. It was two of the sales staff from the oxides and glycol product area, Bob Hain and Stewart Reid, who were entertaining a customer. When we gathered for the formal dinner that evening, I couldn't resist telling Jack Callard, the company's technical director, that I had seen HOC members on the golf course that afternoon. Jack came back at me straight away and said 'What is much more important is that they saw you'!!

I finally was asked to hand over my oxides and glycol product area in March 1968. I had been responsible for the business for four years, and I thoroughly enjoyed leading a team of colleagues covering all business aspects. When I came to leave ICI in May 1974, Maurice Hodgson, now a deputy chairman of ICI presented me with my farewell present from the staff at Millbank. On Wednesday 29 May I wrote in my diary 'Maurice made the presentation to me and did it very well. So honest and straightforward. I was particularly touched by his praise of my work as a product area manager in HOC. This means a lot to me as I become managing director of APV.' I shall always be grateful to Maurice Hodgson for his help, support and encouragement as I learnt to be a businessman.

My departure from HOC Division

At the end of June 1970 we heard that Jack Lofthouse was being promoted to the main board, and John Harvey-Jones was to succeed him. By the end of July John Harvey-Jones told the HOC board that there would be no promotions to deputy chairman of HOC. I asked to see him. As I wrote in my diary on 27 July 'He gave it to me straight that it was unlikely that I would ever be a deputy chairman. It was a real shock. John H-J said I had not carried my colleagues on the board with me.'

From being very much in the first eleven I was now an also ran. It contrasted with what Jack Lofthouse had told me less than two years before when Jack told

ICI Enginering Conference at Paints Division, Slough – May 1966. Left to right: back row: TB Owen, KAG Miller, H West, G Talbot, T Foster, SEM Wright, E Lees, EW Greensmith, GS Jones, DC Harrison, EH Sale, CAC Petrie, C. Vowles, J Hamilton, RH Dibb; front row: FB Wrightson, L Marsden, JD Brown, RE Newell, Sir Ewart Smith, EJ Callard, EF Brookman, N Archer, A Bennett

me that John Harvey-Jones was to be the new deputy chairman at Wilton. I wrote in my diary on 30 September 1968 'Jack went on to say that I was highly thought of, and he expected me to get a deputy's job within two to three years and I was not to rule out the possibility of it being with HOC. Interesting and encouraging.'

So be it. I was now faced with a new chairman who took an entirely different view. I reminded myself of that wonderful poem, 'If', by Rudyard Kipling on advice given to a young man setting out in life, and the quotation is 'If you can meet with triumph and disaster and treat these two imposters just the same . . . yours is the earth and everything that's in it and – which is more – you'll be a Man, my son!'

I was sure that at this point in my career I must get out from under John Harvey-Jones and Arthur Taylor (deputy chairman). Then in mid-November I saw Mr JC Brown the technical director on the main board, known as 'JC'. He offered me the post of engineering adviser to the main board. 'JC' had recently had the post upgraded and there was a degree of promotion in the move. When 'JC' made the offer I noted in my diary for 17 November 1970, 'I saw JC Brown and he offered me the job of engineering adviser in succession to Ted Greensmith. I accepted and gathered there was some promotion. I also saw Jack Lofthouse.' Next day 18 November 'I saw John Harvey-Jones first thing. I got the message that John and Arthur had suggested to Jack Lofthouse that 'JC' should take another engineering director and give me a horizontal move. I didn't give anything away about the scope JC will let me have.' An interesting sideline was that 'JC' sent the written offer in the post to me at my home and not via HOC Division.

So it was I moved to Millbank, and on 1 February 1971 I started to take over as engineering adviser.

CHAPTER 8

Engineering Adviser

THE ENGINEERING ADVISER POST IS A staff appointment reporting to the technical director on the ICI main board. There were excellent functional links to the engineers in the ICI divisions. I was a member of the ICI Engineering Conference – a body comprising all the divisional engineering directors and chaired by the technical director. It met every six months.

With the secretary of the Conference a member of my staff and good relations with my boss, Mr JC Brown, the technical director, the Engineering Conference is a fine body which allowed me to keep my fingers on the pulse of engineering in the divisions. This was helped further by another co-ordinating body, the general purposes committee of the divisional engineering managers. This committee was chaired by myself as engineering adviser.

There are other useful contacts amongst the head office staff. I found Duncan Davies, then general manager – research, was a fellow spirit with whom I struck up a particularly close working relationship. This culminated in an ICI discussion document 'Indicative Plan of ICI's Technical Manpower for the next 15 years', produced in September 1973, and this will be covered in a later section.

An important part of the post was to represent ICI on outside bodies. Some of these I found to be deadly dull and I will not write about them. Others, however, were government sponsored committees set up for a specific purpose, answerable to ministers and supported and serviced by senior civil servants. As well as having an opportunity to put in my views, it was a chance to meet and get to know key top civil servants particularly in the Department of Trade and Industry (DTI). I didn't appreciate it at the time, but this proved invaluable when in 1982 I was appointed the first director general of the Engineering Council.

Committee for Industrial Technologies (CFIT)

In July 1972 I was invited to join the Committee for Industrial Technologies. Gilbert Hunt, managing director of Chrysler United Kingdom Ltd was chairman, and Peter Jost, who led the way with the highly successful development of Tribology (Sliding surfaces and the use of lubricants). Full credit must be given to Peter Jost for this success. He was offered and accepted the deputy chairman appointment. CFIT was now intended to extend this concept to other industrial technologies of (i) terotechnology concerning the total cost of ownership of assets used in the production of goods and services, (ii) corrosion concerning selection of materials and corrosion protection and (iii) material handling, ie getting goods to the right place at the right time and right cost.

Bert Darnell was director of engineering at British Steel Corporation. Bert was in many ways my equivalent in British Steel and from time to time we compared notes. Bert and I were both appointed to this new Committee for Industrial Technologies, and we had lunch together on 1 September 1972 when Bert gave me his views on Peter Jost, the deputy chairman. Peter was a friend of Wedgwood Benn's and Peter had hoped to be named chairman of this new committee. There had been a change of government and he did not have a sufficient power base in the Conservative party. He pressed to chair the management committee. Jost had already persuaded Bert Darnell to be on the management committee and wished Bert to take over the terotechnology committee as soon as possible. I was being sounded out to be on the management committee and to chair the corrosion committee as well and to be part of the Jost team who were really going to run the show. I made the excuse of not being able to spare the time. I was asked by Gilbert Hunt at an early meeting of the main committee if I could suggest the name of an ICI metallurgist to play a key role on the corrosion committee.

I came up with the name of JB Cotton, a metallurgist in IMI. On Tuesday 16 January 1973 I had a phone call from Peter Jost about my nomination of John Cotton and as I wrote in my diary for that day I recorded 'A lobbying phone call from Peter Jost trying to put off a decision on the chairman of the corrosion committee. He tried to quote Sir St-John Elstub, chairman of IMI. I telephoned Sir St-John for his opinion and he spoke highly of John Cotton. I relayed this to Alan Havelock, secretary of CFIT and to Gilbert Hunt the chairman.' I went on in my diary and reported Thursday 8 February 'I went to a Special meeting of CFIT. We confirmed John Cotton as chairman on corrosion. Bert Darnell had a diplomatic absence and Peter Jost arrived as we broke up.' I believe the clashes between Jost and Hunt took some time to resolve. It ended in June 1974 when tribology was declared well and truly launched, and Peter Jost ceased to be a member of CFIT.

Perhaps my greatest contribution to CFIT was to chair a small working panel on 'Financing of IT Centres'. This panel was set up in March 1973. As well as myelf there was Dr Hugh Campbell, industrial adviser at the DTI, who had previously been research manager of the Chloride Group, and we had Frank Warren of the DTI staff as our secretary.

We set ourselves the objective to examine and make recommendations on the financial control and methods of funding Industrial Technology Centres. In particular we were interested in (i) attitudes and motivations of the staff, (ii) the ability of the centre to become financially self sufficient and (iii) the quality of the service offered, now and in the future.

We made contact either visiting or holding discussions with some twelve Research Establishments. Hugh Campbell knew the Chloride Technical Centre and I as ICI engineering adviser had Dr Philip Chipperfield, who was director of ICI Brixham Laboratory, reporting to me. The ICI Brixham Laboratory was extremely well run and their work was greatly valued by the ICI Divisions who called on their services. Both Hugh Campbell and I had experiences of high standards of performance, and this assisted us in setting high standards for the Industrial Technology Centres.

We had a clear dislike for deficit funding. It makes no allowance for the research establishment to build up a trading fund to meet the needs for working capital and other contingencies. We said it should be replaced by a contract between the customer and the research establishment.

There is a clear necessity for each centre to carry out a percentage of long term research and to this end the research establishment should be allowed to build a reserve fund to meet the need of working capital.

In appointing the director, careful attention should be paid to his marketing ability. This arose from our concern that some of the Directors of Government Research Establishments personally denied any need to be market oriented.

This report was accepted by the main CFIT committee on 17 June 1974. I continued my membership of CFIT when I moved from ICI to APV at the beginning of June 1974, and remained on until September 1976. By this time I had been a member for four years and I felt I had made my main contribution.

Indicative plan of ICI's technical manpower for the next 15 years

Duncan Davies, the general manager – research and I both were concerned that with a likely lower level of manpower needs, ICI might have difficulty in achieving a balance between the needs of the business in terms of task effectiveness and costs, and the career expectations of individuals.

We also took the view that while we expected the company would continue to grow in business terms with increased turnover, there would no longer be the increase in staff numbers that had occurred in the 1950s and 1960s.

We independently decided that we each wished to have a mathematical model to describe the numbers and ages of staff at the various levels in the organization. Duncan for the research and development staff, I for the engineering staff.

We started with two separate working parties – a research and development one under the chairmanship of Dr ER Howells and an engineering working party which I chaired. Both were serviced by a common central personnel secretariat. Subsequently Duncan and I agreed that it would be sensible to include production staff and combine the two working parties into a technical manpower working party and Duncan generously agreed that I should chair it. This happened in July 1972.

For the next twelve months, Tony Caston of central personnel and I visited the divisions and obtained unanimous support for the study from divisional directors covering the functions of engineering, research, development, production and personnel in the Divisions of Agriculture, Fibres, Mond, Organics, Petrochemicals, Pharmaceutical, and Plastics. We were greatly encouraged by their attitude and suggestions to improve the company's personnel policy.

We also received informal support from key individuals at Millbank including Geoffrey Gilbertson, the general manager personnel, Jack Lofthouse the personnel director and Maurice Hodgson, a deputy chairman.

'Indicative Plan of ICI's technical manpower for the Next 15 Years'[1] was issued in September 1973 as a document for discussion. We made certain assumptions:

(i) Production manpower would be proportional to the absolute value of fixed assets, allowing for productivity gains.

(ii) Engineering manpower would be proportional to the rate of additions to the fixed assets, again allowing for productivity gains.

(iii) R & D manpower. This was the most discretionary area, and could not be related to fixed assets in any direct manner. We initiated a survey of the divisions of new and existing businesses, and their best assessment of the R & D staff required.

The existing staff were classified horizontally into nine five-year age bands and vertically into six hierarchical levels. A critical part of the input data is the survivor function. This represents the proportion of staff that would remain in the technical population. We used company wastage rates for 1971, and carefully separated the wastage, which the company controlled (redundancies and early retirements) and those which it does not (voluntary resignations, ill-health etc).

Looking forward we considered three scenarios (a) lowest (1½% annual contraction), (b) most likely (½% annual contraction) and (c) the highest (1% annual growth). These were all well below the 3% growth rate of the 1960s. This change from an expanding manpower situation to a contracting one was the single most important pressure bearing on the then current strategies for managing staff.

The modelling showed three critical areas:

(a) low staff inflow leads to an older, more costly, less adaptable, and a less effective population.

(b) low staff outflow leads to the transfer out of good young people, and retention of average to poor older staff within the technical group.

(c) poor career expectations. Promotion rates are notoriously sensitive to overall growth rates and fall immediately to somewhere between 30% and 60% of the 1960s rate.

The report described this as costly stultification and went on to say that existing staff policies cannot cope with these problems by pretending they do not exist.

---

[1] 'Indicative Plan of ICI Technical Manpower for the next 15 years'. An ICI Head Office document for discussion dated September 1973.

This would result in periodic redundancy crises (appoximately in phase with the business cycle) which because of the relative absence of younger people, would be more unpleasant to mid-career people at the next trough (1975–6) than the 1971–2 measures were. Employee insecurity would lead to unhelpful and defensive work and attitudes, contributing to a general fall in the quality of ICI staff, and pressure for unionization at a more senior level.

The Report raised five recommendations:

(i)   Introduce a control system similar to the control of capital to limit recruitment at the peaks of the business cycle.
(ii)   Introduce a form of short term service agreements for staff in their mid-20s.
(iii) Retrain staff over 50 for redeployment in preference to redundancy.
(iv)   Greater emphasis on honest and firm career and performance appraisals.
(v)   Encourage redeployment and retraining rather than recruitment of unknown staff from outside ICI.

By far the most effective of these proposals is short-term contract of employment for five years at the age of 26. At 31 some 20% would leave.

An interesting side-line to this modelling of ICI's technical staff was the effect that the action ICI took in the 1971–2 redundancy was to stop all recruitment of chemical engineers. No doubt other companies were behaving in a similar manner, but word went out to the schools and the numbers of home students starting chemical engineering courses in UK universities dropped from 851 in the academic year starting in 1970 to 499 in 1973. One of my last tasks with ICI at the end of May 1974 was to present a note to the Engineering Conference on the supply of chemical engineers.

We had received some hards words from some of my friends in the chemical engineering department at Cambridge on our ham-fisted effort of cutting out all recruitment in 1971. So on 28 March 1974 Robin Paul, who is himself a Cambridge chemical engineer, working at that time in ICI's Central Personnel Dept and I visited Cambridge and saw John Davidson, Robin Turner, Nigel Kenny and Denys Armstrong. There was an element in our visit of Robin and myself mending fences with some old friends amongst the academics in the chemical engineering department, and indeed we largely succeeded in this. It was also an opportunity to trail to these Cambridge dons the idea of short-term contracts for young graduates, as I reported back to the Engineering Conference in my note on the supply of chemical engineers as follows. 'We tested the dons' view on the use of short-term contracts to meet our chemical engineering technological requirements without committing us to provide subsequent career openings in management. They were surprisingly receptive to this and suggested the undergraduates would accept this as a perfectly valid approach to meet our needs.

Inquiry into the collapse of the Nylon Cooling Tower

At approximately 7.50 p.m. on Thursday 27 September 1973, the cooling tower at the Nylon Works at Ardeer, Ayrshire collapsed in a wind gusting between 56 to 68 mph.

The Nylon Works was operated by my old Division now renamed Petrochemicals Division. Next day I received a phone call from my old colleague Ken Gee, now a deputy chairman of the Division, asking me to lead an inquiry team into the cause for the collapse.

It was clear that there were political implications to this inquiry, and Ken Gee and I were soon certain that I should gather together a strong team including civil engineers of national standing. I consulted widely. I spoke on the telephone to Professor Sir John Baker, Head of Cambridge University Engineering Department and Dr Henry Chilver, Vice Chancellor, Cranfield Institute of Technology, whom I knew well and who had chaired the Inquiry into the collapse of the Central Electricity Generating Board (CEGB) cooling towers at Ferrybridge. I received two recommendations: Professor Ken Kemp, Professor of Civil Engineering at University College, London and Bill Hannah, the Civil Engineer of the CEGB. Both accepted my invitation to join the team and we were very well served by their contributions to our discussions. From ICI we had Lewis Jenkins, the civil group engineer of Petrochemicals Division. Lewis had worked with me closely during my time on Teesside and I had the highest respect for him as an extremely sound civil engineer. As our secretary Alan Frew of Petrochemical Division became our scribe. The committee met on nine occasions between 8 October 1973 and 26 April 1974.

The cooling tower had had a chequered time during the construction period. Design work by Holst & Co started in June 1965. When the CEGB tower at Ferrybridge collapsed on 1 November that year, ICI asked Holst to review their design of the Ardeer tower. Holst then made some design changes, strengthening the bottom 20 feet of the shell with additional steel reinforcement.

A start of the construction was thus delayed until May 1966. Then in September 1966 an ICI inspector reported a 'flat' at 68 feet up on the north-east side of the shell and two days later a second 'flat' started at 75 feet on the south-east side. Early in December a detailed examination of the shell showed contours of the imperfections with irregularities of varying severity. In particular the extremes ranged from plus 15 inches at 38 feet up to minus 21 inches at 275 feet up. As a result ICI insisted that the strength and stability of the tower should be corroborated by an independent authority. Dr J Munro of Imperial College acted as the independent authority. He made certain recommendations to strengthen the tower. These were accepted and incorporated into the tower which was then completed.

When the tower collapsed, the committee had all the information of the contours of the imperfections. We had one important conundrum to solve and that was the knowledge that on 15 January 1968 the tower had successfully withstood a wind from the West gusting to 104 miles per hour, while it collapsed in September 1973 with winds from the same direction gusting at only 68 miles per hour. What had changed between January 1968 and September 1973?

The committee carried out a very thorough examination looking for possible causes. A careful and detailed examination of the debris provided no evidence of sabotage, and this was soon ruled out. The tower had been built over old mine workings, but mining had not taken place since 1924 and when the debris had been removed no measurable movement of the foundations had taken place. Then the shell and columns had been examined and materials of construction were all up to specification. Shell uplift, shell buckling and shell dynamic failure were all considered, but were not thought to be the cause of the failure.

As often happens with hyperbolic cooling towers, Vertical cracks started to appear in the tower shell starting at the base and growing upwards. These are associated with the starting up and shutting down of the tower and are normally of no great consequence as the horizontal hoop stresses are normally in compression. These cracks were reported in September and noted by an eye witness to have grown considerably. The committee considered that in all probability the crack had reached the area of greatest imperfection. The calculations carried out by Professor Kemp and his team at University College showed that with no vertical crack the tower's limited tensile strength could have withstood the 104 miles per hour gusts in January 1968, but with vertical cracks the tower would not have been able to withstand a wind gusting between 68 miles per hour in September 1973. The committee concluded that this explanation satisfied all the known evidence and is the most probable explanation for the collapse of the tower. The full report was published in July 1974,[2] and this was accepted as a reasonable explanation of the cause of the failure of the Nylon Cooling Tower. I am most grateful to Professor Ken Kemp and his team at University College, London for their elegant analysis.

Engineering at my old division (re-named Petrochemicals) as seen from Millbank

One of the important aspects of the engineering adviser's job was to keep an overall watch on the engineering staff resources of the company to carry out the supervision of the design and construction of new chemical plants to meet the company's capital programme, and reporting the position to the technical director and through him to the board of ICI.

In February 1971 ICI's capital programme of sanctions in the UK dropped from a peak of around £150 million in 1968 to about £50 million in 1971. The

[2] 'Report of the Committee of Inquiry into the Collapse of the Cooling Tower at Ardeer Nylon Works Ayrshire on Thursday 27 September 1973.'

problem had shifted from not enough engineers to not enough sanctioned projects to keep the key staff fully employed. In the early months of 1971 I visited all the divisions in the UK and held discussions with the engineering directors of the various divisions. With the ease back on the total load there were strong pressures to have a shared engineering department on Teesside and from June 1972 Lionel Wright, engineering director of Agricultural Division, was in charge. It is a sad reflection on how HOC (now Petrochemicals) had fared since my departure from HOC that I now judged Agriculture Division to have a more effective engineering department. Lionel Wright was not having an easy time. When I saw him about regionalization on Tuesday 21 November 1972 I wrote in my diary 'He is up against it with Arthur Taylor being awkward and three of the Petrochemicals Board following his master's voice.' I was again on Teesside and on 12 December I wrote 'I had dinner with Lionel Wright. Regional engineering will probably not be accepted 100%, but Lionel Wright has a back-up programme.'

At the end of 1972 we heard that John Harvey-Jones was going onto the main board and Arthur Taylor would succeed him as Petrochemicals Division chairman.

By early in 1973 I was concerned about Petrochemicals Division. On Thursday 11 January I wrote in my diary 'I saw JC Brown in the afternoon and gave him the background to my old division's figures on the design load. He takes the point they have under-estimated.'

On Friday 18 April I flew to Teesside. I spent the morning with Lionel Wright and John Hopkins going through the Petrochemicals Division's design load. John Hopkins, while having a reasonable minimum load for olefines VI, is assuming an improved efficiency, which won't be achieved because of all the other pressures.

At the beginning of May 1973 JC Brown retired and Bill Duncan recently in charge of the ICI companies in North America returned to the UK and became technical director. I had known Bill when he was a young engineer at Billingham, and I was confident I could work well with him, and so it turned out.

To return to the Petrochemicals design load. On 16 May I spoke to John Hollingsworth in control group department and he said he was going to put in a paragraph on the engineering staff resources.

My diary entries for the next two days continued the tale. 'Friday 18 May Lionel Wright and John Hopkins arrived first thing and we spent three hours going through their capital programme blow by blow. They do have some staff up their sleeves on nylon, but haven't really got to grips with it. The net effect is that they will be short by eight men for two years, and at long last they have agreed. In fairness to Lionel he had only today come to grips with the detail. I wrote to Lionel afterwards to confirm the discussion. I also spoke to John Hollingsworth and told him of the outcome.'

As was being mooted at that time it had been suggested that Shell Mex and BP might be a partner in Olefine VI. The engineering design load would then be shared and both Lionel Wright and I felt this was an acceptable way ahead. We were getting mixed messages of Petrochemicals' intentions. Some like John Lister and Peter Robinson weren't keen on the joint effort. In June while at Plastics Division I even heard that Arthur Taylor was supporting ICI letting Shell have a share of say 15% of the cracker. Ken Gee told me in October that they would go in with Shell, but it was John Harvey-Jones who did not agree. By the end of October the message was that they might go it alone.

On Tuesday 5 June I had a visit from John Harvey-Jones and I wrote in my diary: 'Tuesday 5 June I had a visit from John H-J re load on Teesside and Design load on Petrochemicals Division. He is claiming he is putting up the case on Petrochemicals being able to do so much better than BP. Although this may have been true in the past I warned against technical arrogance and that others from BP and Shell could learn their lessons. I emphasized the general loading of the economy and engineering firms. J. H-J went off saying I had depressed him!'

A week later I wrote: 'Thursday 14 June John Hollingsworth came to see me about the capital programme and my contribution to the paper to the capital programme committee. John feels Petrochemicals will get their cracker, but something else will be recommended to be put back. I saw Bill Duncan in the afternoon. He, too, is pretty convinced that Petrochemicals will get their cracker and he thinks that having said our piece we should leave it to them to sort out what they cut back on.'

'Tuesday 31 July I saw Bill Duncan. He told me to keep up the work on the capital loading and said that in presenting the progress at the board meeting, Maurice Hodgson referred to my reservations.'

'Friday 12 October Over to Billingham. First a session with Lionel Wright and Ken Coleman on Ag capital programme. As ever in good order, but then I saw Lionel and John Hopkins of HOC Division. Their design resources are stretched beyond the reasonable limit. I wrote down their qualifications to their figures. These are so immense that in my judgement their programme is not realistic.'

'Monday 15 October After work I went to the Lummus cocktail party. I saw Jack Lofthouse there and told him of my concern about Petrochemicals.'

'Wednesday 17 October I had a session first thing with Tony Challis and John Hollingsworth re Ag & Petrochemicals capital programme. They accept my points completely.'

On Wednesday 31 October I recorded in my diary: 'In the afternoon Lionel Wright and John Hopkins came to see me and John Merckx re their programme. They know in their heart of hearts it is not on, but daren't say so.'

'Friday 2 November 73 Tony Challis, John Hollingsworth and I went up to see John Harvey-Jones and really warned him about the Petrochemicals' capital load and our views. He said they were now drawing the line and saying no more, but I reckon they have already gone too far.'

'Thursday 22 November I met up with John Merckx and we saw Lionel Wright and John Hopkins about their capital programme. They have found a whole lot of other staff and have also cut back severely.'

'Wednesday 28 November I attended the pre-meeting of the Petrochemical Policy Group. I was delighted to hear that they are going to cut their capital programme by another £10–15m.

'Wednesday 9 January Lionel Wright came to see me re the three Olefine Plants and gave me a very honest view.

'Thursday 10 January I saw Bill Duncan and briefed him for the capital programme committee. He took the point that Harvey-Jones understated the difference in time needed between the projects. I doubt if he will act on it.

'Monday 22 April The capital programme goes on unabated. I feel I have had so little influence. The divisions get away with murder. I think they are heading for trouble and will sanction far too much for all the wrong reasons.'

The discussions so far were on the underestimating by Petrochemicals Division of the design load. However, they had also been underestimating the capital cost. They had come up with a capital estimate of £105 million for Olefine VI. My own view was that it was too low and at that time I considered the capital cost would be more like £130 million. I also questioned whether the division had taken full account of the effect on the projects profitability of the quadrupling of the price of the main raw material of naphtha. I was told that the market assessment was none of my business as engineering adviser. As I was about to leave ICI, I felt confident enough to speak my mind, and I was no doubt already thinking myself into the managing director's role at APV.

On 1 June 1974 I joined APV as managing director of the main subsidiary the APV Company with a seat on the Holdings Board. As part of my introduction to the Dairy market I paid a visit on 22 August 1974 to Clifford Dairy in Bracknell. I met Gordon Clifford, the old man who had really built up the firm. It was a very worthwhile visit and I learnt a lot about the Dairy Industry. Gordon Clifford and I were clearly getting on well and at the end of lunch Gordon offered to show me his 'white elephant' of a plastics bottle-making machine which he said is now redundant due to the rise in the cost of plastics. I was nearer the mark than I thought possible with my question to ICI about the quadrupling of the price of naphtha.

On Thursday 12 September 1974 I had a visit from Costé Edeleanu, the Agricultural Division metallurgist, and he told me of the rapid rise on Olefine VI capital by £30 million. They were already in an over-expenditure situation.

On Tuesday 24 September 1974, Peter Seligman returned from a business trip to Billingham and he told me that ICI was cutting next year's capital budget down from £300m to £150m. 'Utterly predictable' I wrote in my diary.

Several years later, Bill Duncan told me that Petrochemicals Division came up with an over-expenditure proposal for Olefines VI and the final capital cost had risen from £105 million to £180 million, and that my note on the capital cost had been dug up and quoted. I had to tell myself that there are no bouquets for being right, if you failed to convince your colleagues at the time.

My departure from ICI

JC Brown had asked me to visit the engineering firms who supplied equipment to ICI Divisions and said he would appreciate my views on their competences. In this connection I visited APV on 19 May 1972 and I wrote in my diary 'I drove over to Crawley to see APV. Very good they are too. They also treated me right royally and we had a most useful discussion.' In my report to JC Brown on the visit I said 'I was impressed by the quality of their top men and their sound business approach. They continue to view their subsidiaries as independent profit centres and in one area even allow two subsidiaries to compete with each other for outside business. In the centre they have R & D, and computer development and applications, but keep a very firm grip on overheads'. Later in my report I referred to their own products and said 'APV have their own profitable line of plate type heat exchangers as well as their own designed distillation column trays. You will be interested to hear that Peter Benson, their managing director, fully confirmed that having their own product line made all the difference in their ability to weather the fluctuations in the investment cycle.'

It was 17 months later at the Process Plant Association's annual dinner on 23 October 1973 that Peter Benson approached me about the possibility of joining their group. With this background I was clearly impressed, and I followed it up with a phone call to Peter Benson next day and arranged that I would see him and Peter Seligman, their chairman, to discuss the matter further. We met on 30 October when I gave them a copy of my curriculum vitae and we discussed my experience and the job in APV. Things were moving along in a very satisfactory manner.

By this time I told Bill Duncan that I had had an approach from another company that I must take seriously. I saw Bill again on Wednesday 31 October and I wrote in my diary 'He turned to my prospects in the company. Frankly they are not good. All a bit depressing. Bill was fishing about who had approached me, but I decided to give nothing away as I hadn't been given a firm offer yet.

On 12 November I had a phone call from Peter Seligman. As I wrote in my diary for that day 'He would like to approach Bill Duncan to get confirmation of my management ability. I told him I understood him wishing to know and he said he will hold off, if I didn't wish it. We will discuss it again in the morning. I told him the more I thought about it the more I felt I could make a long term contribution with Peter Benson. Altogether encouraging, so long as Bill and Jack don't let me down.' Next day I phoned Peter back and I told him I was quite prepared for him to talk to either Bill Duncan or Jack Lofthouse, the Personnel Director. Jack was out of the country, but Peter said he would wait and speak to Jack Lofthouse. I knew Jack of old and he would give Peter a fair assessment of me.

On Tuesday 20 November I wrote in my diary 'I saw Jack Lofthouse first thing about APV. He was most reasonable. He thought I could make a greater contribution to the country in such a job than with ICI. He said ICI would not stand in my way, and he would be pleased to see Peter Seligman. It couldn't have gone better. I told Bill Duncan in the afternoon that it was APV and that Jack would see Peter. Bill said it might be difficult to release me, but I just said we would cross that bridge when we came to it.'

A week later Jack Lofthouse phoned me to say that he had seen Peter Seligman yesterday evening and he had clearly given me a good write-up.

On Thursday 6 December I met some of the APV Holdings directors and I wrote in my diary 'I met Madron Seligman, John Jackson, Sir Robert Shone and Stanley Higgins. They quizzed me for two hours. I got the feeling that it all went very well. Afterwards Peter asked my wife and myself to have dinner with him and his wife Elizabeth in about two weeks time. Still no definite offer, but I continue to be hopeful.' Peter Seligman telephoned me next day to say he would like me to see the other two directors and that they would almost certainly make me an offer.

After the ICI Christmas lunch on the 18th, I again saw Peter Seligman. We talked about overseas policy. Peter also said he would have a letter of appointment to give me the following day when we met for dinner with our wives. Excellent. Everything seemed set fair.

And so it was that I left ICI at the end of May. In mid March I heard the rumour from Petrochemicals Division that I would not be replaced. I wonder who started it? In reality Bill Duncan was able to arrange for a high quality successor as engineering adviser in Frank Whiteley, then a director of Agricultural Division who later went on to the main board. I would like to think that I had effectively upgraded the post.

On 14 May I attended my last board meeting of Engineering Services (Wilton) Ltd and at the lunch afterwards Ken Gee, in making a presentation to me, referred to Jack Lofthouse and me and our celebrated arguments. It was interesting that they saw it that way, while in reality Jack and I had the highest respect for each other as we spoke our minds. This was the culture that Jack and I had been brought up on, but it was now becoming more and more foreign to the current Petrochemical Board. It was as if everyone was now obsequious to their superiors and would only tell them what they thought their boss wished to hear.

The 29th of May was my last day at Millbank. I wrote in my diary 'I went round and said good-bye to the chaps in the department. Maurice Hodgson made the presentation to me and did it very well. So honest and straightforward. I was particularly touched by his praise of my work as a product area manager in HOC. This means a lot to me as I become a managing director.'

My last work for ICI was to attend the Engineering Conference which was held at Billingham. On the Thursday evening of 30 May we had the conference dinner and Bill Duncan made the presentation to me. I replied as planned. Duncan Brown, now retired, spoke to me afterwards of the politics in ICI. It seemed to me it was worse than I thought.

CHAPTER 9

APV

D URING THE EARLY MONTHS OF 1974 I had several opportunities to meet the senior members of APV. David Shore, the research director of the APV Company was on the same Chemicals and Minerals Research Requirements Board as myself. When we next met at a Requirements Board on 5 February 74, I noted in my diary that 'David Shore was there and spoke up very clearly – I am impressed'. There was no doubt in my mind I should retire from the Requirements Board and leave David to continue, which he did very well.

Madron Seligman entertained me to lunch at the Royal Thames Yacht Club. Like the chairman Peter Seligman, Madron was a son of the founder of the company, Dr Richard Seligman. Madron was a charming man, an Oxford graduate who in his time was president of the Oxford Union and a personal friend of Teddy Heath. Madron was an extremely good after dinner speaker. He was always very helpful to me.

On 25 March 1974 I had lunch with John Jackson. John was the managing director of APV Paramount, the foundry company, and he was also a member of the holdings board. He was an astute observer of the Group companies. I wrote in my diary of that day, 'I was delighted to hear from John that he saw APV as a non political company'. I was greatly encouraged by this and his comment was fully justified when I became established as managing director of the APV Company.

A very great deal of this was due to the leadership of the Group by Peter Seligman. Peter was a Cambridge engineer and his leadership was to bring out the best of his team. He emphasized the importance of keeping closely in touch with the customers, and to direct the research and development of the company's products to meet the needs of the customers. He had created a climate in the company that was innovative and where new ideas would be allowed to flourish. It reminded me of my early days at Billingham, and made my introduction to APV both enjoyable and relatively straightforward.

Peter Benson the Group managing director was a tough accountant who kept a close watch on the Group's finances. His business judgements were first class, but his judgement of individuals was to my mind too black and white. Fortunately Peter Seligman and Peter Benson worked well as a team. They were very different characters, but they counterbalanced each other.

Managing Director of the APV Company Ltd

My initial appointment on 1 June 1974 was as managing director of the APV Company Ltd. This was the original company on which the Group was built, With other companies joining the Group, APV Holdings was formed in 1962, and became the quoted public company. From this time on the APV Company Ltd became the leading subsidary in the UK. In plate heat exchangers the APV Co Ltd was one of the leading manufacturers supplying the world market and here was second only to Alfa Laval. It had also taken a leading part in developing computer control of dairies and breweries and was gaining a reputation for contracts for complete breweries and dairies.

Peter Benson the managing director of APV Holdings Ltd, had continued as managing director of the APV Company as well. As more companies joined the Group he was clearly overloaded, and with my arrival he was able to concentrate on managing the whole Group.

The climate set by Peter Seligman was of a very friendly co-operative team. Much of this stems from the small company origins, but now with 13,000 employees world wide, I would describe it as a small international group.

The company was a group with a high degree of delegation from Holdings with some strong subsidiaries which were the centre of important products. APV, as I have mentioned, for plate heat exchangers, Crepaco in Chicago for ice cream freezers, Manton Gaulin in Boston, Massachusetts for homogenizers and Anhydro in Copenhagen for spray driers.

My first months with APV were spent meeting the Directors and key staff in the APV Co Ltd, generally obtaining a feel of how the company worked and listening to hear what the senior staff thought were the key problems.

Product and process co-ordinating committees

As I continued to meet staff and have longer talks with the APV directors, it became clear to me that we were already overloading the APV Company board meetings with business decisions which could and should be taken at a lower level in the organization. This was my lead in to introduce a product co-ordinating committee system, with the chairman of each product committee reporting the business activities to the APV Board. This was very much in tune with my own thinking based on my experience of the product area committees in the Heavy Organic Chemicals Division of ICI.

A key point to make the new system effective was to have the monthly financial returns presented on a product basis as well as an industry basis. Ken Grover, the finance director, already produced reliable monthly accounts and his staff very soon presented the financial results on a product basis as well, and this was a vital ingredient to make it happen.

By the end of August the APV Directors had agreed in principle and by early September I had convinced both Peter Benson and Peter Seligman. Peter

Seligman's reaction was particularly pertinent and I recorded in my diary for 6 September 1974 'Peter Seligman gave me his comments on my proposed co-ordinating system. He is basically for it, particularly in the bringing on of bright young men.' Peter Benson didn't show just such a keen interest and I wrote in my diary 3 September 'I had a session with Peter Benson in the afternoon. The Group half year results are good. Peter gave me his views on the co-ordinating committees I had put forward. He is reasonably in favour, though he is not really a committee man himself.'

It was important to have a lively forward thinking director to lead the way. The two Peters, Madron Seligman and I had no doubt that David Shore was our man for the job. In fact I got David's agreement on 12 July to chair a working party on plate heat exchangers, which in due course became the product co-ordinating committee.

Madron Seligman himself took on the 'Contracts and Process Committee', and they had two sub-committees: A 'Cleaning in Place (CIP)' chaired by Norman Garrett, and Ultra High Temperature (UHT) chaired by Granville Starkie. These two bright young men on the sales side were given the opportunity to gain some early business experience chairing these two key Dairy Process committees. Before the year was out an Evaporator Committee with Julian Kemper, the engineering director as chairman, and the Pumps, Valves and Fittings (PVF) with Charles Brissenden the home sales director as chairman, were established.

As I had previously observed about the HOC product area committees. much depended on the quality of the leadership given by the chairman. David Shore led the plate heat exchanger committee superbly, and they tackled with great gusto the development of the new largest ever Industrial Plate Heat Exchanger (irreverently known as BLIP, Bloody Large Industrial Plate exchanger), which was launched at the ACHEMA exhibition in June 1976. Madron Seligman's contracts committee made good progress, too, and two years later I wrote in my diary of 15 January 1976 'I attended the contracts committee. All the more recent contracts are making good money, and the two sub-committees UHT and CIP are with the new chairmen of Granville Starkie and Norman Garrett making very good headway. I had a chat with Peter Benson on how things are going.' Later on 5 July I wrote 'I attended Madron's contract committee. It is going well and they monitored the business plan well'. Thus the two key product and process committees were well launched.

During my first working day at Crawley I met John Brown, the personnel manager of the APV Co Ltd. John was a highly professional operative. Much tougher than most personnel managers and encouragingly outspoken. After this first day I wrote in my diary 'I had a useful chat with the personnel man, John Brown. Even more has to be done than I first thought, but I think he has the right ideas'. John later told me the apocryphal story that when Ealing Studios were preparing for the film *I'm Alright Jack* they modelled the personnel manager, played by Terry Thomas, on the then APV personnel manager. I encouraged John Brown to draft a personnel policy paper including the development of a staff job evaluation scheme. This he did and I will return to it later.

The APV Co Ltd had a monthly board meeting when the normal monthly financial figures were discussed along with any capital proposals. Peter Seligman was chairman and Peter Benson often attended as well.

I had my second APV Board meeting on 8 July. I still didn't feel I really was in control, as the directors tended to bring up the odd items. However, Peter Seligman encouraged me to get my executive directors' meeting under way and this I did. Generally about once a month and a week before the APV Board meeting. I was also determined that this executive was not to be seen as a pre-board meeting, but an occasion when I could discuss matters of new policy as we were developing them.

For example the co-ordinating committee system on a product or process basis was discussed at the executive in August, September, October and November. Re-reading my diary entries thirty years later shows how I was getting the directors' support for the system. In August I recorded 'I had a second executive directors' meeting. They really are making some progress in getting the monthly financial figures presented on a product basis as well as an industry basis. It will make all the difference to our financial and product control.' In September I said 'I got lots of support for my new co-ordinating system for products.' Then in October 'I had my executive meeting and we had further discussions on the co-ordinating committee system'. By the November executive meeting I cleared the details of the committee system. I had in effect been so encouraged by the early reaction of the directors and the two Peters that I presented a paper to the APV Board on 23 September and it was agreed in principle.

Staff job evaluation scheme

John Brown's personnel policy paper with its staff job evaluation system took a little longer to sell. By early September John had given me a first draft of his policy paper. In my diary of 3 September 1974 I wrote 'After supper I read John Brown's policy paper on personnel. Good stuff until he comes to the extra staff. Here I boggle.' John was keen to press on and at the executive on 9 September we had a presentation of the staff job evaluation by Inbucon, the consultant. At the end of that week I recorded in my diary for Friday 13 September, 'I had a long session with Ken Grover and John Brown on John Brown's magnum opus. I accept it in principle, but he will have to take it slower to carry people with him.' This particularly applied to Peter Benson. Rises in staff salaries was to him extra money out from the company. It was always quite a tussle to convince him that if we didn't pay good staff well, we would lose them. This showed itself and on Thursday 10 October I wrote 'I made little impact with Peter Benson on our salary levels and putting the differentials right for the senior staff.' Nevertheless we pressed on and at the executive on Monday 14 October I wrote 'I had my executive meeting. We gave our support to John Brown's proposal for a job evaluation scheme. I had to take a firm line with them.' There were some mixed feelings amongst some of the directors, but John Brown and I pressed on and after the APV Board meeting on 21 October 1974 I wrote in my diary 'We had the APV Board. Peter Seligman was not here, but Peter Benson took the chair and I had a very tough passage getting the staff job evaluation scheme through. I only just made it. The attitude is all for market values and nothing else. It can land us into a major long term problem of a poor quality of staff.' I was nailing my colours to the mast.

Through 1975 there was a certain tendency of some senior staff to try to delay the implementation of the scheme. On 5 June 1975 I wrote in my diary 'After lunch I had a meeting with the executive directors on the staff job evaluation scheme. There are a lot of anomalies, which will have to be cleared, and it was accepted we would not get an answer in time for the July salary review. I think I diffused a potentially serious situation and it's now back on the rails, but I have some chaps who are just not with it on personnel matters.'

On 29 August 1975 I wrote in my diary 'I had a long session with Peter Seligman. He was a bit concerned about John Brown and how I might get my name linked too closely with John Brown's efforts, which Peter felt might not be in accord with APV thinking.'

By September 1975 there were still people dragging their feet, including Ray Vernon in accounts under Ken Grover, such that I wrote in my diary on 17 September 'I spoke first thing to the job evaluation panel to give them some heart to press on with their work on appeals.'

We had set up a new personnel committee and it was serving a useful function. On 21 October I wrote in my diary 'I had the personnel committee in the morning. We had a good discussion on the job evaluation scheme and extending it to the managers. We are making some real progress, but there are some very old fashioned ideas round the building.'

By 5 January 1976 we had moved on, and I reported in my diary 'The groups of jobs into grades has been announced – so far no bad reaction.' Then on 20 January 1976 we had a personnel committee meeting and I wrote in my diary 'I had heard rumours that there would be rumbles about the staff and management job evaluations, but it was all very reasonable with a lot of help from David Shore, Arthur Boyce and Madron Seligman. Charles Brissenden is on the fence and only Ken Grover and Julian Kemper are a problem. I am playing it along gently.' This meeting helped to clear the air.

By 20 April we made some real progress and I wrote in my diary 'We had a directors' meeting on the managers' job evaluation. We made some real progress, but I sat back and let Richard Alston of Inbucon do most of the chairing.' By 25

May I wrote 'After lunch I had the third meeting of the directors on management grading. It all fell into place, which was a great relief to me.'

Thus the saga of establishing a staff job evaluation scheme took almost exactly two years, but we succeeded in the end.

Communications

The APV Company Ltd at Crawley employed a total of about 1800 people, and I was determined we should have good communications down the line so that everyone had a chance to hear how the company was doing.

To this end I arranged to have a meeting every six months of the directors and 40 top managers. I invited Ken Grover our financial director to present the financial results for the last year and I would follow it with a talk on the forward prospects. A week later we had a similar meeting for the shop stewards at which Ken Grover gave the same presentation.

By the second set of meetings in April 1975 I wrote in my diary of the managers' meeting. 'It was a pretty lively meeting and I was very pleased with the general atmosphere and attitude shown by everyone.' At the shop stewards' meeting which followed I wrote 'I think it was a pretty successful meeting. Certainly they asked lots of questions and the works convener did not hog the occasion. In fact he congratulated me on successfully getting all the unions together for the first time ever.' In an exploratory meeting in September 1974 with the shop stewards I noted afterwards that I hoped I had set the scene for some goodwill which I was sure to need in the future. It was to come sooner than I or the shop stewards expected.

Redundancies

Early in 1975 our new orders started to fall away badly. By the time of the board meeting on 29 May we had decided to have a contingency plan to cope with the fall-off in our order intake. I recorded in my diary of that day that 'It is really getting very serious'. On Tuesday 3 June I wrote in my diary 'I went round the stores with Arthur Boyce to see how much final stock is piling up. It was the first round of the payroll wage negotiations. The men staged an hour's walk-out from 3.30 to 4.30 p.m. We are in for a stirring time. I kept Peter Seligman informed.'

At the APV Board on 23 June we decided that we had to go onto immediate short-term workings, and 10% redundancy amongst staff at Crawley. The order intake was so low and the work was just not coming in.

I had discussions with each director in turn. I told them as a group that we required a 10% reduction in the salary bill and I asked that each of them would prepare for me what they would do to achieve an 8%, 10% and 12% drop in the salaries of their department, with the names of who should go. I emphasized that the APV company had grown over the last 17 years and some mistakes would inevitably have been made in staff appointments, and I expected them to put forward the names of staff who hadn't been pulling their weight. At the same time I discussed the matter with John Brown and Miss Windess, the chairman's secretary, who at that time was looking after me as well. There was one classic case of a man in the sales department, whose sole job was to organize the annual APV golf competition. I discovered he only had about a quarter of a job. Somehow his name was not on Charles Brissenden's list. I took a firm line with Charles, and I briefed Peter Benson and Peter Seligman, particularly on the case of the man who only appeared to organize the golf competition, and they both supported me. In the end I settled for 8% cut for the sales staff, 10% for engineering and research and 12% for accounts and administration.

Meanwhile on 25 June, Ken Grover, Arthur Boyce and John Brown saw the payroll unions. Arthur and John were listened to in stunned silence. We had offered the unions a 7½% pay rise with inflation around 20%, on the basis that that was all we could afford. Two days later the mass meeting of the payroll decided to return to normal working from their working to rule which had been going on for some time. This de-escalation was good news.

On 27 June, John Brown saw the staff unions and listened to them, but made it clear we were going ahead with telling the people on Monday 30 who were being made redundant.

On 30 June I wrote in my diary 'The redundancy notices were handed out today. Arthur Boyce had a meeting with the shop floor unions and listened to their case. We will stick at 10%. John Brown also saw the staff unions.'

On Tuesday 1 July John Brown was back from his meeting with the staff unions and I wrote in my diary 'The unions will accept the 10% rise if we withdraw the redundancy notices. I am sticking firm. Later in the day we heard that Healey came out with his 10% limit on salary and wage rises. This is the first bit of sense the government came out with. No doubt yesterday's run on the pound concentrated their minds.'

Next day I wrote in my diary 'I heard from John Brown and Alex Townsend that they had had a good meeting with the staff unions. The full list of the redundancies had a distinct calming effect. On the other hand Arthur had a stormy session with the shopfloor unions. We must hold firm.'

By the end of the week I was able to write in my diary of 4 July 'The staff unions have accepted the 10% rise unconditionally and also accepted the redundancies. At the mass meeting of the workers they turned down the militant shop stewards' proposals and also accepted the 10% rise. This is excellent news.'

The rumblings about the redundancies continued. I had a meeting with Peter Seligman and Peter Benson on 22 August and wrote in my diary afterwards 'A meeting first thing with the two Peters on the treatment of long service men declared redundant. It all arose from two men on production who really had to go. I found myself wanting to be tougher than Peter Benson! Ken Grover was there. He really is sentimental. Nor does he back up John Brown. This was left for me to do. Afterwards I ran through the June results with Ken Grover. I still have a feeling we are carrying too much fat for old times' sake.'

On the face of it, we had come through the redundancies pretty well and we moved on to other matters.

For some time I had been spending the occasional afternoon going round the departments and having informal talks with the young graduates. It was a repeat of what I did in the engineering department of Heavy Organic Chemical Division when I was engineering manager and later engineering director. As on the previous occasions I made it clear to the director concerned that I would not give any instructions, but was there to listen to the young graduates and to hear how they described the work they were doing. Any comments I would hold back and perhaps mention it to the director afterwards. On the whole the exercise was appreciated by the young graduates and I found it very useful in giving me a feel of the climate and atmosphere at the graduate level in the company.

In 1977 I was still finding that one or two of the directors were harping back to the poor atmosphere left by the redundancies. It was just after one of these outbursts that I was having an afternoon chat with three very bright and enthusiastic graduates in research department. Towards the end of the discussion on their jobs, I asked them what was the atmosphere like in their department. Fine they said. I went on 'What about the redundancies?' 'Oh, the redundancies,' they replied 'we looked on that as your pruning exercise.' At the time I must have said that their comments were interesting. At the next executive meeting of the directors I repeated their comment. From that day on there were no more complaints from the directors about the legacy of the redundancies.

There was one other action that I took in the summer of 1975, and this was to insist that David Shore should continue with his normal recruitment of engineers of I think three graduates from universities. I had been shaken in the 1971 recession when we in ICI cut all our recruitment and it had a devastating effect on the entry to chemical engineering departments in the universities (see page 82). I felt I had to tell Peter Benson and I remember his horror. 'Do you mean to tell me that you will make three more members of APV redundant?' 'Yes,' I said. 'This is being done for our reputation in the universities, as we will wish in the future to recruit really good graduates.

Industrial espionage

Early in March 1975 I heard a rumour that there may have been a leak of confidential information to Alpha Laval. At that time a major shortage of work was brewing and the risk of industrial espionage was put on the back burner. However later in the year, Hayden Sayce, one of our most reliable salesmen, reported that an offer he had made to a small company had been matched by an

Alpha Laval offer and he was convinced that the offer which only he and his secretary knew about had got back to Alpha Laval.

This had to be taken seriously. Early in December Denis Usher who was leading the team working on the design of the new large plate heat exchanger (BLIP) came to see me and I wrote in my diary for 5 December 'Denis Usher came in to show me the Alfa–Laval's 1973 report quoted R145 with its old code number which had never been published outside Crawley. There is no doubt we have a leak somewhere.' It clearly had been going on for some time.

With the agreement of the two Peters I consulted Sergeant Joll and PC Hines of Crime Prevention. I said we were looking for a consultant to advise us on the industrial espionage we thought we were up against. They strongly recommended Mr Vincent Carratu. Ten days later I went up to London and in my diary of 12 December I wrote 'I met Mr Vincent Carratu of Carratu Ltd re our security problem. I like the man. He is competent and knowledgeable, while APV are babes in arms at industrial espionage.'

By April 1976 Mr Carratu had drawn a blank on his investigations so far and he then started on a security check for us on the Crawley site. I kept the directors fully informed of these developments and on 28 of April I wrote in my diary 'Mr Carratu and Mr Weatherhead went through the building last night and appeared in my office with a fistful of papers left around. I mentioned it at the APV board and then in the afternoon I saw the directors in turn with the offending member of staff.'

On 30 April I saw Mr Carratu. 'He will submit his report in the next two weeks. Our general security in the office block has been very slack.' I stressed security to staff in regard to taking visitors to the works. However next day I transgressed myself when Hugh Lang of PE Consultants and Dennis Hodges of NEDO visited Crawley. I took them round and inadvertantly walked them past BLIP!

From then on we really tightened our security. With strong support from David Shore's plate heat exchanger product committee, the programme for the latter stages of BLIP's development were speeded up and we met our target of exhibiting it at the ACHEMA exhibition in June. To confuse any inquisitive competitors we labelled the outside No. 2 Evaporator. The exhibition started with a reception on the Sunday evening 20 June and we only took the cover off BLIP on Sunday morning. Alfa Laval must have been in on Sunday, measured up BLIP and discovered it was larger than their A35. It was a small moral victory when Alfa Laval had to ship back to Sweden their literature on their plate heat exchanger, which claimed it was the largest in the world. This showed us that our security was now holding.

I concluded that whoever was responsible for the leak was declared redundant on 30 June 1975 and off the premises by the end of September. Vincent Carratu's investigations didn't start until December 1975.

Queen's Award for Industry

In 1970 the Heavy Organic Division of ICI was awarded the Queen's Award for Industry for the Computer Control of Olefines IV Plant. This reflected extremely well on Guy Shute and his team on instrument design in the engineering department and was a good morale booster.

When I arrived at Crawley I was impressed by the quality of the computer control of the complicated batch processes of dairies and breweries. I judged that this gave us a competitive edge in competing for complete dairies and breweries. I persuaded the Executive of APV Ltd that we should apply for a Queen's award and in late November 1975 I told the two Peters we were going to have a shot at the Queen's Award for Industry.

I was naturally delighted when we heard in April 1976 that we had been successful. It was duly announced on 21 April and I wrote in my diary that 'We had a good write up in the FT.' This was followed on 21 September when the Duchess of Norfolk, as the Lord Lieutenant of West Sussex, came along to the works and made the presentation of the Queen's Award. I wrote in my diary of that day 'It all went off very well. She did her job magnificently and quite charmed all those presented to her.' I seem to remember we had only allowed half an hour in the programme and the Duchess spent a good hour talking to the staff responsible. This was excellent and was a really good morale booster. In mid December HM the Queen and HRH the Duke of Edinburgh held a reception in Buckingham Palace for the recipients. I took Ken Lloyd and his colleague David Lenel from the automation department to the Palace. I had heard that the Queen and the Duke would circulate and they were sure to ask what we had won the award for. It so happened that the development work was done with the Scottish & Newcastle company at their brewery at Fountains Abbey near Holyrood Palace in Edinburgh. When the Duke came to our group and I explained that the practical development was done near Holyrood Palace. At the mention of palaces and breweries the Duke told us that Watney Mann used to have a brewery at Victoria and the smells came over and 'filled this house'. As I looked round at the gilded state room of Buckingham Palace I had a wry smile to myself at the thought of the Duke referring to Buckingham Palace as a house.

Looking back on being associated with these two award winning occasions confirmed my conviction that outstanding technology gave us a competitive edge in the market place.

Hall Thermotank Ltd

This was the last of the Seligman–Benson take-overs. Peter Seligman kept me fully briefed on progress and I was at the APV Holdings board meetings when the two Peters briefed the non-executive directors. It was to me a very good example to see the two Peters in action. The discussions and negotiations took place from mid

July to mid September 1976. The support from the non-executive directors was clear. The relations with Hall Thermotank top staff were excellent.

I played a small part when Peter Seligman asked David Everington the chief executive of APV Parafreeze, our freezer equipment manufacturing company, and myself to visit Hall Thermotank to be shown their new single screw compressor and to report back our assessment of it. I was not to say I was from APV, but just announce myself as Dr Miller to see Archie MacDougall who was fully in the picture about the possible take-over. I immediately took to Archie. He was a Scot and in the general social chat at the beginning he told me he came from Clydebank. I said I had an uncle, Dr Bill Allan, who used to be in practice in Clydebank and did Archie know him. 'Oh yes,' he said, 'he was our doctor – a lovely man.' Bill Allan had married my mother's sister Willis Glen and I was very fond and grateful to Uncle Bill and Auntie Willis. In the early 1950s I had a girl-friend in Glasgow and when I went up to Glasgow for a week-end, Auntie Willis always welcomed me into their home and I invariably stayed with them. Uncle Bill's consulting room was part of the house, with a waiting room with an outside door. Uncle Bill's evening surgery was meant to end at 7.00 p.m., but it invariably ran over, and my aunt was getting concerned at waiting for ever for the evening meal, so at around 8 o'clock Auntie Willis in high dudgeon marched through to the waiting room and locked the outside door, so that no more patients could come in. 'Oh,' said Archie, 'we all knew about your aunt locking the outside door, but that's not the end of the story. As soon as your aunt had returned to the house, Dr Allan went through to the waiting room and reopened it!' Such was the dedication of Uncle Bill to his patients. After that breaking of the ice Archie and I were great friends.

David Everington and I were given an excellent presentation of the new single screw compressor. It was a most elegant design. It had two star wheels on the periphery which counterbalanced each other. The result was that it did not suffer, as normal reciprocating compressors do, with major fluctuating loads on the bearings with every stroke. I reported all this on our return to Crawley.

Chapter 10

Managing Director APV Holdings Ltd

Peter Seligman had made his intentions clear that he would retire at the AGM in May 1977. In preparation for this the Holdings Board agreed in September 1976 that Peter Benson would succeed Peter Seligman as chairman and we would have two managing directors: Ken Fraser to look after the old Hall Thermotank Companies and I would look after the old APV companies. This struck me as a reasonable set up and I had no hesitation in agreeing with it.

David Shore succeeded me as managing director of the APV Co Ltd with a seat on APV Holdings Ltd. This was an appointment I fully approved of and David's subsequent performance fully justified it. What I was not so happy about was Peter Benson's insistence that he was to be both chairman and chief executive. Since the 1970s there have been several classical examples of individuals determined to combine the two appointments, but it can have regrettable consequences and the city now, rightly to my mind, frowns on such arrangements.

Peter Benson's judgement of business situations was absolutely first class, but it was in his appointment of people to key posts that he had a blind spot. In the previous arrangement Peter Seligman supplied to the partnership that understanding of people and how to lead and get the best from them as a team. The combined effort of the two Peters as a team was quite outstanding. I will refer to this subject later both in APV and with my experience with the Engineering Council.

The new top management came into being on 18 May 1977. A great deal of my time in the early months was spent visiting the UK subsidiaries, chairing their Board meetings and generally meeting the local directors and their staff.

During the next five years with APV Holdings some interesting and challenging problems came my way. The first occurred in the summer of 1977, when we had the opportunity to take a minority holding in Holvrieka, a Dutch company, who manufactured dairy evaporators.

Holvrieka Holding BV

In April 1977 APV began negotiations to take a stake in Holvrieka Holding BV, a Dutch engineering company, who manufactured large tubular milk evaporators under licence from DEC, an American company. Holvrieka had a well equipped factory at Emmen in Holland.

Peter Benson and I were dealing with Bill de Waard, the chief executive and Luis Hissink, the sales director. Negotiations went smoothly, although the collaboration on the sale of large tubular milk evaporators did not develop as we had originally hoped. However, we believed we could gain from the fabrication capability in Holland as we had no such factory in Europe. Our personal relations with de Waard and Hissink were good, so on 30 December 1977 we took 30% of their equity shares.

I went onto the Holvrieka Board as a non-executive director. By the time I attended my first board meeting on 25 April 1978, we heard for the first time that Holvrieka had made serious losses in 1977. Peter and I had received reassuring noises on Holvrieka's finances from their auditors the previous June. We were both surprised and not exactly pleased to hear of the true state of affairs. As I wrote in my diary for that day 'The chairman was as concerned as I was by the poor results for last year and our inability to know in time. We expressed our displeasure very clearly.'

By August de Waard stepped down and became a non-executive director. Mr Molengraff was brought in as the new chief executive.

At the same time NOM, the Dutch government Investment Agency, was taking an interest and Mr Wirman the NOM managing director came in on the discussions. By the end of 1978 the Holvrieka results were even worse than I feared and we were being asked to put more money into Holvrieka.

Peter Benson and I had agreed between ourselves that we shouldn't put more money in, and if need be we would let the company go to the wall. We obtained the APV Holdings Board's agreement to this at our board meeting on 11 January 1979 and our non-executives wished us to look into the question of suing – neither Peter nor I thought this was possible and this was confirmed by discussions with our solicitors McKenna & Co.

By the Holvrieka board meeting on 25 January 1979 it became clear that NOM were willing to give Holvrieka a loan of 2 million guilders (nearly £0.5 million) – really to save jobs in Emmen, an area of high unemployment. It was now a matter of negotiating our exit and we could only squeeze 100,000 guilders out of NOM. I was more than ever convinced that we were doing the correct thing for our shareholders when I heard that the sickness rate was as high as 18% for the whole of 1979 and was running at 20% for the first two months of 1980.

It was a salutary lesson to me, and despite the tough things which had to be said to our Dutch colleagues the personal relations were all carried out politely and at the end the directors of the Holvrieka Board sent me a book of *Holland in Full Color* with the inscription 'With a most pleasant memory of the personal contacts with you and great appreciation of your valuable contribution to the work of the Holvrieka Board'.

The Arab boycott

Early in 1978 we heard we were being put on the Arab Boycott list. This had come about because the APV Company's accounts department had answered a routine questionnaire from the Arab Boycott office in Damascus asking if APV had any know-how agreements with Israel. 'Yes' they answered. When it blew up into a full scale boycott, I heard for the first time that although such an agreement had been signed, it had never effectively been implemented and no royalties had been received. It was really a non-event, but nevertheless here we were on the boycott list.

I decided immediately that the problem should be handled by Freddie Cooper, the overseas sales director of the APV company. Freddie was familar with dealing with the arab world. We then appointed a Mr Moukaden as our consultant who, being an Arab, was able to negotiate on our behalf.

I very soon discovered that the Arab Boycott office only knew what we had told them and this was a great help in what we produced in the way of documents to get round this non-event. Nevertheless Mr Moukaden would have to oil some wheels. When I first told the APV Holdings board, I suggested it was likely to cost approximately £70,000. In the end the final bill was around £120,000. I was concerned as I reported this sum to the Holding's board, but the non-executive directors congratulated me on getting away with such a relatively small sum as £120,000. Fortunately this was also comparatively small compared the APV company's profit.

APV Osborne Craig Ltd

APV Osborne Craig was a small company in the Group located at East Kilbride near Glasgow where they manufactured and sold a range of centrifugal pumps. They employed just under 100 people.

In October 1978 I received news of the latest expected outcome for the year, which would be a very severe loss. Peter Benson and I agreed that we should suggest early retirement for the managing director with a fairly generous offer. This was accepted and Alan Wallace, one of the directors, was promoted to be the new managing director and, on John Brown's advice, we sent him on a business course at Cranfield Institute of Technology. By mid August 1980 Osborne Craig were doing well and on 19 August I wrote in my diary: 'To East Kilbride for APV Osborne Craig board. They really have done remarkably well, despite not having a sales manager – £42,000 profit in the first half. I agreed they should extend their workshop and concentrate all the activities in the one location.'

In the annual report of APV Holdings for the same year we reported that 'APV – Osborn Craig enjoyed a record profit with turnover up and the improved efficiencies making themselves felt. Several notable contracts were obtained during the year, including 199 agitators for a new vitamin C extension to the Roche Products pharmaceutical plant at Dalry in Scotland. A good order book is carried over into 1981.'

This good performance continued. It was gratifying to see the tough decisions taken in 1978 bear fruit and full credit goes to Alan Wallace and his team.

Manufacturing Advisory Service (MAS)

In June 1977 I was invited by the then Secretary of State for Industry, Mr Eric Varley, to chair a new steering committee on the development and operation of the Manufacturing Advisory Service. A pilot advisory scheme on the Pump and Valve industries had been lead by Fred Morley CBE of Rolls Royce, then on secondment to the Department of Industry. It was on the basis of Fred's report that the scheme was expanded and developed.

The Advisory Service provided 15 man-days of free consultancy on any manufacturing problem for manufacturing firms employing between 100 and 1000 people. This could be followed by a further 15 man-days consultancy at half cost. The service was managed by the Production Engineering Research Association (PERA), led very effectively by Donald Morgan. A key part of the service was the use, in an executive capacity, of a number of senior industralists who decided, with the top management of the company, what help could usefully be given. Looking back on it, I believe that it was the input of the senior industrialists which greatly assisted each consultancy.

We were able to persuade some key people to join the steering committee. Sir Henry Chilver, then Vice-Chancellor of Cranfield Institute of Technology, Dr George Brosan, Director of North East London Polytechnic from academia, Hugh Lang, chairman PE International Ltd, George Adler, Director of Research, British Hydromechanics Research Association, Ken Cure from the Amalgamated Union of Engineeering workers and of course Fred Morley.

I chaired the steering committee for five years and from the very beginning the service was a great success. In the Steering Committee's report in March 1981 to Sir Keith Joseph, the Secretary of State, we were able to say that the saving to the company was at least twelve times the cost to the Treasury. This was an outstanding performance. To widen the scope we recommended the lower limit of size of company should be reduced fom 100 to 80 employes. This was further reduced to 60 in 1980. The life of the Service was originally expected to be five years from 1977 to 1982, but before I gave up the chairmanship we had obtained agreement for a further four years to 1986.

From the very beginning of my association with MAS I had seen a similiarity between MAS and the Agricultural Development and Advisory Service (ADAS). ADAS had operated for many years and its budget was more than ten times that of the MAS. The steering committee believed the enviable efficiency of British Agriculture may well be due in part to ADAS.

As a postscript I was delighted to hear that MAS was relaunched in 2002 meeting European Community regulations, and in April 2004 Jacqui Smith, the Industry minister at the Department of Trade and Industry, said she thought that the Manufacturing Advisory Service had been a big success. I very much agree with her.

Management motivation

It was Richard Alston of Inbucon who introduced John Brown and myself to Management Motivation on 29 August 1979. Management Motivation is a fairly sophisticated management tool[1] developed by David McClelland, professor of psychology at Harvard University and David Burnham, president and chief executive of McBer and company, a behavioural science consulting firm in Boston, Massachusetts.

The objective is to determine the inner driving forces we all have. McClelland and Burnham have determined that there are three main categories:

1. **Achievement.** Individuals high in Achievement like to outperform others. They set challenging goals for themselves and set high standards of performance.
2. **Affiliation.** In giving Affiliation the individual is positively interested in and concerned for others. On the receiving of affiliation they are concerned about being disliked, disapproved of or rejected. They like to be liked.
3. **Power.** Individuals high in Power are seen as strong and influencing others. There are four stages in the maturity of an individual's power. Stage I is the power of being associated with powerful people. Stage II feeling strong through self control, not letting others control you. Stage III is split into IIIa which is self-aggrandizement, eg exploitative or aggressive. The maturer Stage IIIb power is used for getting something done. It is the power to persuade and influence. It is power to make others feel strong. Stage IV is feeling strong by using higher authority for larger purposes.

The method to determine an individual's profile is to invite them to write a story from being shown a picture of a group of people. By the words they use the experts can determine how strong the individual is in achievement, affiliation and power.

There are also six motivational styles of management: Coercer, Authoritarian, Affiliator, Democrat, Pace-setter and Coach. These styles were developed from research conducted at Harvard Business School.

1. **The Authoritarian** is a strong 'firm but fair' directive leader. He/she listens, sets goals, directs clearly, controls tightly and rewards and punishments are balanced firmly and fairly.
2. **The Affiliator** believes in 'people first, task second'. He/she listens a lot, does not set goals, does not direct task performance clearly, does not give task-oriented feedback, rewards personal characteristics, not task performance.

---

[1] Management Motivation. 'Power is the great motivator' by David C McClelland and David H Burnham, Harvard Business Review Volume 54, Number 2 March–April 1976.

3. **The Democrat** believes in 'participative managers'. He/she listens a lot (holds many meetings), sets goals and standards, does not direct clearly, gives some task feedback, rewards task performance and co-operative behaviour, and doesn't punish.
4. **The Pace Setter** is the 'do it myself' manager. He/she doesn't listen, sets goals by example, Does not direct, but sets the pace, gives some task feedback, rewards good performance, but does not provide warmth of support.
5. **The Coach** is the 'management by objectives' manager. He/she listens, sets challenging but moderate risk performance goals, directs and influences subordinates, delegates responsibility – as much as subordinates can handle, provides frequent task oriented feedback, rewards task performance , but does not overlook failure and responds by helping subordinate to improve.
6. **The Coercer** is the 'all stick and no carrot' manager. He/she doesn't listen, unilaterally tells people what to do, gives very clear direction, immediate feedback – usually negative, motivates primarily by threats, fear and punishment, and rarely praises or rewards.

The optimal Motivational profile and the management style for a particular management post can be assessed by the management consultants in this field. Job characteristics can be used to indicate individuals and their own personal profiles can be matched to jobs. The most important of the posts is that of the managing director or chief executive, and the classic profile is medium level in achievement depending on the type of company. In a fast growing developing area the achievement motivation could well be higher. However the affiliation should be low. The managing director has on occasions to take a tough line and must not be put off by feelings of sympathy. He/she must have considerable power motivation preferably of IIIb maturity to persuade and influence.

In October 1979 We had a Management Motivation course run by George New and his consultancy firm, Omega management consultants. They had been working closely with Richard Alston of Inbucon, and would now be our direct contact. This course was for four group companies.

One of the companies at the course in October, APV Kestner, were doing badly and showing little sign of improvment, so I agreed with George New that he would run a course just for the Directors of APV Kestner. This took place towards the end of February 1980. When I saw George New on 29 February, I wrote in my diary 'George greeted me with a long face. There is simply no one with Stage III power. The objectives exercise was pushed all the way by George and his team. There will have to be many changes.' The current managing director was low in power and what little he had, was at stage II – not letting others control him. The directors of APV Osborne Craig had been assessed by this time and Jimmy Hillicks, the sales director, had 50% stage III power and moderately low affiliation so he moved over to be the managing director of APV Kestner.

In the Group's 1980 annual report and accounts it said of APV Kestner 'During 1980 the company made a loss, partly due to the necessity to increase its provision against obsolescence of stock'. In the following year (1981) the annual group report said of APV Kestner 'In spite of a poor economic climate in their traditional chemical and textile markets the company produced good profits'.

Then in January 1983, after I had left the company, it was reported that APV Kestner had been sold to Derfshaw, a company formed by Mr FH Shaw, a former director of APV Kestner.[2]

Leslie Halling the managing director of APV Paramount was from the beginning keen that his company should take part in the Management Motivation courses. Leslie has the typical 'V' profile for a chief executive, and he had built up a strong team amongst the APV Paramount directors. I wrote in my diary for Saturday 23 February 1980 'I went to Crawley for the last session of APV Paramount's course on Motivation Management. I sat in on the end of the development of their objectives. They have got some first class objectives and Leslie Halling was clearly pleased with how the course has gone. This is good news. George New is pleased too.' The following Monday, Leslie Halling phoned me to say how worthwhile the George New course had been last week. This was a case of a very well run company in the Group improving their performance. In 1980 the Group annual report said 'APV–Paramount's results through the year were satisfactory although orders fell away in the last quarter. During 1980, despite fierce international competition, the company achieved some notable export successes, which amounted to nearly half of the total value of orders taken during 1980.' In 1981 after a number of successful years APV–Paramount recorded a considerable loss, but the following year returned good results. This dip was due to the state of the market. Omega consultants continued to work for APV companies including APV–Parafreeze, who provide capital equipment to the freezer industry, and used them to improve the climate within the company. APV Osborne Craig used them to select Jimmy Hillick's successor. The use of Omega consultants petered out towards the end of 1980 for reasons I will come to in the next section.

On the transfer list

Ken Fraser, the other managing director of APV Holdings, had indicated to Peter Benson that he wished to retire at the age of 60, and in July 1979 Peter called in the headhunters. On 9 November 1979 it was announced that Peter Hamilton from GKN would take over as the other managing director. It was another week before Peter Benson saw me and told me that Dick Morris was coming in as

---

[2] I should add as a footnote that FH Shaw was the finance director of APV Kestner and in his motivation profile showed average achievement, low affiliation. and high power with 38% (stage IIIb). This should have allowed us to consider him to succeed as managing director.

APV Holdings Board – November 1981. Left to right: standing: *Sir Frederick Warner,*
Mr David Shore, Mr R Wright, Mr Ken Grover, Mr Edwin Jones Jnr, USA,
Mr Madron Seligman, Mr Ronnie Middleton; sitting: *Dr Kenneth Miller, Sir Ronald McIntosh,*
Mr Peter Benson, Mr Peter Hamilton

non-executive Chairman, and that Peter Hamilton will be the Chief Executive in twelve months time. I said I was very disappointed and I would have to review my position. It was another case of reminding myself of Rudyard Kipling's poem that 'when you meet with triumphs and disasters you treat these two imposters just the same'.

I could have left the company in a fit of pique, but I decided that worthwhile jobs at my level were not that easy to find, so I decided to stay but clearly determined to review the situation seriously.

Early in January 1980 there was an informal approach by Consolidated Gold Fields to take over APV and Peter Benson said we would resist it and he asked for new five year contracts to drawn up for all executive directors. With the uncertainty over my future I asked that I should have a special clause. On Wednesday 22 January I wrote in my diary 'I saw Peter Benson first thing and put it to him that under all the circumstances I wished to have a clause in my contract which will let me give six months notice. He admitted that from my point of view this was understandable, but the company might not wish to give me a special contract. I said this was up to the company, but if they really wished me to stay, this would be an indication of their good intentions. He said he would have to consult the non-executive directors.'

I took the precaution of seeing two of the non-executives. Ronnie Middleton, a solicitor who was then senior partner of Coward Chance & Co, and Sir Frederick Warner (Ned), senior partner of Cremer and Warner and our technical consultant who attended all board meetings. Both Ronnie Middleton and Ned Warner were both very understanding of my position and as a result I was allowed a release clause in my agreement. I had effectively put down a marker. I had no idea how long it would be, but the more I saw of Hamilton's style of management, the more convinced I was that it was only a matter of time before I departed.

I took George New into my confidence and he gave me invaluable personal advice over the next two and a half years. He also recommended that I should take one of the leading headhunters into my confidence. I had recently had contact with Jim Parker-Jarvis of Spencer Stewart. I left my CV with Jim and he agreed to see what he could do for me. The other action was to speak to Duncan Davies, an old colleague from ICI days, who had left ICI and was now the chief scientist at the Department of Trade and Industry (DTI). I said absolutely nothing of this to my colleagues in APV.

I was still determined to play my full part in directing the affairs of APV, and that no one could say I had a chip on my shoulder or that I was not giving good service to the company. There were too many good friends and colleagues that I couldn't let down.

I was convinced that the cost of management motivation by Omega consultants was fully justified. Unfortunately Peter Benson objected to the immediate costs, and I was unable to convince him of the longer term financial savings. Peter Hamilton saw fit to take the same view, and I therefore had to drop the use of Omega consultants. This to me was a great mistake and indicated to me my loss of influence.

Not surprisingly John Brown found another job with Mecca and left APV at the end of May 1980. On the day he left he gave me his assessment of the four stages of the maturity of power of Benson, Hamilton, Shore and myself as he saw us. In my case he was remarkably close to what the Omega tests had revealed. It was invaluable information for me in assessing how these three colleagues were likely to behave towards me. It was not encouraging.

Hamilton was already reducing the extent of the Group, of which I was in charge, and with the Holding board's agreement I was able to take on the major commitment of being a member of the 'University Grants Committee'.

University Grants Committee (UGC)

Membership of the University Grants Committee was on the invitation of the Secretary of State for Education and Science. I received the formal invitation in September 1980, and attended my first meeting of the UGC on 15 January 1981.

The UGC comprised a full time chairman, then Dr Ted Parkes (now Sir Edward Parkes) and 26 part-time members. Twenty of the members were academic staff from the universities, three were from the schools system, and three were from industry, of whom I was one.

The meetings were held at the UGC's offices, and we each sat in the same seat being the one occupied by the person from whom we each took over. I found myself sitting between Professor Richard Atkinson, professor of Archaeology at University College, Cardiff and Mrs Phyllis Taylor, Head Mistress of Wanstead High School, London Borough of Redbridge.

All groups of people with a common interest very soon start to use acronyms. They are a type of shorthand, and should only be used in conversation and correspondence within the group who know the code. As I was the new boy, it was up to me to learn the acronyms of the university world. Here Phyllis Taylor was very helpful. She suggested we should have a sheet of paper between us and when some initials were used which I didn't understand I would write them down on this sheet of paper and she would write out the full name beside the initials. We were soon onto the second sheet of A4 paper!

The use of acronyms can be very irritating if you are not familiar with the particular one. The same initials can even mean different things to a different group. I found on my secondment to British Rail that BNS to the railwaymen meant Birmingham New Street, while back in ICI it was British Nylon Spinners! To return to the UGC.

I was joining them at a fascinating time. The committee's main task, of advising the government on the distribution of grants to individual universities, was going to be no easy task as government had already indicated that there would be a reduction in the money available for distribution.

At my second meeting on 12 February 1981 Ted Parkes told us that the cuts were coming and the Resources sub-committee proposed to be selective. Several members of the UGC became self-righteous and emotional and were all for sharing the misery evenly across the whole system. I supported the chairman and as I recorded in my diary for that day 'I waded in and said all bodies which had grown over the years grow some surplus and it was up to us to be selective'. In retrospect Ted Parkes did the country a great service by pressing selective cuts between universities and between subjects.

I was very conscious of my experience of the redundancies in APV and how the young graduates in Research saw it as my pruning exercise. The APV company achieved a 10% reduction in their salary bill, after 17 years of steady growth. The universities were expected to achieve a 10% reduction in grants and a 5% reduction in student numbers. After all the growth since the war, I didn't expect any trouble. However I had not appreciated the effect of tenure. This in practice meant more money for redundancies. When Ted Parkes later obtained Mrs Thatcher's agreement he came back to tell us that the Prime Minister had made the comment to him that if she had offered the same terms to the Palace of Westminster she would have emptied the place tomorrow!

Gordon Higginson, the Professor of Engineering at Durham University, chaired the Engineering and Technology sub-committee and I believe that both Ted Parkes and Gordon Higginson did an excellent job. I had known Gordon when I was the Engineering Director of the HOC Division of ICI in the 1960s and we arranged for John Robins, an experienced HOC Design Engineer, to be a part-time design tutor at Durham University's Engineering department. Gordon and I took a quiet delight in the continuing success of the scheme. Professor Anthony Unsworth of Durham University told me in 2005 that there are nine design tutors from eight companies in the North East, and this is a distinct feature of the engineering course at Durham.

The concept of being selective and avoiding the across the board cuts of equal misery meant that the UGC went through every university and every department separately. It was a subjective exercise but, in retrospect I believe it was done conscientiously and thoroughly. Honest, critical and frank comments were made in complete confidence, but in writing this account of our deliberations, I am making one exception. We had been discussing East Anglia and the academic members of the committee were fully aware of the reputation East Anglia had acquired after the student unrest of a decade before, and we were remarkably kind to them. Then the chairman moved us on to Exeter. Phyllis Taylor immediately broke in and said 'Mr chairman, this is the university where my parents like to send their daughters'. What a delightful comment on Exeter!

I recall the impressions I already had of the various engineering departments, based on the experience I had a decade before when interviewing graduates in my ICI days on Teesside. They were generally in line with the views expressed by other members of the UGC. Not that the UGC members were out of date, but that the education system's response to change is on a long timescale.

The formal Grant Letters came out on 1 July 1981, and there was the inevitable howl from those universities who received more than average cuts.

Dr John Ashworth, Vice-Chancellor elect of Salford University, enlisted the support of his Chancellor, the Duke of Edinburgh, and Professor Frederick Crawford, Vice-Chancellor of Aston University, obtained the backing of his Chancellor Sir Adrian Cadbury, the industrialist.

The Duke of Edinburgh had raised the matter of Salford University with Lord Caldecote, President of the Fellowship of Engineering. I had first met Robin Caldecote back in 1954 when he was on the staff of the Engineering department at Cambridge, and interviewed me for a job in the department. So it was that I went with Jack Ferguson, who was another of the industrialists on the UGC and a Fellow of Engineering (F.Eng), to see Robin Caldecote and RB Sims, Group Technical Director of Delta Metals, on Thursday 27 August 1981 at the Fellowship of Engineering.

We explained that we proposed a 10% cut in the total grant from our base year of 1979/80 (being the latest available figures the UGC had to work on) and a 5% reduction in the student numbers. Within these overall figures Engineering and Technology courses had a 2% increase from 1979/80. We were also able to show that the largest Engineering Departments were still the same ten before and after the cuts. On size ranking Aston dropped from largest to third on the list, while Salford dropped from fourth to sixth. There were seven Technology Universities, both before and after the cuts in the ten largest departments.

As I wrote in my note on the meeting on 27 August 'Lord Caldecote was clearly impressed by the +2% in engineering/technology, but was still concerned about the supply of technician engineers and less academic professional engineers'. On this latter point I was able to say that the government had a consultative document 'Higher Education in England and Wales outside the Universities' and I pressed him to get the Fellowship of Engineering to give a view by the deadline date of 30 November 1981.

As we discussed it over lunch, it was felt that Salford would have to decide whether they wished to be (i) a smaller university with a higher quality of average intake of students and carry out more research or (ii) keep with the larger numbers of lower academic quality intake, do little or no research and revert to being a Polytechnic. I had the impression that in replying to Prince Philip, Robin will make these points.

In supporting Salford at a press conference on 27 November the Duke of Edinburgh was reported next day in *The Times* as saying that he refused to be drawn, however, on whether the UGC had been right to make such selective cuts 'They have been made and I think we have to live with them'. In the same article it was reported that 'Salford's senate has just given its overall approval to radical plans that over the next three years it would abolish some 30 degree courses; reduce student numbers by 1,200; close departments of music, physical education, and visual and applied arts; and cut total staff by a third including 140 of the 468 academics.'

It was becoming clear that a battle royal was developing for the hearts and souls of industry to support the beleaguered University of Salford. On 21 July Michael Dixon, education correspondent of the *Financial Times*, reported under the heading 'University seeks industry help against cuts'. This article starts with a paragraph 'A DRIVE to enlist industry in freeing technological universities from domination by the traditional academic establishment was launched in London yesterday by supporters and staff of the University of Salford'.

I was able to make contact with Michael Dixon, and on Wednesday 29 July, the day of the royal wedding of the Prince of Wales and Lady Diana Spencer, Michael Dixon visited me at my home in Oxshott. We spent two hours sitting out in the garden going over the basis of the UGC's grant to the universities.

By this time the UGC had announced details of two important criteria it had used. As a measure of a course's popularity the UGC took the average 'A' level grades of the students joining it. On this basis Cambridge, Oxford, Bristol and Durham were at the top with Aston, Salford, Essex and Keele at the bottom. The other criterion was the total research income the university received from all sources including industry. The ranking by research was also headed by Cambridge.

Michael Dixon and I clearly had a rapport with each other. From then on Michael Dixon did us proud. On 30 July Michael wrote an article ' "Order of merit" basis of university cuts', based on the criteria I have outlined in the previous paragraph and then on 3 August Michael produced another key article 'How grants re-shape the British university system'. By this time I felt we were succeeding in publishing our main criteria and the emotional anger in the press was largely subsiding. I was keen, though, to obtain the support of the Confederation of British Industry (CBI).

On 14 July 1981 I attended a CBI seminar on Innovation and Growth. As I said in my diary of that date 'I spoke to Michael Bury the CBI Director of Education, Training and Technology. He would like me to liaise with the CBI about the UGC. I said I would be very pleased to do so.' I was effectively being asked to take over this liaison between the CBI and the UGC from Sir Donald Barron, chairman of Rowntree Mackintosh Ltd, and an industrialist member of the UGC. Sir Donald was a very effective member of the UGC.

On 26 August I had a useful meeting with Michael Bury and his colleague Maurice Roberts. As I said in my diary, it was 'Very much a meeting of minds'. They said there had been no reactions from CBI members, and only Aston had written to the CBI. They thought Salford had been more skilful in their campaign. Salford went straight to the firms who recruited their graduates. Maurice Roberts who is ex-ICI went back to his old colleagues at Organics Division of ICI and discovered that ICI were recruiting Salford graduates for Technician Engineers' posts, i.e. the support staff to the Chartered Engineers. This led us on to consider the Polytechnics and we all agreed that co-ordination of the Polytechnics is needed. We were fully aware of the government's consultative document on 'Higher Education in England outside the Universities'.

I was invited to attend the CBI's Higher Education panel on 28 September. The discussion centred around the effect of the cuts arising from the UGC's grant allocation and the government's discussion paper on higher education outside the universities. I was able to deflect any criticism from the UGC into support for the need to co-ordinate the Polytechnics.

Although I had been able to uphold the UGC's position at the CBI's Higher Education panel, I was a little apprehensive of the debate at the CBI Conference in November. I had the highest respect for Sir Adrian Cadbury's ability to put over a convincing case for Aston University. I was not at all certain I could do justice to the UGC. As it happened I was called to speak first, and I wrote it up in my diary 'I found myself speaking just after Ian MacGregor and as such before Sir Adrian. I stole Sir Adrian's thunder. Answered his questions before he started and proposed co-ordination of policy. He was left to agree with me. Donald Barron was a great help too, over UGC.'

After I became director-general of the Engineering Council, I had running arguments with John Horlock and John Ashworth who were complaining about my membership of the UGC, claiming I had a clash of interests. I never saw it in this light, since all members of the UGC were appointed in a personal capacity. However as events unfolded and my work with the Engineering Council expanded, I decided that I had made my main contribution to the UGC, and I could no longer afford to spend 10 to 15% of my time on UGC business. It was a great pleasure and honour to have been associated with the UGC over the July 1981 Grant Letter, and the knowledge I acquired with this association was invaluable in a particular episode with the Department of Education and Science, as I will relate later.

My efforts on the UGC were clearly appreciated by Keith Joseph as our exchange of letters on my resignation show very clearly (see Appendix IV).

My departure from APV Holdings

As I mentioned in the section 'On the Transfer List' I was in contact with George New who gave me invaluable advice. He knew my personal profile according to the management motivation tests. George was quite clear that I had the profile to take on a chief executive's role. I won't bore the reader with some of the 'might have beens'. As soon as the possibility arose of the chief executive of a new Engineering Authority arising out of the Finniston report 'Engineering our future', I knew this was a post I really wanted.

I was very touched that Bill Duncan, my last boss in ICI, should put me up for the Fellowship of Engineering (F.Eng). This was formally confirmed at their AGM on 17 February. Then Michael Leonard, the Founder Secretary of the Fellowship, asked me to reply for the new Fellows at the Fellowship of Engineering dinner at the end of March. In my diary of 30 March 1981 I wrote 'A works car to the Apothecaries Hall for the New Fellows dinner. I replied on behalf of the New Fellows and sat next to the Duke of Edinburgh. He was very easy to talk to.' In my response to the toast to the New Fellows, I said 'The economic circumstances of industry are already putting a severe strain on the traditional training of professional engineers, both at university and in industry. So, at a time when the country needs a high quality of engineers, the means to provide them is seriously at risk. It is therefore, to my mind, essential that we have a new Engineering Council established. Many of us believe that this new council must be a strong independent body. Not subservient to the Government of the day in any way, nor to the civil service, be it the Department of Industry, the Department of Employment or the Department of Education and Science. It must be properly and fully supported by academics, by leaders of industry and by professional institutions.'

As I came away I thought that this evening's effort would be a useful step to establish myself in the Professional Engineering circles.

Although Michael Leonard and I had been on Gilbert Hunt's committee for Industrial Technologies (CFIT), we didn't have any contact until I became a Fellow of Engineering. Michael had been Secretary of the Council of Engineeering Institutions (CEI) before he became the Founder Secretary of the Fellowship of Engineering. With this experience he became an extremely useful contact for me, and I will come later to the part he played on the Engineering Council's by-laws.

Matters were moving on for the Engineering Council. In July 1981 Sir Kenneth Corfield, chairman and chief executive of Standard Telephones and Cables Ltd (STC) was appointed Chairman designate of the Engineering Council. The Royal Charter was granted on 27 November and on 10 December Sir Keith Joseph, the Secretary of State for Industry, appointed the first seventeen members of Council.

In mid-December 1981 I received a phone call from Neville Cooper, one of Kenneth Corfield's directors. I had known Neville back in my ICI days on Teesside when he was the education manager at Wilton. Neville inquired if I was interested in the director general's job at the Engineering Council. The result of this was that I saw Sir Kenneth Corfield on 15 December and I wrote in my diary 'After lunch I drove up to London to the STC offices. I had one and a half hours with Sir Kenneth. I think it went very well. We had a meeting of minds on most things and I think he is favourably disposed to me for the director general's post of the new Engineering Council.'

There was then a slight delay as the Engineering Council members felt they should call in the headhunters and chose Spencer Stewart to do the search. In retrospect I considered this strenghtened my position. On 18 March I saw John Sackur of Spencer Stewart and I wrote in my diary 'Up to London to see John Sackur of Spencer Stewart about the Engineering Council job. It went pretty well and I will be on the short list.' I was interviewed by David Plastow, a Council member, and managing director of Vickers Ltd on 28 April and I recorded that it went pretty well. The following day I was seen by Gordon Beveridge, a Council member and head of Chemical Engineering at the University of Strathclyde, along with Sir Kenneth Corfield, and I wrote in my diary for 29 April 'I met Ken Corfield and Professor Gordon Beveridge of Strathclyde. We had a long talk. It really went remarkably well. I was immediately on a good wavelength with Professor Beveridge.' So it was that the Council appointed me to be its first director general at their Council meeting on 12 May.

During this period leading up to my appointment, I hadn't spoken to any one at APV about my future. Peter Hamilton introduced a bureaucratic organization of five divisions and Hamilton and Benson tried to persuade me to take on the Industrial Division, as well as the nominal title of group managing director as Hamilton's deputy. In the end I accepted being head of the Food Division.

Hamilton wanted us to get all the group companies to have a complete balance sheet every month, instead of quarterly, as we had been doing, with a revised estimate of the latest expected outcome (LEO) of the year's final results. The accountants came to me complaining that it would increase their work immensely without any clear advantage. My diary entry for 23 October 1980 reads 'I saw Peter Francis and heard just how much the paper work would increase if we followed Peter Hamilton's wishes. I told Peter Hamilton myself.' Next day I spoke to Peter Benson and said we should have a meeting to discuss it. My diary entry for 24 October read 'I told Peter Benson about disagreement on forms and returns and said I thought we should have a meeting. Shortly afterwards I heard from Ken Grover that Peter Hamilton has completely capitulated and now agrees completely with Ken Grover and our views. After Peter Hamilton had backed down I felt relaxed and confident.'

Peter Hamilton had been chasing Leslie Halling and myself that our notes were too short. Hard to believe, but it was so. There was a Group Strategy Conference coming up in May 1982. On the 27 April 1982 we had the APV Holdings board and I wrote in my diary for that day 'We had the APV Holdings Board. Hamilton was away in Australia, but Ronnie McIntosh was back. Benson was highly critical of all the paperwork and long reports from the divisional chief executives. Even ruder comments about the conference papers. I let them know I had been upbraided for too short a note.'

Later I realized that these nonsenses could only be stopped if Hamilton had a boss who could and would come down heavily, but Peter Benson was fast approaching his retirement.

Postscript to APV

Two years later on 17 July 1984, when we were well underway with the Engineering Council, I found myself entertaining the Engineers Employers' Federation to dinner at the Caledonian Club, and I saw that Astley Whittall was amongst our guests. Astley was at this time a non-excutive director of APV Holdings. I arranged that Astley would be one of my dinner sides. As we sat down to dinner he passed to me under the table a notice that Hamilton will be leaving APV tomorrow. What an irony of fate that I was by chance given an early notice of his departure. As I drove home that evening, I wondered if I could possibly have survived at APV for the last two years and I concluded that no way would it have been possible. In any case, I was in the middle of a wonderful challenge, guiding the new Engineering Council.

I often wondered afterwards if I should have said something to either Peter Benson or Ronnie McIntosh just before I left APV, but at the time any remark from me could so easily have been treated as sour grapes, and in any case I was looking for a satisfactory exit, and indeed had found one.

CHAPTER 11

The Engineering Council

THE ENGINEERING COUNCIL FORMALLY AGREED my appointment as the first director general at their meeting on Wednesday 12 May 1982. The announcement was in the papers on Monday 17 May. In an article in *The Times* the same day Derek Harris wrote 'The job of knitting together the three key areas in engineering – academics, industrialists and professional engineeers – will fall to a considerable degree on the director general and a strong candidate was being looked for'. In the same article Sir Kenneth is quoted as saying 'The calibre of candidates was extremely high, but Dr Miller's qualifications and experience are particularly well balanced.' I was always grateful to Sir Kenneth for this superb introduction.

That same afternoon I was with Sir Kenneth at the STC offices and with the help of Martin Butler, the STC press man, we gave telephone interviews to Maggie Brown of the *Guardian* and Rob Golding, the editor of the journal *The Engineer*.

Maggie Brown did me proud and in my diary of 18 May I wrote 'A very racy article in the *Guardian*. All my hobby horses had a good airing'. In fact Maggie Brown under the heading 'Engineering a revolution in UK industry' started off by quoting me as saying 'I'm an engineer turned accountant'. She went on to say 'he volunteers the view that money is a good scale of measurement when it comes in assessing the performance of a product. His is a no-nonsense commercial approach very much in keeping with brass tacks official government thinking. It is bound to go down well with the powerful industrial companies who have been lobbying hard for just such a man as the first director general, whose stamp will carry on long into the future.' Later in the article Maggie Brown quotes me as saying 'I spend my time preaching at everyone that development must be geared to the market place. It's not very tactful to say so, but Concorde is the classic example of something that wasn't.' She goes on in the article to say

> Dr Miller was the unanimous and popular choice of the Engineering Council's lay members when they met last week because his experience is broad. This is of crucial importance because the Engineering Council, if it is to succeed in the engineering skills renaissance it is expected to achieve, will need every ounce of dipomacy and know-how its director general possesses. In a nutshell he has to persuade other powerful entrenched institutions to see things his way. For example, there are co-operative relationships with the engineering institutions, all of which cater for segments within the professional elite. He is a Fellow of the Institution of Mechanical Engineers and knows the ground well.

117

Second he has a fair inkling of the ways and wiles of Government. Or at least he has observed the Department of Industry while he sat on two advisory committees, first as a member, then as chairman during the 1970s. This quiet behind-the-scenes work may not make headlines, but it marked him out as a diplomatist. He has also served on the National Economic Development Office's process plant committee.

The main thrust of his lobbying will be to argue for resource, money and people to be shifted towards the broad engineering sector. He points to the UGC advice: while university spending was cut overall by 5 per cent, there was a 2 per cent increase in engineering and technology educational spending.

That kind of shift should be taking place wherever government grants, or effort, are being deployed. Second he wants to see far more effort going into applied development and design and making products which have a commercial application.

'Engineering' he sums up 'is all about the creation of real wealth, and that is what I hope we will be doing through the council.'

This article came out on the morning of an APV Holdings board meeting, and I remember Peter Benson exclaiming 'Engineer turned accountant'. I bantered back at him that I had learnt so much from him. He seemed to appreciate this slightly back-handed compliment, and came back to say 'does this make me an accountant turned engineer!'

Rob Golding, the editor of the magazine *The Engineer* inspired an Opinion article. 'Into the future with Dr Who?' The article read as follows:

The announcement that Dr Kenneth Miller is the chosen hero to lead engineers to the promised land was greeted with a chorus 'Dr who?' It has to be said that the 55-year-old Cambridge engineering graduate has not spent much of his life in the limelight and does not quite fit the identikit that has taken shape during six months of speculation about the appointment.

There is no argument about his experience and ability. He has been engineering adviser to the main board at ICI. He is managing director of a £300 million turnover process engineering company. He could have been an engineering don. He has sat on NEDO committees and helped set up the Government's manufacturing advisory service. That all makes him a respected industrialist.

The learned societies must be relieved to learn he is a member and staunch supporter of the Fellowship of Engineering. Academia will have mixed views about his membership of the University Grants Committee.

What APV (Miller's company), the Fellowship of Engineering and the University Grants Committee have in common is hopeless public relations. APV works very hard at its lack of corporate image, the Fellowship of Engineering has been around for seven years and still declines to publicise the achievements of its new recruits. And the UGC – which is now fairly widely complimented for a successful redistribution of resources to universities – got a damning press when the cuts were first announced because of its own poor PR.

Dr Miller contends that years of association with poor self-publicists has not dulled his appetite for publicity. It is vital it has not. Like it or not, communications is a burgeoning technology and controlling it is an increasingly sophisticated art. Engineering and its dilapidated image badly needs a svelte super-hero who can deal deftly with anything from Government select committees to Robin Day's Question Time. The late Sir John Methven had just begun to show mastery of the art.

There is evidence of a drift in the right direction for the status of engineering. The Government is recognizing new technology with grants and responsible ministers. Pay has improved to the point where the brain drain is not a constant problem. Satellites, robots and biotechnology have added some glamour to a profession which is for the majority still represented by the man who fixes the TV.

But it is not a drift that will become an unstoppable force through its own momentum. Dr Miller must forget all about the misplaced modesty learned with the establishment and blaze a new trail. We wish him well.

This was all an excellent start for me personally. We had an initial Council made up of 17 distinguished people. In fact a real power house of experience and ability.

Kenneth Corfield made it clear to me on our first meeting after I joined on 5 July that he only took on the chairman's job on the basis the council appoint a good director general and that they would pay the proper rate. Not long afterwards Kenneth told me that he was the non-executive chairman of the Council and I was very much the chief executive. This was music to my ears and a great relief after Peter Benson in my APV days. Kenneth was as good as his word.

The Policy Statement

Our first priority was to produce a policy statement outlining the future intentions of the Engineering Council. As early as 15 July I noted in my diary 'I went back early to see Kenneth Corfield. We agreed the plan ahead for timing of the policy paper.'

We had, as our starting point, three key benchmark documents (i) The Finniston Report 'Engineering our Future',[1] (ii) National Conference on Engineering Education and Training (CONCEET) held in October 1980 and (iii) The Royal Charter of The Engineering Council, granted in November 1981.

Kenneth Corfield generously made available staff and assistance from STC during these early days. One such person was George Heard, who for over a year was acting Secretary of the Engineering Council. One of his sterling jobs in the early days was to check over our three benchmark documents mentioned above, to ensure that no vital topic had been been omitted from the Policy statement.

On Wednesday 11 August I wrote in my diary 'I had a good go at the draft Policy Statement and have now got it into shape to send out.' Next day I wrote in my diary 'Mrs Hatton, my personal assistant, produced the first draft of the Policy Statement in record time and we sent it along with my covering letter to Kenneth Corfield'. Within 24 hours his comments came back and I noted in my diary 'I received Kenneth Corfield's comments back on the first draft of the Policy Statement. He has clearly read it through very carefully, made some worthwhile

---

[1] 'Engineering Our Future' Committee of Inquiry into the Engineering Profession chaired by Sir Montague Finniston published January 1980.

improvements and added the comment "An excellent first draft". This was an encouraging note on which to go on holiday.' It was while I was on holiday that George Heard did his devilling and cross referencing of the key benchmark documents.

On Tuesday 31 August I returned from holiday and George Heard and I were soon editing a second draft of the Policy Statement. On Friday 10 September we had a Council meeting and as I recorded in my diary of that day 'We had the all day Engineering Council meeting. Onto the Policy Statement – at first it seemed impossible, but Ken Corfield did press them along later and we have the lines settled. At this point it was clear that Kenneth Corfield was taking a close interest in the document as it took shape and there were many helpful contributions from the members of the Council at this meeting which were then incorporated in the text.'

The Policy Statement was launched with a press conference on 30 September. It was well received, almost embarrassingly so, with eight of the chartered engineering institutions strongly supporting us with their own press release. The engineering professional institutions were clearly with us and we awaited the reaction of the national press next day. As I recorded in my diary for Friday 1 October 'Into the office to see the reaction to yesterday's press conference. *Times*, *Guardian* and *FT* all good. Nothing in the *Daily Telegraph.*'

Sir Monty Finniston came on 15 October to discuss the Prince of Wales award and in my diary I also wrote 'Monty thought our Policy Statement was good'. This was praise indeed, coming from such an influential person. Then on Monday 18 October I wrote 'In the late afternoon I drove round to Imperial College for the Fellowship of Engineering Council. The Engineering Council's Policy Statement was on the agenda. It was very well received with lots of compliments.' I felt at the time that the Council was well launched.

Reading the Policy Statement again after two decades, it has stood the test of time remarkably well. An abridged version appears in Appendix V for those who are interested.

I believe this Policy Statement was the launching of the Engineering Council and our subsequent actions and achievements stemmed naturally from this early momentum.

Transfer of titles from Council of Engineering Institutions (CEI)

Our next priority was to persuade the Council of Engineering Institutions (CEI) to hand over the Register and the right to grant the Engineering qualifications. Gordon Beveridge became chairman of the newly formed Standing Committee on Professional Institutions (SCPI). Gordon gave unstinting service to the Engineering Council. He was a tower of strength in the part he played at this crucial time. Gordon would master the details of whatever was under discussion, and with great logic argue the case. He and I worked well together and presented a united front in our negotiations.

Even before I joined the Engineering Council I was invited to a lunch on 7 June when Kenneth Corfield, along with Gordon Beveridge and myself, entertained Gerald Mortimer and Denys Wood, the chairman and secretary of the CEI. In my diary of that date I wrote 'We told them straight. We are taking over.' It was a fairly blunt message.

On 10 June I received a letter from John Lyons, another Council member, who was general secretary Engineers' & Managers Association and Electrical Power Engineers' Association, and he emphasized that I should see Denys Wood early. Later that day I wrote in my diary 'I thought I would link it with ensuring I had Gordon Beveridge with me.' Some instinct told me that I would need his support. Next day I spoke to Gordon on the phone and he willingly agreed and from henceforth we always batted together. I contacted Denys Wood and as I wrote in my diary for 11 June 'I also said to Denys Wood that I would bring Gordon with me. He replied he would have to check with Mortimer. Later in the afternoon Rob Golding of *The Engineer* phoned me to say that the CEI had put out a peevish press release yesterday. I was really annoyed as they had promised on Monday only to say we had met. I gave Rob my views.' For good relations I let the whole incident pass, but it did convince me that Gordon Beveridge and I must always act together in these negotiations.

On 2 July we had our first working party meeting with the CEI. Gordon Beveridge, George Heard and I for the Engineering Council met Gerald Mortimer, their chairman, Bill Eastwood, their vice-chairman and Denys Wood, their secretary. Gerald had had a distinguished career in Consolidated Gold Fields Ltd retiring from the chief executive's post in 1978. At the time of our negotiations he was a Surrey County Councillor, Honorary Treasurer of the Fellowship of Engineering and Chairman of the East Surrey Conservative Association. Gerald's maturity and wisdom did much to assist our deliberations. Dr Bill Eastwood, a distinguished civil engineer had been head of the Department of Civil Engineering at the University of Sheffield and was then senior partner of Eastwood & Partners, consulting engineers. The third member of their team was Denys Wood, a retired Major-General who was the CEI secretary.

In mid September we were indebted for help and support from an unexpected quarter. John Sampson, Secretary of the United Kingdom Association of Professional Engineers (UKAPE), was also an elected member of CEI. John had invited me to be their guest at their Annual Delegate Conference on 26 September 1982. Although this was five days before the official release of our Policy Statement, I was able to assure them that Chartered Engineers would not be swamped by TEngs and Eng Techs as the same ratio of two thirds CEngs on the Council would be carried through in the make-up of the committees through which the profession would be regulated. My discussions with them in the debate and at lunch were carried out in a very friendly atmosphere, and I was delighted a few weeks later when John Sampson invited me to meet the elected members of the CEI Council on the morning of the key Board meeting when the CEI would debate and decide whether they would agree to the transfer of CEI's Regulatory Powers to the Engineering Council.

When I met the elected members of the CEI Board on 11 November their main concern was the non-elected nature of the Engineering Council. We had included in the Policy Statement a brief mention towards the end saying that the 'Council is giving consideration to the possibility of an Engineering Assembly'. Knowing I had the backing of Kenneth Corfield I had no hesitation in agreeing to hold another meeting with the elected members on a later occasion, when we could have a full morning's discussion about an elected Engineering Asembly. I was told later that this undertaking helped persuade some of the elected members to vote in favour of the transfer. At the crucial Board meeting that afternoon the Special Resolution to transfer the Regulatory Powers to the Engineering Council was passed by 25 votes for and 10 against. As a two thirds majority was necessary, it was a close run thing! Next day I wrote in my diary 'Several calls re yesterday's vote. At least two people said I swung three votes at yesterday's pre-meeting. If so, it was crucial as we needed a two thirds vote.'

This was followed by 20 regional meetings which the CEI held with registrants. We in the Engineering Council attended all the meetings and supported them in making the case for the transfer of the titles to the Engineering Council. The CEI then carried out a postal vote of CEI registrants. On 7 February Denys Wood phoned me up to say 42% of those eligible voted and the vote for the transfer was a 92.2% 'yes'. This was good news. The way was now clear for the Engineering Council.

On 7 January 1983 we had the follow-up meeting with the elected members of the CEI to discuss the form of an elected Engineering Assembly and as I wrote in my diary 'There were some useful ideas put out'. All of this was followed up. We developed the Engineering Council's Regional Organization (ECRO) and an Engineering Assembly.

I was pleasantly surprised and touched when early in February Gerald Mortimer invited me to do the honours at Caterham School Speech Day on 9 July 1983. I felt this invitation reflected well on the relationship which Gerald and I built up despite the sensitive and fraught nature of much of the CEI/EC negotiations.

Gerald had been at Caterham School himself, but unfortunately he was in poor health and he wasn't able to be at the Speech Day on 9 July. I wrote in my diary 'We went to Caterham Speech Day. It was a boiling hot day. Sir Olliver Humphreys was in the chair. I made a speech and Dorothy (my first wife) handed out the prizes. It all went very well. We had lunch before and tea afterwards and we took some time to go round the exhibits.'

My speech that day was one of the first occasions I ventured into the field of education. I thought at the time that what I said was pretty straight forward, but I clearly touched on some sensitive nerves. As at all speech days we have three

Caterham School Speech Day, 9 July 1983

separate audiences, the school children, the parents and the teaching staff. I set out to speak to each group in turn.

To the children leaving school I said 'The western world you are going out into has a greater material wealth than has been known at any time in the past. It is also a world that is changing very rapidly.' I went on to be more specific: 'There are certain basic things which I am sure you have already learnt from your time at Caterham School. I start here with the three "Rs", reading, writing and arithmetic. I cannot emphasize too strongly the importance of the written and the spoken word. It is the ability to communicate to other human beings that is so important.' I went on to say 'The other basic I want to mention is mathematics. I am old fashioned enough to believe that you start with simple arithmetic and multiplication tables.' I finished my remarks to the school leavers by saying 'It is not just the academic teaching that you have learnt which will help you through life, but the attitude of mind, the standard of social behaviour which you have also learnt at school that will stand you in good stead as you face the uncertainties of this rapidly changing world.'

To the parents I said 'Give your sons and daughters every chance to develop their abilities whatever they may be.' I went on to say 'No matter what may be our prejudices or hidden desires in perhaps satisfying our own frustrated ambitions, the important thing is that youngsters choose an occupation which they will find satisfying. In the final analysis, the youngsters themselves will have to live with their decision and I think it is essential they appreciate that it is their decision.'

Then to the teachers, and here I clearly touched some sensitive nerves. I started by saying 'I would like to support you in every way in maintaining the high standard of social behaviour, of which I am sure Caterham School is justly proud, going back as it does for over 150 years. To encourage the good habits of hard work and considerate behaviour to other human beings. To develop their interests in outside activities, music, drama and painting.' I went on to say 'I may be preaching to the converted, but speaking nationally we must give a higher priority to maths, science and technology over languages and the arts. In particular we must encourage more girls to do these subjects.' Then I gave a real plug for maths by saying 'I have emphasized the importance of mathematics. The technological developments of the future are highly mathematical. The old descriptive sciences of botany and zoology must give way to the highly mathematical microbiology and biochemistry leading on to the exciting developments in genetics and biotechnology.' I finished by saying 'I must leave you with the thought that to prepare your students of the future to face the world of the future we must move fast to swing the balance from arts to mathematics, science and technology.'

The speech was received politely, and with the Chairman Sir Olliver Humphreys, a distinguished engineer, I was on safe ground. But at the general discussion afterwards I met again with Philip Burns, the head of the History Department, who had been at Trinity Hall with me nearly 40 years before. By lucky chance I remembered Philip's name, but despite this our chat was a little stilted. Philip had played in the Trinity Hall hockey XI, which was captained by Standley Bushell, an old friend of mine with whom I have kept in touch over the years. It was Standley who told me I had put my foot in it at Caterham School. I came to realize that Sixth Form teachers support the narrow specialization in the English Sixth Form. It allows them to teach their subject at a higher level. I will return to view this phenomenon later, and I believe it is one of the key factors in the English school system, which prompted CP Snow in his Reith lecture on 'The two Cultures' in 1959. His full quotation reads as follows: 'A good many times I have been present at gatherings of people who, by the standards of the traditional culture, are thought highly educated and who have with considerable gusto been expressing their incredulity at the illiteracy of scientists. Once or twice I have been provoked and have asked the company how many of them could describe the Second Law of Thermodynamics. The response was cold: it was also negative.'

Recruitment of staff

Kenneth Corfield helped us in those early days with the STC back up on personnel matters, and in particular he made George Heard available to be Acting

Secretary of the Engineering Council. George was a great help in those early days, but he had no desire to be considered for the permanent appointment. It was through STC personnel that I recruited a first class secretary. As I wrote in my diary on Monday 2 August 'My new secretary Mrs Betty Hatton arrived. She shows every sign of being first class'. Jack Levy in the Chronicle of the Engineering Council[2] refers to the appointment of the estimable Betty Hatton as my PA, which she very soon became. Throughout the whole period when I was director general our relationship was strictly business-like. It wasn't until four years after I retired that our paths started to cross again and we began an affair. Seven years later we were married.

Tony Bond, seconded for two years from the Department for Industry, was already in post as Director – Education and Training.

I had four other key directorial positions to fill; Secretary of the Council, Director – Industry, Director – Public Affairs and Director – Professional Institutions.

I was keen that we should use headhunters and also to put all the candidates through the Management Motivation test run by George New and his consultancy firm Omega Consultants. For the headhunters I suggested the Corporate Consultancy Group whom I had used to recruit John Brown's successor as the APV Group Personnel Manager and I had been impressed by their senior partner John Trafford. Kenneth Corfield didn't know them and he very reasonably wished me to check with Council members. By the end of September, Derek Roberts of the General Electric Company, Ralph Quartano of the Post Office and John Faiclough of IBM had given me their full support to use the Corporate Consulting group.

Even before I started to interview, Gordon Beveridge was keen that I should meet Jack Levy. Gordon, Jack and I had dinner on 19 July 1982 at the Caledonian Club. I wrote in my diary that 'We got on very well and he is clearly very interested in the job of Director – Professional Institutions'. He was head of the department of mechanical engineering at City University and was chairman of the Chartered Engineering section, Engineers Registration board of the CEI. Jack was ideal for the job. He knew the background and he was proposed by Gordon Beveridge. Jack was to become a tower of strength and I came to rely on him implicitly.

We started to interview early in October. John Trafford of Corporate Consulting Group and I did the first interviews. Then as soon as I had a preferred candidate for any of the four posts I took them to see Kenneth Corfield. The next step was to put the proposed appointment to the Engineering Council. I simultaneously contacted the Department of Industry and put the proposal to them

---

[2] 'An Engine for Change' – A Chronicle of the Engineering Council by Colin R Chapman & Jack Levy. Published in 2004 by The Engineering Council UK on their Web site www.engc.org.uk

for confirmation. It all went very smoothly and by May 1983 I had a full complement.

Jack Levy was confirmed as director – Professional Institutions. Graham Anthony joined us as director – Industry. He had had his engineering education at Kings College, London, he joined ICI Fibres Division in 1958. After 10 years he joined Ilford Ltd as chief engineer and a decade later became commercial director of Ciba Geigy (UK) Ltd. John Carlill, a recently retired rear-admiral, joined us as secretary of the Council. His last appointment in the Navy was admiral president, the Royal Naval College at Greenwich. The fourth member of the team was Ron Kirby who came as director – Public Affairs from Sime Darby, where he was their European PR manager. Ron had earlier experience as a journalist and knew the press and TV extremely well. Tony Bond, on secondment from the Department of Industry, was already acting director Education and Training. These five full time members of staff made up the team. They came from very different backgrounds and experience. They tended to have the 'V' type personal profile. It was medium to high on Achievement, low in Affiliation, and high on Power. This didn't trouble me. Kenneth Corfield was as good as his word and supported me in my preferences during the selection process, and I obtained the team I requested. I realized full well I also carried the responsibility.

The Engineering Council had already received encouraging support for its Policy statement, and we had an initial success in persuading the CEI to hand over the Register and the right to award the titles of Chartered Engineer, Technician Engineer and Engineering Technician. The final foundation we required was the By-Laws, amplifying the powers conferred by the Royal Charter.

By-Laws

One of the early tasks was to produce and obtain the agreement of the Privy Council for the By-laws of The Engineering Council. Early in 1983 We set up a small working party to carry out this work. Gordon Beveridge again played an important part, as did Jack Levy and John Carlill. I myself found it very hard to raise any enthusiasm in the writing of the By-Laws. I started with no previous experience, but I appreciated their importance and I did have the good sense to ask Michael Leonard to join this small working party. Michael at that time was secretary of The Fellowship of Engineering. He had previously been secretary of CEI and with his background of the Charter of the CEI, was extremely knowledgeable on by-laws, and he was a tower of strength as we developed the draft.

The result was a set of By-laws which strengthened the position of the Engineering Council. For example members of the Executive Group Committees were representatives of their institution as they attended Executive Group Committee (EGC) meetings, but when some of them then sat on the superior body, the Board for Engineers' Registration (BER), the By-Laws stated that they must speak for their Executive Group as a whole and put forward the views agreed at their EGC. Michael Leonard was never fully credited during his life-time for his immense contribution to improving the position of the Engineering Council, but I am pleased that I can do so now.

There was one proposed Clause 17 which would have given the Engineering Council authority to charge Institutions for being a Nominated Body. Gordon Beveridge was very keen that this clause was included, and it was in our first draft. When Gordon and I saw Sir Neville Leigh, Clerk to the Privy Council he made it clear to us that, if as was likely, the institutions objected to this Clause, the Privy Council would almost certainly uphold their objections. We reported this back to Council and they wisely deleted the offending clause. The By-Laws were approved by the Privy Council on 25 November 1983. 'Another landmark' I wrote in my diary.

Engine for change

For the first three years the members of the Council were appointed by the Secretary of State for Industry. He was, of course, strongly influenced by the advice from the permanent secretary, Sir Peter Carey, and the chairman of the Engineering Council Sir Kenneth Corfield. The full list of the members over 1983 to 1984 is shown in Appendix VI.

The result of this was that Kenneth Corfield had collected a galaxy of talent. It was all voluntary, unpaid work and their dedication to the success of the Council was a delight to behold. The chairmen of the three Standing Committees in particular played a significant part in the work of the Council. Geoffrey Hall – Education & Training, Bob Malpas – Industry and Gordon Beveridge – Professional Institutions.

Perhaps the most important action was the introduction by Kenneth Corfield of an annual residential seminar at Highgate House, a conference centre in Northamptonshire. Kenneth Corfield, the Council members and the council's directing staff all attended. The staff included my two PAs, Betty Hatton and my PA seconded from the Department for Industry, the first being Colin Richards.

We would travel through to Highgate House late on a Thursday afternoon or evening. The seminar would start on Friday morning and go on until 5.00 p.m. when Kenneth Corfield would stop the meeting promptly, so that in the next hour, I and the permanent staff could draft out an 'Action list' of what we thought had been decided.

We would then have a formal conference dinner of the Council members and staff, which was invariably a very enjoyable affair. The seminar was an opportunity for the Council members to meet in a relaxed atmosphere and get to know their fellow members.

By breakfast time on the Saturday, Betty had produced a typed first draft, and Kenneth Corfield and I would discuss it over breakfast and would make any alterations we wished. Copies were then run off for the Council members to discuss at a brief meeting that morning. Before we went to the first seminar, I remember Kenneth asking me rather diffidently if I thought the staff could manage this action list, and I had no hesitation in saying 'yes'. I had come across the concept of sleeping on a decision when I had been invited by John Baker, my old professor at Cambridge, to join the Board of Electors for a Cambridge Engineering professorship, and there was an occasion later when we had such a professorial appointment to make and Cambridge had the arrangement that the electors returned next morning to confirm their decision. The concept that the human brain puts matters into perspective after a good night's sleep is a sound one, and I have many times slept on a decision, particularly if it is an important one, and next morning I would make the final choice.

This we did at all five Highgate House seminars that I attended, and I was confident that all the Council members were firmly behind the decisions taken. This proved to be the case. Time and time again I would find that what had been agreed at Highgate House would appear in the public speeches of the members of the Council.

Over the course of time we arranged privately for the same group of staff who attended Highgate House to have a day away from the office to start to formulate ideas for the Standing Comittees to put to the Highgate House Conference. For this we went to Chartridge. The combined effect of Chartridge and Highgate House was a very effective way to develop the Council's strategy.

English Culture and the Decline of the Industrial Spirit

During the Christmas break in 1982, I read Martin Wiener's book *English Culture and the Decline of the Industrial Spirit 1850–1980.*[3] This objective study by Martin Wiener of Rice University brought home to me the deeply rooted causes of Britain's industrial decline, and I became convinced that the problem we had to address was the English culture which developed in the second half of the nineteenth century.

In the early months of 1983 I started to include in my speeches a brief description of the case Martin Wiener makes. One such example was the talk I gave to the Engineering Professors Conference on 28 March 1983, when I said:

> From the thoughts we have developed so far, we are convinced that the reasons for our relative decline as an industrial nation are associated with the cultural climate and social institutions in this country. Many of them go back to the early stages of the industrial revolution.
>
> Martin Wiener, in his recently published book *English Culture and the Decline of the Industrial Spirit,* paints a devastating picture of a cultural blight on our industrial

---

[3] *English Culture and Decline of the Industrial Spirit 1850–1980* by Martin J Wiener of Rice University published by Cambridge University Press 1981.

activity. Wiener sees this as the aristocratic opinion-formers harking back to the idealistic splendour of rural England and the cultural academics playing up the worst aspects of the social upheaval of the industrial growth. The materialism of the money-grabbing businessmen was downgraded in public esteem in preference for the caring professions. It was socially much more acceptable to be a clergyman, doctor or don at Cambridge than a successful businessman. Engineering did not escape criticism and *The Times* in an editorial in 1856, whilst commenting on Robert Stephenson's presidential address to the Institution of Civil Engineers, sneered at Engineers and Engineering as the causes of the railway financial problems.

According to Wiener, the industrialists were encouraged to become country gentlemen and they and their offspring carried on their business in a half-hearted manner. Stanley Baldwin was quoted as the archetypal example. Those that remained as industrialists tended to be conservative (with a small 'c') and their prime objective was to maintain the status quo. This meant an inclination to share markets against fierce competition from America, Germany and Japan. Many of the same points were made by Dahrendorf (at that time director of the London School of Economics) in his TV programme on Britain. He, too, saw the gentrification of the business-class as a major factor, but goes on to criticize the Institutions. In particular he saw our propensity to set up rival bodies with a built-in conflict. The electoral system with two parties locked in mortal combat, each determined to undo the actions of the other when they return to power. The management and unions in industry are equally in an adversarial situation – not talking with each other but at each other.

Taken to its logical conclusion, if we in Britain continue to cling on to our increasingly outmoded social institutions, we will go the way of Venice and Spain as major trading nations, who eventually turn into historic backwaters.

To my mind these analyses miss out on the ability of the British to pull back at the eleventh hour from the abyss. We still have the natural ability and we do have a highly educated professional class. We have in the last three years accepted a rate of change which would have been unheard of and corporately unacceptable to our institutions five years ago. The economic pressures have forced changes on manning levels, both in the office and on the shop floor. Many restrictive practices dating back over many years are being eliminated. We have a government that is determined to have financial discipline both on itself and on industry. The risk is, however, that large tracts of industry have become so weak that they may have gone beyond the point of recovery, but the seeds for this decline were generally sown some ten, fifteen or twenty years ago.

From what I have said so far, you will gather that I believe that we must carry out a cultural change and at the same time not be afraid to change our social institutions. This is what we in the Engineering Council will be endeavouring to do.

The previous week I had spoken at The Careers Research and Advisory Centre's (CRAC) conference in Cambridge on 'The Role of The Engineering Council' and included the the same section on Martin Wiener's book. I wrote in my diary for 23 March 1983, 'I gave my talk to the CRAC conference. It went down well. John MacGregor the minister (Parliamentary Under Secretary of State from D of I), also spoke. He, too, referred to Martin Wiener's book.

There was another government reference to Wiener in 1985. There had been a government reshuffle, and David Young was taking up the appointment of

Secretary of State for Employment. As I drove to work I heard him being interviewed on the 'Today' programme. It struck me at the time as pure Wiener. Later in the day I was talking on the phone to Roger Dawe, a deputy secretary in the Department of Employment, and said I had heard his new Secretary of State on the radio and it sounded very much like Martin Wiener's views. 'Yes,' said Roger. 'We have all been told to read his book.'

When Nicholas Edwards, then Secretary of State for Wales, opened our second Engineering Assembly in Swansea on 17 July 1986, he, too, quoted Martin Wiener. I had the chance at lunch to ask him how he had heard of Martin Wiener, I gathered he had been given the book by his family as a Christmas present.

There was no doubt that I wasn't the only person who had been impressed by Martin Wiener. I realized, too, that the standing and influence of the engineering profession has been greatly influenced by the culture and priorities of the English education system, as it has developed since the middle of the nineteenth century. Nor was there any simple solution, but a long, slow business which would take decades to correct. It did, however, give us an indication on where we should start and what our priorities should be.

I hope in the sections which follow to give an indication of the related work we did during the main part of my time with the Engineering Council.

Resources for engineers' education

The idea of a switch from Science to Engineering came up in the Autumn of 1983. In the evening of 19 September 1983 I went to the Institution of Civil Engineers' reception and wrote in my diary 'I had a useful talk with Lord Gregson and Sir Alan Muir-Wood on the need to swing more resources from Science to Engineering.' Next day Kenneth Corfield and I had a key meeting and I wrote in my diary 'A quiet morning and then Kenneth Corfield and I attended the meeting with the two Secretaries of State, Sir Keith Joseph (Education and Science) and Cecil Parkinson (Trade and Industry). They had Peter Brooke (Education and Science), Kenneth Baker (DTI) and John Butcher (DTI) there and a host of Civil Servants. Ted Parkes and Peter Swinnerton-Dyer from the UGC, John Kingman from SERC and Christopher Ball of NAB were also there. We had a field day. Support for four year courses and funds to be made available. Training places in Industry came up and Cecil Parkinson made my case for me. I pressed for a major swing: Science to Engineering and again said it needed earmarking – a good day's work.'

This was followed by the first Highgate House seminar and the action List of Saturday 24 September 1983 included the following action 'Follow-up letters to Secretaries of State for Education and Industry to confirm understanding of what was agreed at the 20 Sept 83 meeting re: a) additional money for four year courses, b) funding of training places.'

By March 1984 the Department of Education and Science were dragging their feet, and as I recorded in my diary for 7 March 1984 'Later in the afternoon I phoned Kit Farrow (an Engineering Council member) to hear how the National Economic Development Council (NEDC) meeting went. Reasonably well – everyone agreed we needed more Engineers, but the DES are now trying to argue that there has been a massive increase of Engineers. This to my mind is ridiculous.' Next day I wrote 'Thursday 8 March A letter came in from Sir Keith Joseph to Kenneth Corfield confirming my worst fears. I believe they have got the statistics wrong. I went to a NEDO meeting on shortage of Electronic Engineers. Again we had civil servants sitting on the fence.'

On Wednesday 14 March 1984, Kenneth Corfield and I went along to see Sir Keith Joseph and we were accompanied by Vivian Brown from the DTI. Sir Keith and Sir Kenneth greeted each other as long lost friends, but their body language suggested to me that they feared the outcome of the meeting. The DES officials had produced the argument that there had been increases in the number of engineering students but whenever they increased the number of places there were not enough students with suitable 'A' levels coming forth compared with other subjects. This gave me the opening I needed, to present a table of the average 'A' scores of students entering universities. On the scale of 5 for an 'A' Grade, 4 for a 'B' grade and 3 for a 'C'. For three 'A' levels there is a maximum of 15. I was able to show that six years ago the engineers and technologists had an average score of 8.7 out of 15, compared with science at 9.2, architecture at 9.6, arts and languages at 10.2 and medicine at 11.3. The latest figures, with admittedly higher competition to get places and higher average results all round, engineers' average score stands at 10.6 now level with science, and had overtaken architecture still at 9.6 and arts courses at 10.0. It was only slightly behind languages at 11.0, but still behind medicine at 12.1. These figures were all taken from University Grants Committee papers. It was an impressive argument. As I wrote in my diary 'Sir Keith hadn't seen the "A" level results'. Clearly the officials had not chosen to include them in his brief. Now Sir Keith was well known as a very open-minded politician who was always prepared to hear a well-reasoned argument. Kenneth Corfield and I had clearly won the day, and at the end of the meeting Sir Keith turned round to his officials and asked if the officials had anything they wished to say and they all chorused 'No minister'. I naughtily relished their 'No minister'.

All seemed to be going smoothly. On Monday 26 March 1984 I wrote in my diary 'Vivian Brown sent me a copy of the minutes of the meeting we had with the DES. Keith Joseph and the DES really are coming round', and on 18 April I wrote 'Kenneth Corfield told me, he has had a telephone call from DES and the DES are going to back the swing to Engineering. This is good news.'

On 4 July I spoke to John Cassels, then Director-General of the National economic development office (NEDO) and I wrote in my diary 'John Cassels sounded depressing about the Switch. Has to be with DES money. We will have to press government at the highest level.' Our fears were confirmed when on 19 November I received a phone call from Richard Bird of DES and I wrote in my diary 'I heard from Richard Bird. The switch is not going ahead – at least there is no extra money.'

Then out of the blue, I received a phone call from Robin Nicholson, who at that time was chief scientific adviser to the cabinet office. I wrote in my diary for 11 February 1985 'After lunch Robin Nicholson of the cabinet office phoned. The Switch looks as if it is going ahead and they want to sort out who gives advice.'

On Tuesday 19 March we were listening to the Chancellor of the Exchequer's budget speech and I wrote in my diary '£43 million from other departments to be made available for more Engineering and Technology places. Sir Keith Joseph to speak later in the debate.' Ron Kirby then showed us just what he could do. He immediately left my office, and before the Chancellor sat down Ron was back, with a copy of the DES press release. He looked at his watch and said we had 20 minutes to make a statement and catch tomorrow's papers. This we did and sure enough I was the only person commenting on the £43 million. The *Daily Telegraph* included the following: 'The Engineering Council welcomed the announcement. Dr Kenneth Miller, director general, said he was delighted the government has listened to our advice over the past 12 months. Dr Miller said Britain needed more highly qualified engineers and technologists in order to become more competitive in world markets.' This was a classic example of Ron's outstanding professionalism. It was the moment, too, when I felt the Engineering Council had arrived on the national stage.

Awareness campaign

During the summer of 1984 the Engineering Council decided to have a modest advertising campaign for the outlay of £170,000. Several visual schemes were considered, and Kenneth Corfield and senior Council members including Bob Malpas and Detta O'Cathain had crucial inputs. The result was three highly successful advertisements developed by Wight, Collins, Rutherford, Scott.

The first was of a boy dreaming in a field. He dreamt of being a tennis ace defeating McEnroe, or a Prime Minister going to war or a doctor finding a cure for a disease which had bedevilled mankind, with the punch line 'He wouldn't dream of being an engineer, of course.'

The second advert was a view of a corner of Westminster Abbey with the caption 'Why isn't there an Engineer's corner in Westminster Abbey'. We took the precaution of checking who was honoured in Westminster Abbey. There were several engineers so honoured and for a brief period I feared we couldn't use this advert, but we soon confirmed that most of them died in the Victorian age, and the latest to die was Sir Henry Royce of Rolls Royce in 1933. As this was over 50 years ago, I was pleased to go ahead with the advertisement. We also checked on those who had died during the last 50 years and discovered they included the poets John Masefield, WH Auden, Rudyard Kipling, TS Elliot and Dylan Thomas. Among the musicians are Sir Adrian Boult, William Walton, Vaughan Williams and Benjamin Britten. Two actors are there too: Dame Sybil Thorndike and Noël Coward. We therefore had the complete answer. Just as well because the *New Civil Engineer* tried to claim in their journal that the Engineering Council was confounded. It was an opening for me to reply, which I did with some gusto. I finished my letter to the *New Civil Engineer* as follows 'Our advertisement was about today's attitudes and how today's society fails to honour engineers. As a final thought, you may care to ponder that a plaque commemorating Thomas Telford, born over 200 years ago, has "President of the Institution of Civil Engineers". Our case rests.'

The same advertisement stimulated Wendy Cope to write her tongue-in-cheek poem 'Engineer's Corner'.

> We make more fuss of ballads than of blueprints
> That's why so many poets end up rich,
> While Engineers scrape by in cheerless garrets,
> Who needs a bridge or dam? Who needs a ditch?

Wendy finishes with these verses:

> While well-heeled poets ride around in Daimlers,
> You'll burn the midnight oil to earn a crust,
> With no hope of a statue in the Abbey,
> With no hope, even, of a modest bust.

> No wonder small boys dream of writing couplets
> And spurn the bike, the lorry and the train.
> There's far too much encouragement for poets –
> That's why this country's going down the drain.

The third advertisement was entitled 'Once more the world is beating us at our own game and it isn't cricket'. The advertisement comprised nine batsmen being bowled out, and each carried a caption such as 'In 1900 Britain made 60% of the world's shipping – now we make 3%' and 'Britain made the first practical computer. We now have only 5% of the Information Technology market.'

These three advertisements had a major impact. Ron Kirby reported that the post-campaign survey showed an increased level of awareness of the Engineering Council to 37% amongst the readers of the three national papers which carried the advertisement namely *The Observer, The Telegraph* and *The Times* to the general public the awareness has risen to 28%. We also had an excellent response of appreciative letters, too, from a wide range of the public.

I recorded in my diary of 29 November 84 'I went to the CBI Conference on Innovation and Co-operation with Higher Education. Sir Keith Joseph came

Launch of 'WISE' Campaign, 17 January 1984. Left to right: back row: *Dr Kenneth Miller, Sir Kenneth Corfield, Ms Nancy Knight, Ms Mandy Fisk;* front row: *The Baroness Platt of Writtle, Professor Daphne Jackson, Mrs Joanna Kennedy, Ms Yvette Hitchin*

along and when I asked a question, he started by congratulating the Engineering Council on our advertisements. Lots of compliments in private; John Gregson, Ken Durrands from Huddersfield Poly, Geoff Holroyde from Lancaster Poly and Brian Street of Air Products.' It was another example of Ron Kirby's excellent leadership of our Public Relations.

Women into Science and Engineering (WISE)

I had only been with the Engineering Council a short time when I received an invitation to a meeting with Baroness Lockwood of Dewsbury, the then chairman of the Equal Opportunities Commission.

I had had one previous encounter with the redoubtable Betty Lockwood. It was during my APV days back in September 1976, when I was invited to attend a dinner at the Mansion House given by the Lord Mayor for the Prime Minister, Jim Callaghan. It wasn't a large gathering – only about 20 of us in all. I found myself with Baroness Lockwood as my dinnerside. We had hardly sat down and she began 'What does APV do for Equal Opportunities?' On the spur of the moment I decided that attack was the best form of defence. So I replied gaily 'We are all for it. Now, how about both sexes retiring at the same age?' The change was immediate. 'Oh you wouldn't bring it in straight away,' she replied, rather subduedly. 'Oh no,' I replied graciously, 'we would spread it over several years'. After that the conversation moved away to other topics, but I was just a little afraid she would remember when we met up again. So I took the precaution of getting some female support and who better than our one lady member of the Engineering Council, Beryl Platt, Baroness Platt of Writtle.

Beryl very kindly agreed. So along with Tony Bond, we visited Baroness Lockwood of the Equal Opportunities Commission on 10 November 1982. As I wrote in my diary for that day 'It all seemed to go well', and my brashness of six years before was not referred to. The two ladies clearly knew each because, as we broke up, Betty Lockwood asked Beryl to stay behind as she had some other things to talk about. It was only a matter of days before it was announced that Beryl Platt was to be the next chairman of the Equal Opportunities Commission. Beryl was then in a wonderful position to take the lead for women engineers.

On 17 January 1984 the Engineering Council and the Equal Opportunities Commission launched the WISE '84 (Women into Science and Engineering) Campaign. Kenneth Corfield and Beryl Platt held a press conference. Sir Keith Joseph, the Secretary of State, supported our joint efforts. Perhaps symptomatic of the time, the *Daily Telegraph* published a sneering article on the use of the word 'WISE'. The article goes as far as to say 'Why should Sir Keith who is supposed to be a Conservative join with the fatuous, future-frenzied technology-crazed propagandists of the Equal Opportunities Commission in this nonsensical bit of crystal-gazing?' I responded with a hard hitting letter to the editor, which I am glad to say they published. After pointing out that the Campaign was a joint initiative, I went on to say 'I find it sad that you should have such a negative view of the nation's prospects. For its part the Engineering Council is quite clear that for the foreseeable future the United Kingdom will be dependant for the major part of its wealth creation and consequent standard of living on its engineering-based manufacturing, process and construction industries.' I finish the letter by saying 'We have neglected the fact that engineering is just as suitable and exciting a career for girls as for boys. Something like a miniscule one per cent of our professional engineers are women compared with, for example, the United States' nine per cent. The WISE '84 campaign, embracing 200 individual projects, is intended to help redress the balance for girls by opening up the possibilities of a career in engineering that parents, teachers and parts of the media all too often fail to appreciate.'

The WISE campaign went from strength to strength. The Engineering Council set up a Career Break Working Group with John Shrigley of the Marconi Company as chairman. They produced a report in December 1985, which was directed to persuade engineering companies to organize career breaks for women

The Rt Hon. Mrs Margaret Thatcher launches the 'WISE' Bus, 25 July 1984

engineers. Not surprisingly women engineers now tend to delay having children until they are professionally qualified. This in practice tends to be around the age of 28.

Another innovation of the WISE campaign was the introduction of a double decker bus equipped as a school laboratory which visited schools that did not have permanent labs. The first bus was launched by Mrs Thatcher in July 1984 in Downing Street, and it was followed by a second WISE bus in 1986 launched by Beryl Platt and Linda Maynard, President of the Women's Engineering Society.

In the four years after the start of the WISE campaign there was an increase from 7.8% to 10.5% in the number of women entering engineering degree courses.

Survey of chartered engineers' salaries

When we were contemplating the WISE Campaign, Beryl Platt phoned me up and said we really should know what is the percentage of Chartered Engineers who are women. To get a quick answer, I had look at the 1983 Salary Survey of Engineering Functions which the CEI had been collecting and which the Engineering Council took over. This reported that 2.3% of the sample were women engineers. I immediately phoned Beryl back and said our starting point is

2.3%. Shortly afterwards I was talking to John McKenzie the secretary of the Institution of Civil Engineers, and he rather apologetically said the Civils had only 1.0% women. I then phoned Howard Losty of the Institution of Electrical Engineers and Alex McKay of the Institution of Mechanical Engineers and found that both of them were down around 1.0%. I immediately phoned Beryl back to tell her of the lower starting point.

I then looked into the basis of CEI salary review, and because they did not have the addresses of the chartered engineers, they sent out copies of the questionnaire to all chartered engineers via their institution's journals. They reported 22,275 returns out of a total of 201,407. This is only an 11.1% return which really is not good enough for statistical work. In such returns there is an inclination to be self selective. For the erroneous figure of 2.3% for women chartered engineers it was hard not to conclude that women were 2.3 times more likely than men to fill in this questionnaire!!

I then awaited with interest the next bi-annual survey of salaries in 1985 which was now under the Engineering Council auspices. We used the same firm, Remuneration Economics, to conduct the survey, but unlike the CEI we now had all the addresses. We selected every seventh name and along with the questionnaire we sent them a prepaid envelope. The result was an overall response rate of 43.7%. The report showed that the median salary for chartered engineers had risen from £12,600 to £16,000. This rise of 27.0% was made up 11.5% inflation and 13.9% genuine increase of income. In my opinion the figure of 1985 was not a genuine increase but a re-adjustment due to the inaccuracy of the 1983 figures. These salary reviews showed a wide range of salaries. Somehow, from then on, there was much less moaning about low salaries.

Change of chairman

I got the first indication in June 1984 that Kenneth Corfield did not intend to go on as chairman after the AGM in 1985. By August we had another discussion, and I wrote in my diary for 2 August 'In the afternoon I saw Kenneth Corfield. He is very taken up with the STC takeover bid for ICL. I got him to agree the Highgate House agenda and the question of Chairman. So far we agreed he would stay on until April 1985 and we needed a good well-known industrialist to succeed him.'

The chairmanship was discussed at Highgate House in mid September. I wrote in my diary for the first evening at the start of the annual seminar on Thursday 13 September 'After supper Kenneth Corfield told them all he definitely wished to go. He suggested a sub-committee to recommend the name of a possible chairman to the Council.' The following evening at the formal dinner the Council had a useful discussion on possible names for chairman.

Sir Francis Tombs' name was coming to the fore. I had heard Frank give an excellent key note address at the first day of the Cambridge Manufacturing Forum on 4 July 1984, and I felt very relaxed as Frank's name seemed to become front runner.

The small sub committee met on 1 November and I wrote in my diary for that day 'In the afternoon we had the first meeting of the ad hoc panel to select a new chairman. Kenneth Corfield, Bernard Crossland and Detta O'Cathain. With the two absentees Bob Malpas and Gordon Beveridgae supporting Frank Tombs, we all came to the same view. Sir Kenneth will now sound out Frank Tombs.'

On 26 November 1984 I wrote 'Kenneth Corfield phoned me late in the afternoon to say that Sir Francis Tombs will be delighted to succeed him as Chairman of the Engineering Council. This is good news.'

At the Council meeting on 15 January 1985, the Council formally appointed Sir Francis Tombs to succeed Kenneth Corfield as chairman of the Engineering Council. Frank took over on 1 May 1985. That same evening The Council gave a farewell dinner at the Caledonian club in honour of Kenneth Corfield.

In making a presentation to Sir Kenneth I said:

This is the occasion to pay tribute to the immense contribution which Kenneth Corfield has made to the Engineering Profession and Industry during his Chairmanship of the Engineering Council.

When I accompanied Kenneth a few days ago for his farewell chat with Sir Keith Joseph, I was very touched at how Sir Keith reminded Kenneth of the occasion back in the Summer of 1981 when, as he said, he had to 'twist Kenneth's arm' to persuade him to take on this task of Chairman of the new Engineering Council. I could not help but be aware of the satisfaction Sir Keith obviously felt at the result of a decision well taken. Not that this is the every-day lot of politicians!

It was an enormous and perhaps daunting task which Kenneth undertook in July 1981. It was eighteen months since the Finniston Report had been published, and articles which appeared in the press during that period did not encourage the lay reader to believe that the Engineering Professional Institutions were exactly welcoming with open arms the birth of this new body.

Kenneth received a Charter which gave no guarantees that the Council would inherit the existing Council of Engineering Institutions' Register and be able to grant the CEng title. He had a modest promise of some money from the Government, and I believe in the 'arm twisting' period Kenneth persuaded the Govenment to increase its offer of £1 million spread over three years to £1 million each year for three years. This three-fold increase reflected Kenneth's feel and understanding of the task ahead. I need hardly dwell on the contrast of these early days with the position we are in today, and I would wish to pay particular tribute to Kenneth's great contribution to this.

In the early days it was essential for us to have the backing of the professional engineering institutions to gain their confidence. Kenneth achieved this with great aplomb. I remember well the conversation we had in September 1982 when we were wondering how we could possibly secure the support of the two thirds majority of the old CEI Council with their elected members. In his quiet way Kenneth suggested to me that we really must have some sort of consultative elected assembly, and this became the key that made it all happen. As the months passed it became not just a political ploy, because Kenneth, with his clear foresight, saw this assembly as a vital means of communication between the Council and the grass roots of the Profession.

Kenneth insisted on our thinking through what we had to offer to industry and industrial firms, and how sound he was in pressing us to go for a subscription income, rather than charitable donations. We now see this coming to fruition. But Kenneth will no doubt be the first to remind us that there is still much to be done, not least for Technician Engineers and Engineering Technicians, something which I know is very dear to his heart. I would like to assure him that although our progress here has hardly started, it is high on our list of priorities for the months to come.

Everyone here has sat round the Council table under your chairmanship. We have been fortunate to have as Council members some very distinguished people from very different backgrounds, expressing very different opinions, often with great conviction. With immense patience and understanding of your colleagues' points of view, you have allowed important topics to be talked through to decisions which the Council could embrace. I know, on occasions, your patience went beyond what some of your colleagues might have thought to be the call of duty, but I believe they, too, have in the long run appreciated the worth of the policies which have evolved.

I believe that as the Engineering Council develops a public reputation it will rest on the worth of these policies, be it on professional standards, education and training or the industrial importance of technology, and we will all continue to value the foundations which have come from your leadership.

We could not let this occasion pass without giving you two small mementos to remind you in later years of this epic period.

The first is your Registration certificate as a Chartered Engineer, duly recorded as Certificate No. 1, and the second is something to which you gave much thought and contributed greatly to its design, and that is the Coat of Arms of the Engineering Council, and here we have a framed print for you. Kenneth it gives me the greatest of pleasure to present these small gifts to you with the very best wishes of the members and staff, past and present of the Engineering Council.

Funding of engineers' training

Early in 1984 the Engineering Council produced reports both on 'Resources for Higher Education' and 'Funding of Training Places'. The first of these reports led on to the highly successful 'Resources for Engineers' Education' described on page 130.

The funding of training places had a much more chequered path to tread. Both documents were launched at a press conference on 29 February 1984 and I wrote in my diary 'We had the press conference on our two documents on 'Resources for Education of Engineers' and 'Training Places for Industry'. We seemed to get a good response from the press, but we must await tomorrow's papers'. Next day I wrote in my diary 'The *FT* gave us good coverage, but *The Times* only a little and the *Telegraph* none.'

However when Kenneth Corfield and I saw Norman Tebbit on 2 April 1984 I had to write in my diary 'At 5.00 p.m. Kenneth Corfield and I went to see Norman Tebbit the Secretary of State for Trade and Industry. They went straight in about our finances and were pretty damning about what we would get from them. No money in the budget etc, urging us to get industry to pay. It was all a bit depressing.'

This was fully confirmed on 5 April 'Michael Cohen of DTI phoned me to say that the minister will not be sympathetic. We must get money from industry or the city.' and again confirmed by Jonathan Solomon on 10 April 'In the late afternoon I went round to see Jonathan Solomon at his request. It was still about financing. They are pressing that we attempt to raise money from industry. We will clearly have to have a go, but I have severe reservations about our success.' The same answer came from Oscar Roith on 22 June 1984.

So matters rested until we had the success of the extra £43 million the government provided on our advice for Engineering courses in the universities. Mrs Thatcher called a meeting of senior industrialists including our new chairman, Sir Francis Tombs, for a meeting at No. 10 on 21 May 1985. Mrs Thatcher told Sir Francis and the industrialists that she expected industry to put more resources into Engineering Training and she would have a meeting with them in six months time when she expected them to report what they were doing.

For this follow-up meeting we and the industrialists had a good story to tell and the Department of Education and Science agreed that industry had spent a futher £26 million on training. With this encouraging story we were effectively being asked to raise with the PM other projects which might require additional funding. The two projects which we in the Engineering Council had in mind were (i) The shortage of Maths and Physics teachers in the schools and (ii) Manufacturing Systems Engineering courses in the universities and polytechnics.

In fact I went to a meeting on 11 February 1986 with David Hancock, the Permanent Secretary at the DES, and Robert Clayton of CBI, to discuss the draft agenda and possible press release after this second meeting with the Prime Minister. It was all going our way with our two projects to the fore. In a jocular tone and with tongue in cheek I said 'Isn't this rather like Sir Humphrey?' David Hancock took it seriously and replied 'That is what No. 10 said.' I reported this back to Frank Tombs, and he, too, was amused. So much so that at the pre-meeting of industrialists on 19 February they supported our two projects, Frank couldn't resist telling them of the draft press release I had been involved with a week before.

Sure enough, it all went through as we hoped. I found myself invited to chair a Steering Group on Manufacturing Systems Engineering. This group's report was presented to Kenneth Baker, Secretary of State for Education and Science, in February 1987. Then Frank Tombs, Jack Levy and I had a meeting with Kenneth Baker on 4 March 1987 and I wrote in my diary 'we met up with Jack Levy to see Kenneth Baker the Secretary of State. It went well. George Waldren and Angela Rumbold were there, as were David Hancock and Richard Bird. At first they said no, but in the end, Kenneth Baker saw a three-way possibility. (i) industrialists doing more sponsoring, (ii) new money and (iii) a squeeze on UGC.'

In December 1987 we were able to report to the Council that the National Advisory Body (NAB) who fund Polytechnics, has formally announced that it will fund 309 additional Manufacturing Systems Engineering (MSE) places at 15 polytechnics starting in the academic year 1988/89. News from the university sector is expected in early February 1988.

Recruitment of industrial affiliates

When Kenneth Corfield and I saw Norman Tebbit on 2 April 1984 he made it clear that there would be no funding for Training but he also intended to get the message over that there would be no further government grants towards the Engineering Council's overheads when the £1.0 million a year came to an end in mid 1985. This was further confirmed to me by two civil servants, Michael Cohen on 4 April and Jonathan Solomon on the 8th. The message was clear – the government expected us to raise money from industry.

In the meantime our industrial members of the Council and the chairman were pulling long faces on how difficult it will be to persuade industrial companies to pay us. The Finance and General Purposes (F&GP) committee were reviewing the forward projections for 1985 and beyond. Ralph Quartano, the chairman of the F&GP committee, feared we could be heading for a deficit of between £300,000 and £800,000.

Tony Bond was due to return to the DTI later in the year and I was having discussions with John Trafford of Corporate Consulting Group about recruiting a replacement director of Education and Training.

We then started discussions on the possibility of not replacing Tony Bond and spreading his portfolio of duties between the other two directors responsible for developing policy. Between mid-May and early July I had long chats with several members of Council. The solution at which we finally arrived was that work on higher education in universities and polytechnics would be part of Jack Levy's directorate, while activities in the schools, and Continuing Education would go to Graham Anthony's directorate. This was formally agreed at the Appointments and Salaries Committee on 16 July. Although this seemed a blow at the time, it was a cloud with a silver lining. Linking schools with industry paid handsome dividends, which I will come to in due course. I had already warned John Trafford that I may have to abort the recruitment of the director of Education and Training.

At the Highgate House Conference in September 1984 the main topic was how we should approach companies to become industrial affilitates and support the work of the Engineering Council. In the action point at the end of the conference we recorded under Approach to Industry.

1. It was agreed that the central theme in selling ourselves to industry was that we would be lobbying Government on their behalf and that we carried sufficient 'clout'.

2. We should consider the feasibility of providing services for industry, for example an information service.
3. The director general would endeavour to set up a staff liaison committee with the senior civil servants in the Department of Trade and Industry, Department of Education and Science, Department of Employment and Manpower Services Commission, which would meet regularly.
4. Consideration should be given to the optimum subscription rates for small companies. (we had previously agreed £10,000 per annum for the larger companies with more than 40,000 employees in the UK).

It was now important to get cracking on the actual recruitment of Industrial Affiliates. I pressed members of Council to support our recruiting campaign. By early October support was coming in. On 5 October 1984 I wrote in my diary that 'Derek Roberts has sent me a letter fully committing GEC'. Then on 12 October I wrote 'Bob Malpas came to see me first thing. I spoke about writing to ask Industrial members of the Council to join the Industrial Forum. Later Bob phoned back to commit BP. I now have four companies behind us worth £35,000 income.'

In mid-November Bob Malpas, Graham Anthony and I went to Teesside. We were put up at Wilton Castle, the Guest House and Senior staff club of my old Division of Petro-Chemicals. I should explain in those balmy days each division had their own equivalent. Billingham division had its Norton Hall, and earlier I referred to their senior staff smoker when the mickey was taken out of the directors. Alkali Division had their Winnington Hall in the centre of the Winnington factory. This was generally thought of as a London club put down in the middle of a chemical works, but even so dinner in their Octagon Room was a treat worthy of any London club. Wilton Castle came with the purchase of the Wilton site after the 1940–46 war. As Bob Malpas, Graham Anthony and I had breakfast at Wilton Castle, we each commented that we had in our different times worked at Wilton during our ICI days. Bob Malpas recalled that he and his wife Josephine had had their wedding reception at Wilton Castle and reminiscing I remembered Wilton Castle for the butler, Mr Gillard. He was a real 'Jeeves'. The apocryphal story is told that when one senior divisional director of the Wilton organization had made some flippant comment about Wilton Castle, Gillard drew himself up and said 'Sir, this is Wilton Castle – not the Elephant and Castle'. My own encounter with Gillard was much more mundane. I had been entertaining some guests at Wilton Castle on a cold winter's evening. As Gillard helped me on with my heavy overcoat he said in his most deferential voice 'Perhaps, Dr Miller, you might let Mrs Miller know that one of your overcoat buttons is loose.'

We then had an interesting day on the Wilton site and I wrote in my diary for Friday 16 November 'The morning session at the Wilton Site Centre was with Industrialists. Bob Malpas, Hamish Orr-Ewing and Malcolm Harker did their stuff. Again more than we expected – a good 78. After a buffet lunch by ICI we had a session with the graduates to whom I talked. Equally lively.'

By 4 December we had been working hard on the sales letter and fact sheets and in my diary of 4 December 84 I wrote 'In the late afternoon I had a session with Bob Malpas and Jim Stevenson on the sales letter and fact sheet. Useful – we are getting somewhere.' Next day I redrafted the sales letter and by the 12th I wrote in my diary 'We had a good director's meeting at which we laid out the programme to make our approach to industry. We also decided the key items we would put on the agenda for the meeting with the deputy secretaries in January.'

At the Council meeting on 15 January 1985 Bob Malpas reported that nine companies had so far pledged their support for three years to the total sum of £55K annually. The immediate aim was to increase this to some £250K with the long term target of £800K.

The Council had already prepared the way for this approach to employers of Engineers. In 1983 the Council produced two booklets 'Appraising the Technical and Commercial Aspects of a Manufacturing Company' and 'Technical Reviews for Manufacturing, Process, and Construction Companies'. Both these documents were well received by industry. These booklets were reprinted in 1985 following sustained demand. Two further booklets were added to the series 'Managing Design for Competitive Advantage' in 1986 and 'Trade Up your Technology' in 1987.

In February 1985 our recruitment of industrial affiliates went forward and it made encouraging news. On 7 February I wrote 'I saw Archie Forster of Esso. He will join us as an Affiliate. It was interesting that he thought our position would be a strong independent voice. I found all of this most encouraging.'

On 11 February Rolls Royce came on board. Then Vickers on the 13th and Glaxo on the 19th. By the Council meeting on 20 February 16 companies had promised £101,500 per year. A further 20 companies were in play and another 15 companies were still to be approached. At the end of the discussion it was minuted that 'The Campaign had got away to an encouraging start'.

So it went on and as the list of affiliates grew I always had an up–to–date list with me when I visited a new company. When I visited Sir Ronald Ellis of Allegheny Int. on 11 July, he said with that list he couldn't afford not to join. So it was that we could hardly believe our good fortune. Much of the credit for this must go to my old sparring partner of our ICI days, Bob Malpas, who spent a great deal of time and his good judgement in helping us to improve our fact sheet and the covering letter which made up our approach to Industrial companies.

We had been so successful that we had something approaching a 100% success rate in our approach to companies who employed engineers. Then we thought the financial companies who invested in engineering companies might feel it was in their interest to become Industrial Affiliates. Here success was nothing like so assured or successful, but I cannot resist telling the story of how we came to recruit the four clearing banks, Barclays, Lloyds, Midland and National Westminster.

It was back in October 1984 that I was invited to chair the morning session of a conference for WISE year organized by the 300 Group. They are, as you probably know, a group who have as their objective 300 women MPs in Parliament; that is virtually equal numbers of both sexes as MPs. When this invitation arrived, my PA Betty Hatton suggested that as it is the 300 Group don't you think I should accompany you? 'Agreed'. And so it was that on 31 October Betty Hatton came with me to the 300 Group's conference. As the conference broke up for lunch, Betty told me that there were four very bright girls from Wycombe Abbey school that I really should meet. Betty had already drawn them out and it transpired that their Science mistress was not at all keen that they should attend, and it was only because one of the girl's fathers had spoken to the school that they were here at all. So it was that Betty and I had lunch with these four very bright girls. They were in the Science Sixth Form, and had been allowed to come on their own. It was very refreshing to hear them chat away.

After we got back to the office, Betty suggested that I wrote to Miss Lancaster, headmistress of Wycombe Abbey school, and say what a pleasure it was to meet the four girls. Betty added she had the names of the girls. I asked Betty to draft a letter for me to sign. It was a very good letter – what a credit they were to the school etc. I had no hesitation in signing the letter as it stood.

When Miss Lancaster received my letter, she was so pleased with it that she showed it to the chairman of her Board of Governors. At that time her chairman was a Gordon Adam, a director of Barclays Bank. When he saw the letter was from a Kenneth Miller, he wondered if this was the Kenneth Miller he knew over 40 years ago at Upper Canada College (UCC). So Betty had a phone call from the school and I duly confirmed that I was the same person. I naturally invited Gordon along to have a sandwich lunch and as I recorded in my diary for 6 February 85, 'we had a nostalgic lunch'. Gordon came back to the UK from Canada and after a degree at Queen's University, Belfast, he went on to Trinity Hall my old college. Gordon had an article in the UCC *Old Times* in January 1950 entitled 'From Cambridge' and he said

'I was to find that UCC is remarkably well-known and wherever known is accepted without reservation. At the time I personally applied for Cambridge fewer than one in twelve applicants were being admitted: for forty-five vacancies in this college over a thousand waited. After some correspondence I was taken in without so much as an interview. This was entirely due to the reputation left of my old school by the personal records of two comparatively recent Old Boys who were at Trinity Hall just before me. To the Cambridge man, with all respect for Rugby, the main sport is undoubtedly Rowing and I am proud that "the Hall" is one of the outstanding Rowing Colleges in either University: on the boards at our boat house, rowing for the great first Trinity Hall eight in 1945 were these two Old Boys at 4 and' 5 respectively KAG Miller and PLP Macdonnell, Stewards of Upper Canada. Both went down from Cambridge with first class honours degrees as well. Ken Miller was lecturing at University College, Aberystwyth, and is now with Imperial Chemicals;

Macdonnell is at the Bar in Toronto. When Mr McKenzie visited England two years ago he stayed with the Master of Trinity Hall when in Cambridge. Such links were fortunate and happy for one coming afterwards.'

After this, it was not surprising that Barclays Bank was the first bank we recruited as an industrial affiliate. Once we had one clearing bank enlisted the other three were soon to follow and so the Engineering Council's income was increased by £40,000 a year. All starting from the good contact Betty Hatton made with the four girls from Wycombe Abbey and the excellent letter she drafted for me to sign. I was not at all surprised that her true worth was appreciated when in 1997 she was awarded an MBE.

By mid 1988 we had recruited all the major industrial companies, Oil and Chemical companies, the nationalized industries, and from the city the four Clearing Banks. By the end of 1988 the number of Industrial Affiliates had risen to 510 and their subscriptions of around £500,000 represented some 16 to 17% of the Council's total income.

Engineering Council's Regional Organization (ECRO) and Engineering Assembly

In the initial Policy Statement of the Engineering Council we said that consideration would be given to the possibility of an Engineering Assembly. This was followed by the promised meeting with elected members of the old CEI, which I held with them on 7 January 1983. I recorded that some useful ideas were put forward, though they themselves had no clearly agreed views.

Nevertheless their thoughts were very helpful and we put out a consultative document in June 1983 proposing an elected Engineering Assembly and an Engineering Council Regional Organization with twenty regional constituencies each of which would elect four Chartered Engineers and two Technician Engineers. This was followed by a Policy statement a year later and culminated with elections in the Spring of 1985.

The first Engineering Assembly was held at the University of Birmingham at which the Prime Minister, the Rt Hon Mrs Margaret Thatcher gave the opening address. With the knowledge of hindsight I look back on the start of the Assembly and the Regional Organizations as a vital link in establishing direct contact between individual engineers and the Council. It is an extremely important component of the strength and standing of the Engineering Council amongst the individual members who make up the Engineering Profession.

The Prime Minister gave us a rousing send off and finished by saying 'I am here today for one reason: to show the importance this Government attaches to your work, your profession and your role in our future. Our country's success needs you!'

The engineering assembly became an annual event and for my remaining years as DG it was held first in Swansea opened by Nicholas Edwards, the Secretary of

State for Wales; In Edinburgh in 1987, with Lord Sanderson, Minister of State in the Scottish Office, and finally in Belfast and opened by Tom King, the Secretary of State for Northern Ireland.

Over the years the quality of the debates at the assembly have improved immensely – helped and guided by Sir Robert Telford, a Council member who became chairman of both the assembly committee and the Engineering Council Regional Organization Co-ordinating Committee (ECROC). Sir Robert played a most valuable part in developing both of these committees, ably supported by Graham Anthony – director industry and regions. I attended the first meeting of both committees. On 15 January 1986 I wrote in my diary for that day 'Back to the office in time to join the ECRO chairmen. They have had a good first meeting with presentations from Graham Anthony and Ron Kirby.' Then on 26 February 'We had the first meeting of the assembly committee under Sir Robert Telford's chairmanship – it went well.'

My last visit to an ECRO was on 18 May 1988 when I wrote 'Off to Slough to speak to the Thames Valley ECRO. A good turn-out of about 70. I had a very lively and successful session.'

I will return to the importance of the ECROs when I come to my final chapter on Federal Systems.

CHAPTER 12

Schools and Qualifications

Y OU WILL RECALL THAT on page 130 I concluded that the industrial decline of Britain and the relatively poor standing of the engineering profession had been brought about in the second half of the nineteenth century by the social climate which had evolved in the education system in England. This made such an impact on my thinking that I became convinced that it was essential that we in the Engineering Council must play our part along with politicians, civil servants, educationists, industrialists and many others by altering the climate in the English schools, so that technology and industrial success become highly respected activities. It will take several decades to achieve it. In this chapter I will describe our activities on the schools' front.

Mathematics and physics

The shortage of maths and physics teachers was raised at the second meeting industrialists had with Mrs Thatcher on 24 February 1986. Just before I retired, the Engineering Council, jointly with the Headmaster's Conference and Second-ary Heads Association, produced a report 'Securing the Future − The shortage of mathematics and physics teachers' produced in June 1988.

John Williams, the Engineering Council executive responsible for projects involving schools, was responsible for this report. He did an excellent job and made useful recommendations, but at that time we didn't dare mention differential salaries in favour of teachers in shortage subjects.

Design and make projects

Design and make projects are introducing the young to the very essence of engineering. It involves what I call the 'Design Cycle', and it applies to the development of all new products and the improvement of existing products.

First think of an article or process you wish to design and make. Then design the first prototype as best you can. You subsequently build it, and test it. The chances are it will have lots of limitations, so it is back to the drawing board to design prototype No. 2, build No. 2 and test it. This cycle of design, make and test can be repeated many times.

The Engineering Council had inherited the Young Engineer for Britain competition. One of my most satisfying days at work each year was to attend the finals of this competition. It was a real delight for me to go round the stands and talk to the young engineers themselves. To hear in their own words what they had designed and made. They were quick to show you earlier prototypes and how they had modified and changed them for a later version.

Their choices of subject were interesting, too. There was clearly a strong element of wishing to help the disadvantaged – kitchen scales specially adapted for the blind or flashing light door 'bells' for the deaf. Some of their ideas were quite brilliant. One lad, Adam James of Y Pant Comprehensive, Pontyclun tackled plaster castings for broken limbs. Often the affected arm or leg is very swollen when the plaster casting is applied. Then as the swelling subsides a gap appears between the casting and the limb. Adam James had the idea of placing a pneumatic 'tyre' between the arm and the outer support, which no longer has to be a heavy plaster casting. Then as the swelling subsides it is possible to pump up the tyre to maintain the support of the broken limb. Adam sold his licence to a Dutch hospital and it is now widely used.

Adam James won the Young Engineer for Britain in 1996. He has since attended Loughborough University, where he obtained a first class honours degree in Engineering. He is now completing his PhD at Imperial College, London in 'Perceptional Intelligence' associated with robotic surgery. Adam is setting up his own company and I am sure he is all set for a fascinating career in what I call 'Medical Engineering'. By 1996 when Adam James won the Young Engineer for Britain Competition, it was now run jointly by The Engineering Council and the Standing Conference on Schools' Science and Technology (SCSST). At that time in my retirement I was deputy chairman of SCSST and I was at the finals on 18 September 1996 when Adam James received his award from the Duke of Kent.

We had a fortunate break as a new Design Technology 'A' level was created which included a 'Design and Make' project. This sounded wonderful, but in practice there was a dire shortage of teachers who were capable of teaching the subject. It was at this point that Graham Anthony came up with the brilliant idea of engineers from industry going into the schools part-time to help the teachers and pupils with 'Design and Make Projects'.

Graham raised this idea at a Chartridge consultation of the directors on 9 June 1986, and he suggested they should be called 'Neighbourhood Engineers'. I remember I was rather doubtful at the beginning of the discussion, but after we had all given Graham our views, I suggested that Graham should raise the idea with Bob Malpas and the Standing Committee for Industry. If they supported the idea then Bob might raise it at the Highgate House Seminar.

This all happened and in the Autumn of 1986 the Neighbourhood Engineers scheme was launched. This was indeed Graham's baby. He was responsible in his directorate for schools, industrial affiliates and the regions and they all became involved with the development and projection of Neighourhood Engineers and Graham must take the lion's share of the credit for launching this very worthwhile scheme. By the end of 1996 there were 13,000 Neighbourhood Engineers going into 2,369 secondary schools and 230 primary schools.

My contribution to the education debate

Over the period I was with the Engineering Council, I made several speeches to audiences of school teachers. You will recall I first experienced this in 1983 in my speech to Caterham school at their prize giving when I was critical of the narrow specialization in the English Sixth Forms. I was again treading on some sensitive issues when I spoke to a conference of school teachers on 'Changing Technology in the Engineering Industry' at Bromsford school in Basildon on 6 March 1985. I again went for the over specialization in the Sixth Forms and quoted the German experience and said in this speech 'In 1960 West Germany decided to follow the English system of specialization in their secondary schools. Then in 1980, they found they had a major problem of a shortage of engineers. They looked back at the pre-1960 figures and found that 20% of the students then studying Engineering and Science had done classics at school, but had kept enough Maths and Physics going to take the decision at 18 to read Engineering. So with typical teutonic thoroughness the German Chancellor decreed that they were going back to the broadly based secondary school curriculum. England and Wales cannot afford to perpetuate specialising at such an early age.'

I then tackled the theoretical nature of the physics curriculum and said 'The Department of Trade and Industry carried out a study of "O" Level physics papers and discovered that only 3% of the questions in 1981 had any practical application. It improved to 5% in 1984. It is all very well for perhaps the top 5% of the population to be taught in philosophical terms, but it is, I believe, the root cause of why so many of our school-children get "switched off" and want to leave school as soon as possible. The government paper on "Competence and Competition" showed that only 60% of our 16 to 18 year olds remain in full-time education compared with 86% in Germany and 96% in Japan. I can think of no more damning indictment of our education system. We must raise the education and training of the whole ability range to match the upward demand of job skills and to allow our manufacturing industries to compete internationally.'

Finally I put in a plug for more girls to enter engineering degree courses by saying 'We also believe that as a nation we have neglected the female half of the community. Only 1% of Chartered Engineers in this country are women. In the United States the figure is 9%. Along with the Equal Opportunities Commission we launched a campaign: "Women into Science and Engineering" (WISE) and we are certainly doing our utmost to encourage more girls to take up engineering as a career.'

The discussion period afterwards was very lively and as I wrote in my diary for that day 'With the teachers on strike, they were very sensitive and I was skating on thin ice telling them so many home truths. One teacher asked me afterwards if I had to slap them across the face with a wet fish.'

On 26 January 1986 I spoke in a very similar vein to a National Council for Educational Standards Conference 'Educating for Prosperity' and I wrote in my diary 'I went up to the Festival Hall to speak at the National Council for Educational Standards. I was first on followed by Sir Keith Joseph. My speech went down well. I met Rhodes Boyson and David Emms of Dulwich. I spoke to Sir Keith about long lead times. Beryl Platt and David Emms spoke in the afternoon. We are all pushing in the same direction.'

On 29 April 1986 I spoke to the Assembly of masters and boys at Manchester Grammar school. I was, of course speaking to a very bright audience. The message wasn't greatly different, but the reaction was very much better as I recorded in my diary for that day 'I spoke on Industry Year to the Assembly at Manchester Grammar School. Then a 20-minute talk on engineering as a career to about 100 Sixth Formers. Both seemed to go well.'

My next speech was the prize giving at Dame Allan's school in Newcastle on 15 October 1986. My views hadn't changed, but were clearly more in tune with the audience and I wrote in my diary 'Early dinner with governors of Dame Allan's Boys School. I handed out prizes and gave an address. It seemed to be well received. Met lots of parents at reception afterwards. Interesting bunch. I seem to have said the right things.'

There was no doubt in my mind that many of us concerned with the quality of our education were moving in the same direction. Two years later I gave a talk at Dartington Hall in Devon on 11 March 1988 to a group which included 17 head teachers and I had the temerity to suggest differential salaries for shortage subjects and said 'I have to mention differential rewards for shortage subjects. I know it is anathema to the common room, but other walks of life have come to accept it, as an acknowledgement of the real world of supply and demand. I am told even now that salary scales are used to try to meet the market situation, so the principle is as good as accepted. Now we must put it into more effective practice.' I also mentioned career breaks, as we were introducing them for engineers. I wrote in my diary for 11 March 'I had a good reception though I had some tough things to say. Geoffrey Constable of the Design Council also spoke. We then had a good dinner and a discussion afterwards. Altogether a lively evening.'

I said at the beginning of this chapter that it would take decades to alter 'the thinking' behind the education of our children and young adults, and I have tried to describe my limited contribution to the debate.

Engineering qualifications

I outlined on pages 67–71 my management philosophy. I believe in delegating to the greatest extent possible and creating a climate whereby my colleagues will not only report to me all news, good and bad, and they will also be prepared to suggest new ideas and new ways of working. This last point seemed to me to be particularly important in starting the Engineering Council. This does call for a high quality of staff.

I was extremely fortunate in the appointment of Professor Jack Levy as the director – Professional Institutions. Jack came to the post with a knowledge of engineering qualifications, having been chairman of the chartered engineering section, Engineering Registration Board in the CEI. Coming from City University, where he was pro-vice-chancellor, and head of the department of mechanical engineering, he knew the academic world well, and he was soon to show his diplomatic skills in handling the foibles of the engineering institution secretaries.

After the CEI had agreed to hand over the registration and the granting of the C.Eng and other engineering titles, I naturally assumed that we would take over the other CEI activities including representing the UK on overseas professional engineering bodies. I was wrong and on 22 June 1983 I recorded in my diary 'I had a very poor meeting on international affairs with the three major secretaries of Institutions'. They were trying to suggest it should be in the control of the Institution of Civil Engineers. Their case was extremely weak as all the leading Engineering Institutions had many engineers working abroad, and they had previously given the co-ordination of international affairs to the CEI.

On 2 September 1983, I recorded in my diary 'Jack Levy and I are all set to take a firm line with the institutions over the secretaryship of international affairs. At the end of the day we received a letter signed by Secretaries and Presidents to Kenneth Corfield saying the Civils should do it. This is a nonsense. I saw Kenneth Corfield at 5.25 p.m. He is backing us up on all I have done in the last month.' When I reported all of this to the Engineering Council at their meeting on 5 September one of our non-engineering members from industry said 'If this behaviour became public knowledge, the engineering profession would deserve its poor reputation'. At the next meeting with the four Secretaries, I told them of this reaction, and they certainly took it on board. At the same time Jack Levy came up with the proposal that the new British National Committee for International Engineering Affairs (BNCIEA) would not obviously be part of the Engineering Council, but would have separate notepaper. The Chairman would be a member of the Engineering Council and Jack Levy, as well as being the Engineers' Council's director – professional institutions, would be secretary of the new committee. I was glad to find that this diplomatic proposal by Jack was accepted by the institutions. The Engineering Council, through its Board for Engineers' Registration, was still firmly in control, so I was well satisfied. No doubt the secretaries could put their own slant on it of a new body with a new name 'British Committee for International Engineering Affairs (BNCIEA)' and new notepaper.

The Engineering Council set up five Executive Group Committees (EGC). Group 1 for institutions in the mechanical engineering area, Group 2 for institutions in the field of civil and structural engineering, Group 3 in the field of electrical engineering, Group 4 in the field of process engineering, and Group 5 in the field of transport. As Jack Levy and Colin Chapman outlined in their *Chronicle of The Engineering Council*[1] on page 18 'Although members of the EGCs were representatives of their institutions, as at EGC meetings, when any of them then sat on the superior Board for Engineers' Registration (BER), the by-laws required them to speak for their EGC, not necessarily for their own Institution, and put forward views agreed by all institutions within that ECG.'

Kenneth Corfield and Frank Tombs found themselves reminding Council members that they were on the Engineering Council as distinguished engineers and not as a representative of their professional institution.

With the new committee structure now in place, the three professors; Gordon Beveridge, chairman of the standing committee on professional institutions (SCPI), Bernard Crossland, chairman of BER and Jack Levy, director – professional institutions, all worked extremely closely to produce the first edition of Standards and Routes to Registration (SARTOR).

On 19 December 1984 we launched SARTOR and I wrote in my diary 'We had the press conference to launch SARTOR. Gordon Beveridge took the chair. Fortunately the press questions widened beyond SARTOR and I hope we get a good press. Certainly the indications were we would do so.' Thus was laid the foundations for the quality standards for the whole engineering profession. It was a magnificent achievement by the three professors.

There were, of course, the occasional rumblings from the major institutions, but they rarely reflected well on the behaviour of the secretaries of the institutions and I will refrain from going into this, but I must relate one incidence when I put my foot in it.

On 22 April 1986 the *Daily Telegraph* printed an article which I had written. It was headed 'Cash boost for major growth sector' and covered the successes to date including extra £43 million for engineering places in universities, industry spending more on training, large companies becoming industrial affiliates, and more girls taking up careers in engineering under our WISE campaign. However there was one error, when I inferred that the British Computer Society, which had been recently nominated, had been authorized to accredit the educational courses and training required in its area. I was clearly ahead of myself and was presuming success. This could easily cause offence amongst the institutions. Ron Kirby very soon informed me that the *Telegraph* would not consider a correction as the public would not understand or consider the matter of any consequence. I therefore decided to send an immediate letter of apology to all the presidents of the chartered engineering institutions, and had the letters biked round that very morning. When I saw Frank Tombs next day he clearly approved of my actions and complimented me by saying with a smile 'There is nothing quite like baring your bottom!' Needless to say that was the end of the matter.

---

[1] 'An Engine for Change' – A Chronicle of the Engineering Council by Colin R Chapman & Jack Levy. Published in 2004 by The Engineering Council UK on their Web site www.engc.org.uk

I referred earlier to the British National Committee for International Affairs (BNCIEA). James Stevenson and later George Adler as chairmen, ably supported by Jack Levy, did a superb job in convincing our European colleagues in the Fédération Européenne d'associations Nationales d'Ingénieurs (FEANI) that in determining the details of a professional engineer qualification, it should include the three elements of (i) academic education, (ii) practical training and (iii) responsible experience. The whole made up a seven year package. This effectively meant that British chartered engineers were able to apply for European Engineer and use the Eur.Ing title.

I have a personal note to add to this. My son Ian obtained a very respectable 2(i) degree in the Engineering Tripos at Cambridge in 1979, and decided to go straight into the computer world in Cambridge and was involved with consultancy work. While I was director general, Ian was making no effort to become a chartered engineer and I kept very quiet about it. Then some time after I retired he phoned me up one day and said that he thought I would be pleased to hear that he had decided to apply for membership of the British Computer Society, which was now a fully nominated and accredited engineering institution. He said 'You see, Dad, when I become a chartered engineer I can apply for the Eur.Ing qualification. My German clients will be more impressed by Eur.Ing on my visiting card than by MA (Cantab).' I now address my letters to Ian as Eur.Ing Ian Miller.

National Council for Vocational Qualifications (NCVQ)

In April 1985 The Manpower Services Commission, the Department of Education and the Department of Employment set up a committee to 'Review Vocational Qualifications' (RVQ) chaired by Oscar De Ville, and Jack Levy was invited to be a member of this review group.

The original intention was to review vocational qualifications at Levels I, II and III. Level III being approximately engineering technician. The membership of the review group reflected this remit.

It wasn't long before Jack Levy was telling me that there was strong pressure for the review group to go beyond their remit and consider qualifications at Level IV (approximately incorporated engineers) and Level V (chartered engineers). In their press release of 23 April 1986 it was claimed they would go 'right to the top professional levels'. By this time Frank Tombs and I realized that Lord Young, the Secretary of State for Employment, was the person behind the extension to the higher levels. So we arranged to see him on 6 May 1986. As I recorded in my diary for that day 'Frank Tombs and I saw Lord Young. Lots of accord on maths and physics teachers, continuing education and practical training, but we gave it to him hard about the De Ville committee going beyond its remit.'

It wasn't just that Oscar De Ville was going beyond his remit, but the body they intended to set up had no means of carrying out the final professional review to judge whether the candidate had carried out a job of sufficient 'responsible experience'.

On 8 May I wrote in my diary 'We completed our draft press release on the Review of Vocational Qualifications. I also phoned the secretaries or chief executives of 10 other leading professional bodies (Law, Medicine etc) about the vocational qualifications paper and they are sure to make warning noises when they get our the press release.'

On 9 May I gave a telephone interview to Alan Pike of the *FT* and Derek Harris of *The Times*. Both quoted me extensively. Alan Pike's article appeared in the *Financial Times* on Monday 12 May. He quoted our statement 'that the working group had not only exceeded its terms of reference, but had done so without consulting the leading professional bodies involved. Derek Harris in *The Times* quoted me as saying 'They are stirring up a hornet's nest among the professional institutions. The government must be cautioned about this.'

On Wednesday 14 May I went to a 3i's cocktail party and wrote in my diary '3i's cocktail party. Six cabinet ministers. Keith Joseph told me I was out on a limb on my own re RVQ. I must check up to see if the government is nobbling the other professional bodies.' Sir Keith meant his remark to help me, but I was taking no chances and on 15th I wrote in my diary 'I again phoned round the professional institutions (Law, Medicine etc). No lack of support. I got over the message that the government is rushing again and the professional bodies should be prepared to act quickly. It could be a bit nail biting if the government came out in full support of the De Ville committee. I must hope that the ministers get the message that the major professions will object, and that the government will hold back and take some time over the decision.'

The pressure was still on us. On 23 June I wrote in my diary 'I went to the Education for Capability Conference as it might apply to higher education. I saw John Cassels. He complained about our action on RVQ. I made it very clear we were not against it at the lower levels and referred to Frank Tombs' letter to David Young. George Tolley, chief officer of RVQ, was there and sheepishly admitted the letter had arrived.'

Then on 2 July the White paper from the Department of Employment came out and I wrote in my diary 'The new NCVQ was announced. It will cover levels I to IV & only have discussions with the higher levels.' Our efforts have had some effect.

Two other things happened to strengthen the Engineering Council's position. In December 1987 the Engineeering Council joined the UK Interprofessional Group, comprising representatives of the General Medical Council, the Law Society, the Bar Council, the Institute of Chartered Accountants, the Royal Institution of Chartered Surveyors, the Royal Institute of British Architects, the Chartered Institute of Patent Agents, the Royal College of Veterinary Surgeons and the General Dental Council. After our intervention in May, we were welcomed with open arms.

In fact this goodwill rubbed off on me. Four years into retirement I was invited by the British-American-Canadian Associates to go on a lecture tour to Canadian and American universities, and one of the topics I was asked to speak on was 'Challenge to the Professions: Self Regulation versus Public Control'. The chief executives of the leading professional bodies all gave me the benefit of their opinions.

What struck me very forceably was that every one of the professional bodies have quite independently developed the same three elements in the formation for their top professional qualification. These three elements are (i) academic education normally a university degree, (ii) practical training – student apprentice, articled clerk, pupillage, or for doctors clinical work in hospital, and (iii) some two years of responsible experience. This latter stage is judged in each individual case by senior members of the profession. The National Vocation Qualifications did not have this final hallmark which requires the backing and support of the professional body. In 1988 I viewed the NVQs as fundamentally flawed on this account.

International comparisons

The United Nations Educational, Scientific and Cultural Organization (UNESCO) produced a UNESCO Statistics Year Book. In collecting the figures for this Year Book, they allowed each country to interpret the definitions for their own country. This meant there were many interpretations in the definitions of various groups.

The Engineering Council came across this phenomenon when the DES produced a UNESCO comparison which appeared to show that UK produced as many engineers per population as Germany and USA, and nearly as many as Japan. When David Hancock, the new permanent secretary at the DES, quoted this report to Frank Tombs and myself at lunch on 4 June 1985, we said 'don't be ridiculous', but he persisted and it took another four years to lay this nonsense to rest.

Unbeknown to us the DES were instrumental in arranging for an interdepartmental working group of statisticians from the Department of Education and Science, the Manpower Services Commission (MSC), the Scottish Office and the Department of Trade and Industry (DTI) with Mr PH Richardson of the DTI in the chair.

Kevin Clarke of DES sent me a letter dated 27 August 1987 saying 'an Interdepartmental Working Group in International Comparisons of Higher Education Output in Engineering has produced an interim report and Ministers have approved publication of it'. He enclosed a copy and was writing now to invite the Engineering Council's comments on the findings. He did have the honesty to draw my attention to the qualification the group made in their last paragraph by saying 'The signification of the figures in table 1 will not be clear, therefore, until further work is done on the comparability of the levels of qualification and subject group allocations in different countries. This needs further study using expertise outside the competence of the working group.' Even in the report's introduction they have another qualification when they say 'They have also agreed that the conclusions which can be drawn from international comparisons are limited by difficulties over comparability of various levels of qualifications in different countries and that it would be valuable for further work to resolve the question to be initiated.'

In my reply of 9 September to Kevin Clarke I said 'We note that this interim report is a statistical exercise based on acknowledged inadequate information, and we are not surprised that it reaches facile conclusions.' At the end of my comments I finished with this paragraph 'We believe it would be irresponsible and nationally counterproductive to publish the dubious information in this report. A superficial reading of the report as it stands could send totally misleading signals through the Higher Education system of this country and engender a degree of complacency which would have no justification. If the Minister does proceed to publish this report at the present time, the Engineering Council would have to respond with a vigorous and appropriate statement. We feel sure that our views will be supported by industry'.

On 10 September I wrote in my diary 'I spoke to Richard Bird of the DES about my letter on International Comparisons and he said he would get hold of it. I rather sense that they might not publish if we come out strongly. I also spoke to Geoffrey Holland (Head of MSC) and he is 100% behind us.' On 18 September I wrote in my diary 'The DTI statistician who chaired the working party knows about my letter. Also the DES man Troedoen says no decision has been taken on when to publish! Apparently notes are flying up and down the DES amongst the officials right up to David Hancock.

We were starting now to prepare the ground for our own study of the statistical data and on 12 October I wrote in my diary 'Jack Blears of Liverpool University and Barbara Bonwitt came to see us. I gave them the problem to check up further on the Japanese Comparisons.' Next day I made contact with Professor Prais of the National Institute of Economic & Social Research. He came to see me with Mrs Hilary Steedman. We had a useful talk and they confirmed that the DES are quoting incorrect figures.'

Despite our best endeavours to save the DES from themselves, I heard from Donald Libby, Under Secretary at the DES, that they would be publishing this report on 1 December with an embargo until 9.0 p.m. on 2 December. I spoke to John Banham, director general of the Confederation of British Industry (CBI) and Jim McFarlane, director general of the Engineering Employers' Federation (EEF). They both helped us with strong press releases. John Banham said 'This is an arid statistical job by a few civil servants. On its own showing the report is based on unreliable information.' The EEF in their press release said 'It is indisputable that there is a shortage of trained engineers in this country. This is a fact and anything that tends to obscure it, including dubious international comparisons, is a damaging diversion. The Engineering Council is entirely justified in its severe criticism of the special feature in the December edition of the *Employment Gazette*.'

Ron Kirby obtained from the Department of Employment Press Office a copy of the *Employment Gazette* on Tuesday 1 December, and then called a press briefing for the morning of Wednesday 2 December. As it happened I saw Donald Libby of the DES at a dinner at Lancaster House on the Tuesday evening. I told him our Press release would be out next day with the same embargo time as theirs of 9.00 p.m. The look on his face made it clear to me that they had hoped that that we could only respond twenty four hours after their publication. Ron Kirby had already received the same impression from speaking to the DES's press office.

On Wednesday 2 December we held our press briefing attended by *The Times*, *The Guardian*, *The Financial Times*, *The Independent* and the BBC. We were able to quote from the DES's draft of the report and thereby did not break their press embargo. I gave a recording to Wendy Jones of the 'Today' programme which was broadcast in prime time at 7.44 a.m. on Thursday morning. Altogether we were well satisfied.

Next day Thursday the 3rd it was all in the public domain. First it was announced on the 7.00 a.m. news on BBC Radio Four and they added that no minister was available to comment. I knew immediately that we had won this particular skirmish. Then as I was driving to work I heard on the car radio my interview with Wendy Jones. It came over as good hard hitting stuff and the full transcript is in Appendix VIII.

The press had a field-day with our press release. *The Times*, *The Independent*, and *Guardian* all quote me as saying that publishing the report is irresponsible and nationally counter-productive. No paper supported them. In retrospect I think the strong and effective backing from the CBI and EEF was particularly effective. When I arrived at work and had time to read all the press cuttings which were all in our favour, I had a few words with Peter Brittain my PA seconded from the DTI. I told Peter we had some fences to mend and could he get onto his opposite number in the DES and make encouraging noises that we still wished to work with them on other matters. A couple of weeks later I had another few words with Peter. He said he thought that it would be all right, but referred to my crack on the Today programme when I said 'Well there's a very good TV programme called "Yes Minister". And the more I see of the workings of Whitehall, the more convinced I am that "Yes Minister" is alive and kicking.' This comment of mine had really hurt them.

There was indeed an encouraging change in the DES's attitude. Kenneth Baker was to have delivered a speech at a CBI conference on 7 December and as he was involved with a Russian leader's visit, Mr Robert Jackson, the Higher Education Minister read the speech. There was one paragraph which referred to the interdepartmental report which is much more conciliatory and reads as follows 'Here I might say that there has been some anxiety caused by a report by an interdepartmental working group of statisticians, to the effect that the Higher Education output in engineering in the UK might not compare unfavourably with our main competitors. There will be follow up work commissioned on the subject, and in any event let me confirm the government's determination to develop an education system which produces the people that industry needs, with the right skills and in the right numbers.'

At the same time we in the Engineering Council judged Japan to be the pace setter that Britain should aim to match. In October 1987 we had set Jack Blears and his colleague Barbara Bonwitt to do a statistical study of engineering education between Japan and the United Kingdom.

On 24 February 1988 I went with Peter Brittain to a meeting at the DES. I wrote in my diary 'In the afternoon Peter Brittain and I went along to Donald Libby's meeting to discuss the follow-up work on International Comparisons. DES, DTI, MSC and Dept of Employment with lots of statisticians there. We get the definition of Project to my liking with IT included. They will make a real meal of it – desk study review. Cost around £100K. They asked us to contribute one fifth. I made the usual noises and said our study with Blears might be our contribution. This will surface in two months. Clearly they want it to report after I retire.'

The DES didn't take up my counter offer of Jack Blears' work as our contribution and it was left for the Engineering Council to proceed with the Blears/Bonwitt consultancy. At the Council meeting on 5 April the Council agreed to publish, and to send copies to the Department of Employment and MSC as well as the DES and DTI.

The Engineering Council's report 'A Comparison of the Statistics of Engineering Education – Japan and the United Kingdom' was published in May 1988. The report showed that

(i)   There was a serious omission of the output from Japanese Special Training schools (Senshus) in the UNESCO figures.

(ii)   The per capita Japan/UK output ratio for engineering Bachelors, whose disciplines are most directly associated with manufacturing industry, are considerably higher than the overall average. for example, for electrical and for mechanical engineering in 1983 the ratio was 3:1, for chemical engineering it was 5:1, and for production engineering 9:1.

(iii)   The Japanese educational system appears to have been designed to make engineering the most attractive of all professions. For example: the pool of Japanese school leavers with acceptable mathematics qualifications is of the order of ten times higher than that in the UK.

At the time I thought this would be the end of the matter and we would all get on with our efforts to improve the education and training of prospective young engineers, but I had reckoned without the DES.

On 18 November 1988, some three and a half months after I retired, it was reported in *Hansard* that Mr Anthony Coombs MP for Wyre Forest: 'To ask the Secretary for Education and Science how many people achieved recognized engineering qualifications at degree or post degree level in Britain in 1987; and what the comparable figures were for France and West Germany.' Mr Robert Jackson in his reply quoted the now discredited UNESCO figures. At least they did not include the Japanese figures!

I gathered from Sigbert Prais of National Institute of Economic and Social Research (NIESR) that he was working on a full study of craftsmen, technicians and engineers of UK, France, Germany, Japan and the USA, going back to the statistics published in each country. His paper 'Qualified Manpower in Engineering'[2] was published in the NIESR's Review February 1989 and showed very clearly that the UK was at the bottom of the league. In Appendix VII I have taken a print of the figures given in the Minister's reply to the parliamentary question and superimposed another column giving the NIESR figures in italics. The total higher education qualifiers per thousand population now read: France 56.3, West Germany 70 and the United Kingdom 45.7.

Sigbert Prais obtained excellent press coverage on 28 February. The *Guardian* article was headed 'NIESR warns of skills crisis', *The Times* headed their article 'Sweeping changes in engineers' training needed says expert', the *Independent* headed theirs 'Britain must expand education for engineers' and the *Financial Times* were perhaps the most perceptive with their heading 'Craftsmen shortfall is "most serious worry"'.

Sigbert had been keeping me informed as his work developed. So much so that I knew that advance copies of his paper were in the hands of the DES by the time they prepared their answer to the parliamentary question of 18 November 1988.

It was early in 1989 that I started to read *The Insolence of Office*[3] by Caroline Cox and John Marks. Baroness Cox of Queensbury and Dr John Marks carried out a research study of the academic performance of 350,000 fifth-year pupils in 1981. They found that pupils at secondary modern and grammar schools obtained more O-level passes than pupils at comprehensives both nationally and within the same social class groups – between 30–40% more O-level passes per pupil nationally and nearly 50% more in areas for which the social class mix was near the national average. Secondary modern schools did particularly well (page 11 of *Insolence of Office*).

---

[2] 'Qualified Manpower in Engineering, Britain and other Industrially Advanced countries' by SJ Prais, *National Institute Economic Review* – February 1989.
[3] *The Insolence of Office* by Caroline Cox and John Marks published by The Claridge Press 1988.

When their work was published in 1983 they were subjected to a sustained campaign attacking and discrediting their work, based on errors, distortions, smears and character assassination (page 27 of *Insolence of Office*). In the end, they were fully vindicated and in November 1983 Sir Keith Joseph made an unprecedented statement in the House of Commons which vindicated their research.

I made contact with Baroness Cox. On 16 February 1989 I drove to London to meet her and John Marks at the House of Lords. I wrote in my diary for that day 'to London to meet Baroness Cox and John Marks at the House of Lords. It was a real meeting of minds. I told the story of International Comparisons. We agreed an approach to No. 10 is essential. Baroness Cox believes we should go through Brian Griffiths. She will make a date for us to see him and hopefully he will pass it on to "Mrs T".'

On 23 February I wrote in my diary 'Baroness Cox's girl gave me a message on her phone call to Brian Griffiths. He was not ready to see us and said publish first.' The following day I spoke to Baroness Cox on the phone. She was all for us taking a strong line.

Then I received a confirmatory letter from Caroline Cox in which she said 'Thank you for your draft letter to the Prime Minister. If I may say so, without sounding patronizing, I think it covers the points very clearly. I believe it would be best for it to come from you personally as your position is so well respected and as you carry such authority from your experience with the Engineering Council. I could always keep my powder dry and support you independently in any subsequent initiative.'

This was the green light to send my letter to the Prime Minister with its two annexes. Annexe I is a statement on 'The International Comparisons of Engineering Manpower' and Annexe II is on an 'Education and Training Department'. A full copy of my letter and both annexes I sent to Baroness Cox, copies of Annexe I I sent to Denis Filer, my successor at the Engineering Council, Jack Levy and Sigbert Prais. Copies of my letter to the PM with the two annexes and her reply are in Appendix IX.

After making some serious criticisms, as I have done in the main letter, I believe it is important to make some positive suggestions on how matters might be improved and these are in Annexe II. I suggested that the Education and Science Department should be split and the Science Research Councils should go to the main user departments as follows:

(a) Medical Research Council to Department of Health.
(b) Science and Engineering Research Council to Department of Trade and Industry.
(c) Agriculture and Food Research Council to Ministry of Agriculture, Fisheries and Food.
(d) Natural Environment Research Council to Department of Environment.

(e)   Economic and Social Research Council to Home Office.

At the same time Education and Training should be put together in a new Department of Education and Training.

I also suggested that the teaching profession should have a professional body ie a General Teaching Council, similar to the General Medical Council.

No doubt other folk considerably more influential than myself have suggested the same things.

In John Major's time education and training were put in one department. A General Teaching Council has been created, but the civil servants and the politicians have not released the control of the standards of entry to the profession. The Research Councils have all gone to the Department of Industry.

I am sure it was quite by chance that Sir David Hancock retired early from the civil service. The *Times Higher Educational Supplement* reported on 12 May 1989 that 'Mr John Caines, the senior civil servant at the Overseas Development Administration is to succeed Sir David Hancock as permanent secretary of the Department of Education and Science in July. Sir David's sudden departure comes after six years at the DES. A former Treasury official he is to be an executive director of Hambros Bank.'

Therafter there was no further reference to the highly questionable UNESCO figures and Sigbert Prais' figures stand.

Second change of chairman and my retirement

Frank Tombs retired as chairman of the Engineering Council at their Annual meeting on Tuesday 17 May 1988. The Council and directing staff entertained him to dinner that evening at the Caledonian club and I proposed Frank's health. It was a very pleasant occasion. As I looked back on the three years of his chairmanship, I felt we were on the same wavelength on all matters of any importance. Frank was extremely busy with the privatization of Rolls Royce, but he still found time to back Jack Levy and myself over such key issues as the National Vocational Qualifications (NVQ) with the Department of the Employment; our arguments with the Department of Education and Science on International Comparisons; and many skirmishes with the secretaries of the four leading engineering institutions. Frank had a very clear understanding of the exercising of power and influence. I will return to this in my postscript on Federal Systems. My own retirement came at the end of July 1988, just over two months after Frank's departure. My relations with his successor Sir William Barlow, were good from when he first appeared and I made a point of giving him very full briefing on all the key issues.

In the Engineering Council's *Newsletter* of March 1988 which went out to all engineers on the register, I was able to give my views on 'Major priorities for the future' and amongst other things I said 'Major priorities will be the implications of a single market in Europe by 1992 for engineers and industry generally, the development of all three sections of the Register and our vigorous recruitment campaign for Industrial Affiliates, in association with the growth of the regional activities.' I went on to say 'The Council will place an increasing emphasis on Technician Engineers and Engineering Technicians. It is hoped that the change of the Technician Engineer (TEng) title to Incorporated Engineer (IEng) will be achieved in the near future; this will overcome the problem of confusion between the two existing titles. When this is done the Council will mount a campaign to recruit many more Incorporated Engineers and Engineering Technicians to the register.

'The Council will also be looking at Industry's requirements for Engineering Technicians and will undertake a fundamental review of their education and training.

'In addition the Council will be running a vigorous recruitment campaign to persuade more companies, particularly small and medium sized enterprises, to become Industrial Affiliates, and to become associated with the Council's regional organization.

'There have been many pioneering projects by the Engineering Council in the past five years. We have many projects now under consideration with more to

CBE presentation at Buckingham Palace, 8 December 1988

come and we have been very encouraged by the response to our work from industry, individuals, professional institutions, educationists and Government over these years.

'The next five, taking us through 1992, will depend upon our broadening our base through the number of Registrants and of Industrial Affiliates and taking up new opportunities.

'We all have a part to play in advancing the cause of the engineer, industrial competitiveness and the nation's well-being. We have the opportunity once again, as engineers, to lead the way. Let's take it.'

In the same *Newsletter* Sir Francis Tombs had some kind words to say about me when he said 'Kenneth Miller deserves the thanks of the whole engineering profession. He has been the Council's lynchpin during its formative years and the vital link between members of the Council and the staff team. He created a wealth of enthusiasm within the team resulting in a variety of projects major and minor which have been accomplished following policy decisions by the Council.

'Dr Miller has helped in no small way in the success of positioning the Council as an important national body which individuals and organizations turn to as the central source on many facets of engineering and technology. The Council will miss his contribution.'

I was honoured to be awarded a CBE in the Birthday Honours of June 1988.

Of the honours which have come my way in the course of my career the one I value most was to be made an Honorary Fellow of my old college, Trinity Hall in 1992. I was joining a very distinguished company; including Rt Rev David Sheppard, Bishop of Liverpool, Robert Runcie, recently retired from being Archbishop of Canterbury, and Professor Stephen Hawking, Professor of Mathematics at Cambridge. Then following after myself The Rt Hon the Lord Howe of Aberavon, the politician.

CHAPTER 13

Postscript on Federal Systems

IN RETROSPECT I BELIEVE that the history of the Engineering Council can be best understood if it is viewed as an attempt to establish a strong federal system embracing the engineering institutions. It was in May 1994 some six years after I retired from the Engineering Council that I read Charles Handy's book *The Empty Raincoat*.[1] Charles Handy gives an excellent insight into the workings of a Federal System: and here I quote from his book.

> Federalism is designed to create a balance of power within a group of related institutions. It seeks to be both big in some things and small in others, to be centralized in some respects and decentralized in others. It aims to be local in its appeal, but national or even global in its scope. It endeavours to maximise independence, provided always that there is a necessary interdependence; to encourage differences, but within limits; it needs to maintain a strong centre, but one devoted to the service of the parts; it can and should be led from the centre, but has to be managed by the parts. There is room in federalism for the small to influence the mighty, and for individuals to flex their muscles.

Charles Handy makes it quite clear that 'Federalism is not an easy concept to understand or make to work. Its only justification is that there is no real alternative in a complicated world.'

Charles Handy goes on to say that the key concepts of Federalism are Twin Citizenship and Subsidiarity. Twin Citizenship might be described as the loyalty of the individual to the local group and a wider loyalty to the overall organization. Subsidiarity can be considered as the willingly reverse delegation of appropriate activities by the parts to the centre.

In the case of Engineering the citizens are chartered engineers, incorporated engineers and engineering technicians. They have a twin citizenship, firstly to their engineering institution (local group) and secondly to the central body namely the Engineering Council (now the ECUK). Subsidiarity is the agreement of the institutions to delegate upwards to the central body certain activities best done in the centre for the good of the whole.

A federal system is not easy or comfortable to operate, but in very many organizations in a complex world, we have no alternative. In my view this certainly applied to the Engineering Council with the engineering institutions (some 36 nominated bodies and 13 Engineering Council professional affiliates).

---

[1] *The Empty Raincoat* by Charles Handy, published by Hutchinson 1994. The Federalist Idea is explained on pages 97–128.

The first citizenship of individual engineers is to their professional engineering institution. In this respect it has to be said that the institutions could have done better, since they have only managed to attract barely half of the engineers eligible for membership.

In engineering, one of the keys to a successful federal system must be the building of second area of citizenship of the individual engineers to the Engineering Council.

To this end the Engineering Council:

1. Insisted on having the addresses of all registrants, so that the Engineering Council could communicate with them and did so with a six monthly newsletter.
2. Set the level of fees for individuals to register and have the right to use the CEng, IEng and EngTech titles.
3. Set up an Engineering Council Regional Organization (ECRO) with 19 regions covering the United Kingdom. Each region elected six members to attend the Engineering Assembly which met annually. In power terms the assembly resembled Strasbourg, but it was also a valuable line of communication.
4. Strengthened engineering links direct with individual members when large numbers of them became neighbourhood engineers. By the end of 1996 there were 13,000 of them, but when the management had been passed to other bodies the numbers fell to 8,000.

These actions were key ingredients in developing the second citizenship for individual engineers, and with it a loyalty to the central body. As Levy and Chapman recognize in their account of the history of the Engineering Council (*An Engine for Change*), the dismantling of the ECROs was a grievous loss to the profession. The demise of the Northern Ireland ECRO, as pointed up by Sir Bernard Crossland on pages 119–120 of this book, is a frightening example. The Professional Engineering Institutions (PEIs) run by the engineering institutions, were meant to replace the 19 ECROs, but they have withered away to a miserable three.

In all federal systems the underlying tension of relative power will always be there. When the Engineering Council was established, there were, of course, all the stresses and strains of a new body being seen to usurp the powers of the independent sovereign states.

The relationship between the Engineering Council and the engineering institutions requires a high degree of subsidiarity. The two best examples of subsidiarity I can recall are (i) acceptance by the Institutions of SARTOR, and (ii) the Engineering Council taking the lead with FEANI and obtaining the right for British chartered engineers to the Eur.Ing title. Action at the centre for the clear advantage of the whole.

In September 1994 I sent copies of my paper on Federal Systems to the first four chairmen of the Engineering Council. Frank Tombs, now The Rt Hon the Lord Tombs of Brailes, fully understood what it was all about. Copies of our exchange of letters are in Appendix X. In his reply of 9 October 1994 he said: 'You and I are at one on this. I had little sympathy with Monty's solution on the grounds that it would anyway result in the loss of much that was good. Latterly I tried, unsuccessfully, to dissuade John Fairclough from pursuing a similar path. The necessary weight has to be put, and has increasingly been put, behind a federal solution – unglamorous though that may seem. The success of the Engineering Council owes much to your efforts to bring that about and we must now look for a renewal of those efforts.'

It was at this point that I fully appreciated how well Frank Tombs understood the whole basis of the balance of power and influence between the Engineering Council at the centre and the professional institutions. It showed clearly in the well judged support Frank invariably gave Jack Levy and myself in our dealings with the professional institutions.

I personnally have no doubt that the engineering profession requires a federal system. It allows the whole dynamic system to evolve over the decades and allows new institutions with new technologies to become fully fledged members of the family of engineering institutions. In my lifetime the British Computer Society has become a nominated body. I remember the Council meeting on 16 January 1986 when the Council agreed to this, and John Lyons made the astute remark that the Engineering Council needed the British Computer Society more than they needed us. I am sure that within the next two or three decades there will be a worthy institution for genetic engineers with all the ethical and moral standards which society will expect of them.

But to return to the Engineering Council. The Fairclough Initiative and the revisions of the Engineering Council charter which followed raised high hopes that a new relationship would come about. This was not achieved. All that happened was that the balance of power between the Engineering Council and the engineering institutions was altered quite dramatically and the influence and prestige of the Engineering Council withered away. This was highly regrettable. Regulation and Registration continues under the auspices of the Engineering Council (UK), and there is every indication that this is successful.

The initiative of the Hawley report of 2001 had the admirable intention of encompassing the wider community of 2 million scientists and professional engineers and for the new Engineering Technology Board (ETB) to lead them.

However, unlike the original Engineering Council the ETB has no real power base. It is neither statutory nor chartered, so has an almost impossible task to achieve a position of power and influence, not only in relation to the engineering institutions, but also to win the hearts and minds of the individual engineers and scientists in the wider community.

Betty and I last saw John Fairclough and his wife, Karen, at a Pilgrim's visit to George Washington's ancestral home, Sulgrave Manor on 17 May 2002. John raised with me the topic of the engineering profession. He as good as acknowledged that his initiative had been a failure and he held out little hope for the Engineering Technology Board. I was inclined to agree with John.

This is a sad note on which to end, but once again I console myself with Rudyard Kipling's poem 'If' that 'when I meet with triumphs and disasters, I treat these two imposters just the same.'

Letter from Mr LM McKenzie, Principal of Upper Canada College, to author's father

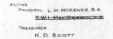

UPPER CANADA COLLEGE,

TORONTO 12

July 5th, 1943.

Dear Dr. Miller:

Early in August Kenneth should receive his certificate from the Department of Education. Therefore the College is not sending out a school report at this time, but is sending this letter instead.

This year has been a successful one for Kenneth. While he did not have to work hard, he always did more than was expected of him. He was a very good R.S.M. in the Battalion: while reserved, he was keen and efficient. As a Prefect and Steward he was most reliable. He is a very thoughtful person, even tempered and with a delightful sense of humour.

I wish him well for the summer and for the future.

With kind regards,

Yours sincerely,

L. M. McKenzie.

Principal.

Dr. Allan F. Miller,
41 Watford Rd.,
Croxley Green,
Rickmansworth,
Herts, England.

Some Comments on the Management of British Railways
by KAG Miller 12 April 1960

1. Introduction

In this report I am making some comments on the management of British Railways under the headings of Staff, Organization and Modernization Plan. They are very much my personal opinions, and are not necessarily the official views of the British Transport Commission, the London Midland Region, or Imperial Chemical Industries Ltd.

I shall always be indebted to Mr Blee, the general manager of the London Midland Region, and to Mr Pearson, the assistant general manager, for the way they launched me in the Region. The arrangement they made for me to join in meetings of the chief officers gave me a rare opportunity to see the senior management at work. Officers, both of the London Midland Region and of the Commission, have very willingly given me their views on a variety of matters dealing with railway management. In doing so, they have often called on experience gained on other parts of British Railways.

Much of what I have to say has been said before by many senior members of the railway staff. In particular, there is a 'Report to the railway general managers on entry into the railway service and training of persons for senior posts in the future,' now being presented by a committee of assistant general managers headed by Mr Pearson. My comments on recruitment and training of staff largely echo the views expressed in their report.

2. Staff

It is regrettable that the importance of having first-class men in all ranks of management has not been fully appreciated. This neglect, at the time of nationalization, by both the Government and the Opposition, has left the nationalized industries with a painful legacy, and I fear it may take several decades to correct this situation. There are other legacies, too, which go back to the organization and traditions of the old railway companies.

2.1. Calibre of present staff

Despite many adverse circumstances, there are still some outstanding men in the railway service. The regrettable thing is that there are so few of them, and that they have been held up by the limitations of many men of lesser ability.

The immediate post-war loss of young staff now aged 35–50 due no doubt to the uncertainty of nationalization and the unsettling effect of war service, has left an unfortunate gap in the age structure of the organization. The opinion has been expressed to me that those who left included some of the best men of that age group. The full impact of this loss will be more heavily felt when the present 'over 50s' have retired. These older men were too far committed in pension schemes to leave the service in 1946–1950, and are now carrying the bulk of the load of middle and top management. It must be remembered, too, that these older men grew up in the inter-war years when the railways were on little more than a care and maintenance basis. These same men have in the last six years set in motion the virtual rebuilding of the railways, at a pace which would stretch the capability of the most progressive industrial firm. It is not surprising, therefore, that there is a shortage of men of imagination and foresight, who can grasp the essentials of any problem and not get lost in a welter of detail.

There is a regrettable tendency for staff to be limited in their outlook by the confines of their own department. Far too often I have heard chief officers express a narrow parochial view. The fact that the departments are so large, and that chief officers arrive at the head of their department towards the end of a long career spent entirely within this one department, no doubt contributes greatly to this extreme departmentalism.

I am convinced, too, that officers who have had a professional training, be it in a branch of engineering, surveying, or architecture, place far too much emphasis on being a professional man, and not enough on the management of men and affairs. This is particularly unfortunate in the senior ranks and shows itself in weak administration within departments. It also contributes to the frequent expression of a limited view.

I have no doubt that senior staff in a department must develop a wider concept of the activities of the whole organization, and appreciate the true position of their own department within it.

The extreme professionalism often causes chief officers to discuss details which should clearly have been settled at a much lower level. On occasions the matter may well have been discussed and agreed at the lower level, but the senior officer is not prepared to accept the professional opinion of his own staff. This inability to delegate, with much back-checking of minutes, tends to make the large organization even more cumbersome. It will no doubt be claimed, with some justification, that the calibre of staff at the lower level is such that considerable checking and supervision is necessary. I would not deny this possibility.

In formulating this criticism of the calibre of the present staff, I have been greatly helped by the willingness of the staff themselves to be forthcoming in their views. On occasions I have been surprised at the readiness with which they have criticized each other and the organization. This does not reflect credit on the morale of staff, but against the background of widespread public criticism it would have been superhuman for them to have behaved otherwise.

If an organization is to remain alive, it must change with the times, indeed ahead of the times. This can only come about with lively intellects in all ranks of management. New ideas in a highly technical industry come best from bright young brains who are in touch with the real work of the undertaking. The senior staff must actively encourage innovation from below. It only takes one weak link in the management chain to stifle a good idea at birth. Management is not unlike a chain. It is as strong as its weakest link.

In general there is a crying need for a better calibre of staff at all levels. The Fleck report (Ref. i) on the organization of the National Coal Board, page 23, paragraph 107, speaking of the coal industry said 'We have come to the definite conclusion that one of the industry's greatest needs is better management at all levels; in other words more people of ability . . .' The same is true of the railways.

The railways are such a highly technical and specialized industry, that I do not think the importing of first class men with experience in other industries will offer any effective solution. I am convinced the long-term salvation must rest on the recruitment of young men of ability, for a career in the railway service. They must be given the right training and experience to develop the necessary qualities, so that in 20 years time there will be enough of them in all ranks to ensure a strong, lively management.

2.2. Recruitment

There is a fair measure of agreement amongst the railway staff I have spoken to, that they are not getting their share of the talent of the country. I am certain this is correct.

2.2.1. Factors affecting recruitment

It has been put to me that the more important deterrents to recruitment to the railway service are:

(i)   The poor financial position of the railways
(ii) The impact of politics on the organization
(iii) The relatively poor prospects of remuneration in the middle period.

While I agree that all these points have a considerable bearing, I think the heart of the problem is the third point, i.e., the salary prospects in the middle period. Young men in their twenties are much more interested in their prospects in ten years' time, than the possible prospects in their fifties. This applies to both initial recruiting and also in the keeping of staff. The chances of losing staff over 35 who have accrued 15 years or more of pension rights are slight. It is in the crucial period from recruitment up to the early thirties, that staff must be retained against the attractions of other industries. Official figures which have been quoted to me recently, of the number of traffic apprentices who have reached £2,000 per annum at 40, confirms the general impression of the salary prospects which I had obtained by talking to members of the staff; so although the exact figures are not published, it is certain that the impression is well understood amongst the younger members of staff, and has got back to the universities.

It would not be so bad if the salary prospects were only 10–15% lower compared with private industry, but unfortunately they would appear to me to be more like 50% lower, i.e. only half the salary.

The static or contracting position of the railways has a bearing on the relative prospects in the middle period. Young men are well aware that an organization which is expanding creates middle management jobs in the process and this can have a big effect in giving early promotion to some. I know at first hand how the rapid expansion of ICI on Teesside since the war has given early promotion to a considerable number of young men.

The dead hand of promotion by seniority can have a disastrous effect on prospects in the middle period, and this will scare off ambitious able young men more quickly than anything else. I have formed the opinion that the effect of advertising vacant positions, combined with the alacrity with which the staff union is prepared to take up the case of the unsuccessful, but senior candidate, does produce a tendency for the election board to take the easy way out and promote the senior man. This, I understand, is more prevalent at the lower levels of the organization, but it is important, as under present circumstances, that all staff have to pass through this mill.

The impact of politics on the organization and the public reputation of the undertaking, cannot be ignored. The railways had their comparative greatness in Victorian days, and although they still have a vital part to play, they must now compete with the glamour of the Atomic Energy Authority, and other modern industries. The publicity given to all the organization's troubles does not help recruitment. The railways have all the problems of 'bigness' and the young undergraduate is, I think genuinely afraid of the large organization – 'a cog in a large machine' springs glibly to his tongue. This is something which all large organizations have to counter, and it must be done by convincing the young graduate that despite the bigness of the organization, he will always be treated as an individual.

These are the deterrents to railway recruitment as I see them. Before passing on to my recommendations, I feel some comments are necessary on the source of recruiting talent in the future.

2.2.2. Source of future talent

The railway tradition has clearly been to look within its own ranks for its traffic apprentices, and the ratio of three internal candidates to one external candidate has become accepted by both management and unions, and formally agreed. I have no doubt that in the times of the railway's heyday this proved a highly fertile field for recruitment. There is now, I think, an interesting shift in the number of young men of high quality who will be available to come up the 'hard way'. Continuing expansion of the universities means that more and more young men of ability are going to university, and the percentage of men of good calibre who miss a university education will continue to get less. I think this process has already gone a long way since before the war. So much so that the quality to choose from now within the railway service for traffic apprentices will, I fear, be lower than compared with 30 years ago. On top of this, the buoyancy of industry compared with the 1930s increases the demand all round for young men of calibre, and more and more firms are recruiting graduates for management careers.

It has been said that since 1951 there have been few resignations from ex-traffic apprentices, and the ratio of internal and external candidates has been maintained. I would not recommend any complacency about this. There is every reason to believe that since the war the quality of traffic apprentices has dropped. The quality of internal candidates has declined due to the educational trend mentioned above, and the prospects offered certainly do not attract outstanding graduates. I think that after a time any organization gets a calibre of man to match the prospects offered. Equilibrium is then reached and the number of resignations drop.

I am convinced, therefore, that the railways have some radical rethinking to do in their staff policy, and that if they wish to get their fair share of the future talent for top management, they must look more and more to the universities. This reassessment must not be blighted by any outmoded prejudice left over from an age when a university education was limited to a wealthy minority.

As R Kelf-Cohen so rightly points out on page 225 of his book on nationalization (ref.ii), 'through the educational opportunities created in the last generation young men and women of all classes of society have received first-class education in a manner unknown thirty years ago. Selection through the education system means that industry must look more and more to the universities for potential leaders.' This is not recommending the exclusion of men coming up the hard way, but a realistic acceptance of the fact that a greater proportion will in future have to come from universities.

2.2.3. Preferential entry

Like the selection of university graduates, preferential entry rouses the same social and class prejudices. The reason for such a form of entry is obvious. Within the limited number of years of a working career there is not time available for future leaders to spend years struggling through the lower ranks. The Civil Service have the administrative class and large industrial firms have their equivalent. It is, of course, necessary to gear the organization to cope with the introduction of bright young men who have been trained to think, but who must learn the practical side of the industry. Such an approach does not merely give the service a chance to attract first-class men, but it will mean that some of them will reach commanding positions in the middle of their careers, and be able to direct the affairs and policies over a worthwhile period of time. Contrast this with the all too common railway spectacle of rapid promotion to the top flight during the fifties, and a succession of caretakers in key jobs.

2.2.4. Contact with universities

The general demand for men of high calibre is so great that if the railways hope to get their share, they must go out and sell themselves to the universities and the undergraduates.

Five or six years ago the Billingham Division of ICI was experiencing great difficulty in attracting good graduate engineers. To overcome this an eight-week summer vacation course was started, and relatively recent graduates were appointed as liaison officers at universities, to interview undergraduates for these vacation courses, and generally keep in personal contact with Appointments Boards and Engineering Departments.

There is no doubt that all of this has paid handsome dividends. By talking to graduates already in the company, undergraduates have been able to judge for themselves what the firm is like. The personal contact of a graduate from your own university coming along to interview you, goes a long way to dispel the fear of bigness. In this connection it would help very considerably if recruitment was done by the Regions.

All of this is, of course, salesmanship and it is only really successful when it is backed up with something worthwhile to offer. I therefore come back to prospects in the middle years. This will not be put right by just increasing salaries all round, though some increases are clearly called for. Training, experience and promotion policy all have a bearing on long-term prospects.

2.3. Training, experience and promotion policy

The basic concept of the traffic apprentice training is sound, and there are no grounds for altering this as the starting point for a new administrative class. The organization must, however, be adjusted so that in the first five to seven years after apprenticeship, young men are moved round to a series of jobs in different departments giving them wide experience, and at the same time giving them some real responsibility. Early acceptance of responsibility will bring on future leaders quicker than anything else, and the holding down of several jobs in different departments will give them an understanding of how these departments really work, and will go a long way to prevent departmentalism in later years. I would recommend a deliberate policy of moving ex-traffic apprentices round the Operating Department, Commercial Department and Motive Power Department in a variety of jobs in their first five to seven years after apprenticeship. The difficulties of carrying this out under present regulations have been pointed out to me. The advertising of jobs and the large number of salary levels with incredibly small differentials, all add to the difficulty of trying to co-ordinate and plan some sort of continuity to the careers of young men in this period. The size of the whole undertaking is so great that individuals can so easily get lost sight of, and the undergraduate's worst fears realized. I would recommend that, like recruitment, transfers in the early part of the man's career should be limited to his own Region. Limiting the moves to the one Region will make it possible for future leaders to be spotted early in their careers by Regional management and given early promotion to the ranks of middle management. I am convinced that it is only by treating this on a Regional basis that the matter can be kept within manageable proportions. Enough younger men must be promoted to the middle ranks in their thirties so that there is an adequate selection available for the final choice of top management. To give top Regional management adequate scope, the number of salary levels in the Region must be drastically reduced. The method of advertising jobs and the staff unions approach must be radically altered before the dead hand of promotion by seniority can be eliminated. I do not in any way underrate the magnitude of this problem, but to attract outstanding men, promotion must be by merit and not by seniority.

There is a lot of truth in the old adage that a young man must choose his boss wisely. We are all affected by the behaviour of our colleagues and young men learn by precept and example. It is just as easy for them to pick up bad habits as good ones. It is therefore not good enough to feed in good young men at the bottom of the organization and hope that in 20 years time that they will have worked wonders. Present staff at all levels have a very great say in the moulding of the next generation. There are strong grounds for early retirement of many ineffective people, not only because of their inability to hold down their present posts, but for the incalculable harm they can do in training and promoting of younger staff. If such a policy is carried out, reasonable compensation must be paid and, as the Fleck Report says on page 60, paragraph 317, 'the money would be well spent'.

The widening of the outlook of future leaders is helped by staff courses and the Staff College at Woking is clearly a move in the right direction. It can, however, be questioned whether the course is not too long. Fifty-six men through the course per year is not many for an organization employing three quarters of a million people. It has also been suggested to me that because of the length of each course, Regions are reluctant to lose some of their best men for so long and second-raters get nominated.

The railways lost some really good ex-traffic apprentices after the war. These men went into private industry, often as transport managers for industrial firms. Their background knowledge of the railways has no doubt been invaluable to them and their firms in striking commercial bargains with the railways. In the current shortage of really good men, is there not a case for trying to attract some of these men back into the railway service? It has been pointed out to me that there is a union agreement that they would have to start again on the bottom rung, but the advantages to the railways are so great in having some such men in senior positions on the commercial side that I think it would be well worthwhile pressing the unions to rescind the particular agreement.

3. Organization

Any solution to the staff problem must inevitably be a long-term one and in the meantime the organization must continue to function. I think that good staff can make a poor organization work, but a poor organization in the hands of lesser staff can come to the verge of breakdown.

3.1. Present organization

The British Transport Commission is an immense undertaking employing approximately three quarters of a million people. All the organization problems of 'bigness' are magnified. There is the legacy, too, of the organizations of the old railway companies. It is very much easier to create a new organization where none existed before than to reshape and re-organize an existing one.

Some of the giants of private industry, both in this country and the USA, had the good fortune to have their amalgamation of smaller firms in their early days and then enjoyed a long period of expansion when a new esprit de corps was developed and the pangs of reshaping dulled by the compensations of growth. The railways have not been so fortunate: the 1923 amalgamation, the 1947 nationalization and the further reshaping of the 1953 Transport Act all took place when the industry had already grown to its full size. The result has often been the superimposing of a new organization without adequate removal of the old, resulting in a cumbersome, unwieldy body. One only has to look as far as the present General Staff of the Commission and the Railways Central Staff for an example of this.

The pattern of the organization of the four railway group companies was on balance towards a general manager as chief officer responsible to the Board supported by functional heads of departments. In all but the LNER, the responsibility was through the district and divisional officers to the head of the department and through him to the general manager. I am convinced that this long-established tradition is one of the causes of the present extreme departmentalism. The size of the organization and of the departments themselves make this problem very much greater than it would otherwise be. Specialization in a highly technical industry is indeed necessary and with it must come departments, but the unit of any group of men with the one functional interest must be kept to a manageable size. I am convinced the present functional departments within a Region are too large. The emphasis placed on their profession by chief officers and their career history of experience only within their own department, tends to make them oblivious of the points of view and requirements of other departments.

I have not observed any sense of corporate responsibility amongst the chief officers. This places an incredible responsibility on the shoulders of the general manager and his assistant general manager. The Fleck Report on the Coal Board, while reporting on the organization of Divisions employing on average 90,000 men, discarded the idea of a general manager by saying on page 37, paragraph 190: 'We are satisfied that the responsibility is too great to place on the shoulders of one man.' I am certain that this applies equally to the Regions of British Railways and the responsibility must be shared by an executive level of management who have a corporate responsibility and authority, as well as individual responsibility for their various functions. Such an organization calls for 'line and staff' policy.

3.2. 'Line and staff' policy

I am certain that 'line and staff' policy must be accepted as the basis of the organization. There has been much controversy over it and I can do no better than quote Kelf-Cohen's definition of it from page 220 of his book on nationalization: ' "Line" is the chain of administrators responsible for deciding on policy and its execution; 'staff' are the technical advisers to each level in the 'line'; they advise on the best technical means of carrying out the policy decided by the "line" '.

The use of functional channel between the functional head at one level and his functional counterpart at the next level below must be clearly understood and it must in no way undermine the authority of the line management. The present organization and relation between the Commission and the railway Regions is, I think, intended to have 'line and staff' policy as its basis, but it has gone sadly astray.

To start with, the line authority has not been clearly defined. The line authority through Area Boards to general managers has been greatly weakened in practice by a parallel path to the general manager from the general staff, not to mention the activities of the British Railways Sub-Commission. The Grey Book of January 1960 does little to clarify a position of self-inflicted complication. (Ref. iii) In organization there is nothing like simplicity and one, and only one, line of executive authority should be clearly defined.

Regrettably there is evidence of British Transport Commission's Railways central staff using the functional channels to the Regions for executive control. The professionalism and departmentalism, so rampant amongst senior technical officers, does not help, nor does the Commission's retention of certain detailed matters of railway management. Section VIII of the Grey Book defines these as:

(a)   design, manufacture, procurement and standards of maintenance of rolling stock, permanent way, and signalling equipment and some electrical equipment for British Railways
(b)   the policies and principles to be adopted in railway operation
(c)   overall control and allocation of rolling stock on British Railways.

I am convinced that greater decentralization of functional responsibility and authority to the Regions must take place. In a period when senior staff have a bias to place too much emphasis on functional matters, line management must be staffed with the strongest personalities available and the supremacy of 'line' over 'staff' exaggerated. There may be a loss of some standardization between Regions as a result, but this will be a small price to pay to give the organization some direction and speed in operation.

The line of direction to and control of the Regional Management, be it from the Commission or direct from the Government, must basically be a financial one, though I appreciate the size and nature of the railways' activities will inevitably raise national issues of policy. However, the volume of business conducted by the level of Regional Management is so great that they have not time to delve into details and must expect details of technical proposals to be discussed and agreed at a lower level. There is a tendency in a period of vast capital expansion, when top management suspects that the proposals are too lavish, to be tempted themselves into chasing the detail. This rarely produces results. Large industrial firms have the same problem and I am sure the solution can only come from a greater degree of cost consciousness further down the line. I will return to this point on the subject of developing capital proposals.

3.3. Some suggestions on organization

What I am about to propose are merely my own ideas of the framework of a Regional organization. I personally think that the top Regional Management should be a Regional Board, comprising a chairman, two or three managing directors and several directors – the latter mainly full-time executives with a few part-timers who are eminent men in private industry. This Regional Board would cover the activities of the present Area Board, general manager and his chief officers. Some of the directors would indeed have functional responsibilities and be the executive head of one or more departments. The Board, too, should have a considerable amount of the authority at present retained by the Commission. It must have some real teeth and not just be political window dressing.

Below the Regional Board there should be further levels of management. The Region could reasonably be split into the present geographical Divisions and each put under the command of one man responsible to the Board. I know in the case of LM Region the splitting of the operating department's activities under the six divisional managers is questionable because of the geographical form of the Region and certain operational control must clearly be retained at Regional headquarters. However, I would go so far as to recommend that the technical department's staff responsible for the maintenance of the railway should come under the new divisional managers and only have a functional link to their headquarter's departments. The headquarters organizations under, say, an engineering director on the Regional Board with, say, a civil engineering manager, mechanical and electrical engineering manager and signal engineering manager, would retain responsibility for design, procurement and construction for all major capital schemes.

This introduction of 'line and staff' policy would, I know, be revolutionary for the present technical department officers, but it would bring general management experience down to a lower level in the organization. I can think of no better way of reducing professionalism and departmentalism.

I appreciate that these suggestions are quite revolutionary and it may be questioned whether the organization could withstand such drastic surgery, bearing in mind that the Regions must continue to function, manned largely by the present staff.

4. Modernization plan

In order to give the public the transport service called for in the second half of the twentieth century, the railways must be re-equipped and modernized. The decision to press on with a major modernization plan is, I am convinced, fundamentally correct. It is, however, necessary to consider whether this capital expenditure is being carried out in the correct manner, and that the most suitable schemes are put forward at the right cost, and at the right time.

4.1. Development of schemes and plans

I am sure the concept of presenting proposals to top management in the form of a financial assessment based on receipts, working costs, capital costs and shown as a return on capital is the correct one. Ideally, figures used must be the most accurate available, and the basic scheme studied, examined and reshaped to give the best overall return. This calls for a high calibre of staff imbued with foresight and imagination, and using the best management techniques such as market research, operational research, work study, etc. One might inquire how often market research techniques have been used to assess future traffic receipts, or operational research to reduce requirements put forward by operating people. How often have these requirements been critically examined using work study techniques, and alternatives costed? Just how cost conscious have the technical departments been in developing their engineering standards? I am certain a greater degree of cost consciousness is required in all ranks of departments of the Regions. The management techniques of work study and operational research must be applied to new schemes and plans for capital expenditure. This means having enough trainee specialists to do the actual analysis, and all levels of management fully aware of the usefulness of having facts presented to them in the correct form before taking decisions. This is an ideal which is not often achieved in practice. Flexibility of operation and insuring against a risk, are the grounds for many of the decisions; I have known managers of chemical plants insist on excessive storage for raw materials and final products. The facts have not been presented as a calculated probability. Instead the manager relies on his judgement and experience, which may be blurred by personal prejudice, and a desire to play safe, since he will be held responsible for the operation, and not for the overall cost. This is such a universal problem and the capital schemes are so vast, that I am certain to ensure that the best possible schemes are put forward, top management must see that the most up-to-date management techniques are appreciated and used by all levels of management, and that all decisions are taken against an alive appreciation of cost–consciousness. It must be added, however, that in practice it is often better commercially to have a good scheme in operation in two years time than the best scheme in five years.

It is with these basic views that I have come to look at the London Midland Region's performance on the electrification of the Euston main line.

4.2. Progress on electrification

It has been put to me that the LM Region have been working against the clock in trying to develop their schemes and proposals for electrifying the Euston main line. There has been incessant pressure from above to produce answers yesterday, and to put it rather bluntly they have been told to get on with the physical job before the financial case has been fully made out. This is little more than putting the cart before the horse.

I have regretfully come to the conclusion that if the main electrification is to be completed and in service by the autumn of 1964, there is not time available to carry out work study and operational research analysis of the present proposals. Even if there was time available, I do not think that men of the right calibre are available to carry out such a method study. From my experience of the critical examination of capital proposals in the chemical industry, it is necessary to have bright, intelligent young men who have a critical mind and have plenty of initiative. They should have no more than a few years experience of the industry, otherwise they will be too influenced by traditional methods of working. First-class men just out of their traffic apprenticeship, who are given a short work study course, are really required. They should be put to work to examine critically the scheme proposals under the direction of the operating staff responsible for them.

The operating department, which is primarily concerned in developing the scheme, have had the added strain of carrying out this work during a period when they have been in the throes of reorganization caused by creation of Divisional Traffic Managers' organization. In the light of all these circumstances, I feel they are hard pressed men who are pushing ahead conscientiously with an immense task.

The presentation of the overall proposals to the Commission in the form of replanning the plan, raises some interesting points. The electrification project, costing approximately £150 million, and spread over five or six years, cuts across Treasury's control of capital expenditure of the nationalized industries which Government tries to use on a year-to-year basis as part of general control of the economy. Although the Commission may not be prepared because of this to authorize the full amount, they have in practice as good as committed themselves to it by allowing work to start. We now have the Gilbertian position of putting up submissions to the Commission for the work bit by bit without showing a return on capital for each unit: The major point of top financial assessment is now lost.

The necessity to co-ordinate submissions and the carrying out of the work of electrification has rightly brought into being the posts of planning officer and chief electrification project officer. The general manager's staff clearly requires strengthening to cope with the volume of submissions which require to go up for approval. Electrification, too, differs considerably from earlier railway schemes in that for the first time new fixed assets on the line are divided between the three technical departments. This calls for a degree of inter-departmental planning and co-ordination unheard of before.

The planning and co-ordinating of interdepartmental activity will be no easy task. They are still all very parochial and the chief electrification officer will have his work cut out to weld them into a team and persuade each on occasions to forego his own advantage for the common good. I feel the system of inter-departmental programming and progressing which we have set up, stands a good chance of delivering the goods. It will require close contact and agreement between the chief electrification officer and the planning officer, and all the drive and initiative they have to keep technical departments on the straight and narrow. Final success, too, will depend on technical departments each doing their own internal planning to ensure that staff and resources will be available to carry out their part of the work at the correct time. To do this the techniques of organization and methods must be used. This internal planning is a function of management of the departments, and rightly remains the responsibility of the chief officer concerned.

In general, I feel that on completion of the main line electrification the LM Region will have a technically good railway. It may be more expensive and lavish than might be necessary, but to have it in time it can hardly be otherwise. There is every chance that with the new inter-departmental organization to co-ordinate the job, it will be completed on time. It will, however, depend on the internal planning of resources within each technical department.

5. Conclusions

5.1. Staff

I consider the railways' greatest need is better management at all levels. This calls for more people of ability. To solve the staff problem, the recruitment and training policy must be altered. Better prospects in the middle years, planned careers and promotion by merit should improve recruitment. To keep the problem within manageable proportions, I consider recruitment and early experience should be treated as a region's responsibility, and I am convinced that the Regions will have to look more and more to universities for young men of ability. The number of salary levels, advertising of jobs, staff union approach, early retirement of some staff, and re-engaging of commercial staff should all be under review. It will take a long time to solve the staff problem, and it will be uphill work against the public reputation of the industry.

5.2. Organization

I am certain that 'line and staff' policy must be accepted as the basis of the organization. One and only one line of executive authority should be clearly defined. At a time when there is a bias for senior staff to place so much emphasis on functional matters, the supremacy of 'line' over 'staff' should be exaggerated. I am convinced that greater decentralization of functional responsibility and authority to the Regions must take place.

5.3. Modernization plan

In the development of the schemes, I feel more use should be made of the management techniques of work study, operational research etc., and all levels of management must become more cost-conscious. I appreciate that the London Midland Region has been up against the time element in developing their schemes, and in order to meet their completion dates it has not been possible to do this critical analysis. The electrification of the Euston main line calls for a degree of inter-departmental co-ordination not experienced before. This need has rightly brought into being the posts of planning officer, and chief electrification project officer.

5.4. General

Although these views have been gleaned from my time at Euston, I am certain from my discussions with staff who have worked in other Regions that the basic staff problem of departmentalism and professionalism is common to all Regions. The organizational problem is associated so closely with the Regions's relationship to the British Transport Commission that all regions are clearly in the same position. Only on the development of modernization plans has it been put to me that the London Midland Region may have lagged behind other Regions.

KAGM

April 12th 1960

6. References

Ref. i. *National Coal Board – Report of the Advisory Committee Organization* – 1955
Ref. ii. *Nationalization in Britain* by R. Kelf-Cohen 1958
Ref. iii. *The Organization of the British Transport Commission* 1 January 1960 (*The Grey Book*)

Personal Report on my Secondment to British Transport Commission

1 September 1959–2 September 1960

1. Introduction

In this personal report I am summarizing briefly the work which I have been engaged on during my year's secondment, and I am recording the great value it has been to me.

I shall always be indebted to Mr Blee, the general manager of the London Midland Region, and Mr Pearson, the assistant general manager, for the way they launched me in the Region. The excellent start they gave me increased immeasurably the use I was able to make of the short period of 12 months.

2. Work engaged on

During the year at Euston I have been engaged on a variety of jobs. I have been asked to attend many meetings, not just as an interested observer, but I was encouraged to take an active part in the deliberations. I was not slow to take advantage of this, and my interventions were very well received, despite the controversial nature of many of them.

As I had been sent along to Euston to assist the planning officer in the electrification of the Euston main line, most of my time in the early days was spent on the electrification project. I was invited to join the working party which at that time was replanning the electrification project.

When I arrived at Euston the Planning Office had only recently been set up, and the post of chief electrification project officer had yet to be filled. I found myself in on the discussions of how these two officers and their staff would co-ordinate the carrying out of this vast project.

In the early stages I found myself chairing a working party which was entrusted with dividing the work into geographical areas. Later I assisted the chief electrification project officer in the discussions with the technical officers to get their agreement to a system of programming and progressing the work both in the drawing office and on site. As we developed a system of programming and progressing, I attended many of the planning and progress meetings and some area project party meetings on site, to gauge for myself how the mechanics of the organization were taking shape and working. I also attended the general manager's electrification meeting which at that time he was holding weekly with his chief officers. To keep myself abreast of the Planning Office work on allied submissions, I often attended the Birmingham New Street and Euston Station working parties which were developing and writing the submissions for these two major schemes.

After about six months, when the new organization to handle electrification was well under way, I had time available to turn my attention to other matters, and the assistant general manager asked me to comment on and examine the general merchandise freight traffic. The LM Region had called in Martech Consultants Ltd, and they had submitted two excellent reports to the Region. Not only did I have the opportunity of reading these reports but I had a chance to hear the opinions of the railway officers on them. After some extremely useful discussions with various officers, I felt able to give the assistant general manager my assessment of these reports and my opinion of the general merchandise freight position, both in regard to the development of the London–Manchester business for high density full load traffic, and to the long-term prospects of a door-to-door service.

Towards the end of my stay a regional working party was set up to study the Martech report on door-to-door transport of freight by rail, and I was asked to join it. Although I have not been able to see this part of the work through to completion, I have had the opportunity of putting my views to this working party at their first meeting.

In connection with reorganization of the Traffic Department, I was asked to chair a small group in a study of how the development of the traffic aspects of new capital schemes should be undertaken in future. We have just completed our joint report, and if accepted this will possibly be the most far-reaching and lasting outcome of my stay at Euston.

I have been very pleased to give my opinion on a variety of subjects and in particular staff matters. Mr Pearson very kindly showed me an early draft of a report on 'Entry into the railway service and training of persons for senior posts in the future.' I was pleased to be able to give him my comments on it, calling where I could on my experience in ICI.

3. Value of secondment

I have no doubt that I have reaped many benefits from this secondment. I have had the rare opportunity of seeing at first hand another large organization at work. All the many railway officers with whom I have come in contact have been most helpful. They have willingly given me their opinion on a variety of topics. They have accepted my questioning with singularly good grace, at a time when many of them have been sorely tried. I am conscious, too, that the period of my stay at Euston has coincided with a time of much heart-searching, of upheaval and public concern, and I feel I am all the more privileged to have listened in, and on occasions taken part, in some of the discussions of the railway's present problems.

Perhaps, however, the greatest advantage to me has been that I have been able to get outside my own company, and view it from the outside. It is this aspect which I will value most when I return to ICI.

Above all else I have been able during this period to study many management problems, such as staff policy, and the development of capital schemes.

KAG Miller

Exchange of Letters with Sir Keith Joseph

On my resignation from UGC dated 22 February 1983
and Sir Keith's reply on 22 March

PRIVATE AND CONFIDENTIAL

Fairfield,
4 Montrose Gardens,
Oxshott,
Surrey, KT22 OUU.

The Rt. Hon. Sir Keith Joseph, Bt, MP,
Secretary of State for Education and Science,
Elizabeth House,
York Road,
LONDON, SE1 7PH.

22nd February, 1983.

Dear Sir Keith

Now that the Chartered Engineers have given a strong vote confirming that The Engineering Council will take over the supervision of the Engineering Professional Institutions, the way is now clear for The Engineering Council to embark on its major role of forwarding the Engineering Dimension.

This is therefore an appropriate moment for me to review my activities as Director-General of The Engineering Council. In order to be able to concentrate on these important activities and be seen to be in an independent position, I have come to the reluctant conclusion that I should resign from the University Grants Committee.

I have discussed this with Sir Edward Parkes and we agree that in proffering my formal resignation to you, this should be effective at the end of March 1983.

I would like to say that I have considered it a privilege to have served on the University Grants Committee during the last traumatic two years and how much I have appreciated the wise counsel and direction which we all receive from our Chairman, Sir Edward Parkes.

I hope that the helpful and supportive relations which I have enjoyed both with the university Grants Committee staff and the Department of Education and Science will continue into the future.

Yours sincerely

Kenneth Miller

K. A. G. Miller.

DEPARTMENT OF EDUCATION AND SCIENCE

ELIZABETH HOUSE, YORK ROAD, LONDON SE1 7PH

TELEPHONE 01-928 9222

FROM THE SECRETARY OF STATE

Dr K A G Miller
Fairfield
4 Montrose Gardens
Oxshott
Surrey KT22 OUU

22 March 1983

Dear Dr Miller,

I was sorry to receive your letter of 22 February conveying your resignation from the University Grants Committee.

I accept your resignation only with regret because Sir Edward Parkes and I have much appreciated both your personal contribution to the work of the Committee and the valuable link which your membership created with the Engineering Council. But I recognise that your responsibilities as Director General of the Engineering Council are considerable and increasing, and in the light of this I am particularly grateful for your willingness to serve on the UGC until now.

The Department and I certainly share your wish that existing good relations should be maintained and strengthened, and we shall do everything in our power to secure this.

Sincerely,

Keith Joseph

APPENDIX V

Original Policy Statement
(abridged) – September 1982

Introduction

The performance of engineering in the United Kingdom is paramount to the nation's future industrial, economic and social prosperity. The revenue earned from the products we make, the services we supply and the business we generate, relies extensively on the quality of our engineering expertise and the development of our manufacturing capability.

It is against this background and in response to the recommendations in the Report of the Finniston Committee of Inquiry into the Engineering Profession that the Engineering Council was established under Royal Charter. The principal aim of the Council is to advance education in, and to promote the science and practice of engineering for the nation's benefit and to promote industry and commerce in the United Kingdom.

The Council acknowledges that its primary objective is to encourage and improve the efficiency and competitiveness of British industry and commerce. It has taken its Charter as the basis for its activities. The Council is also aware of the long term nature of much of its work and has taken note of this in setting its priorities.

The Engineering Dimension

The Engineering Dimension encompasses all factors and activities associated with technological capabilities and expertise in order to improve the competitive performance of industrial or commercial enterprises. In developing this concept the Council is conscious of actions resulting from the Finniston Report and the recommendations from the National Conference on Engineering Education and Training (CONCEET October 1980) broadly related to the formation of Engineers. In the light of these initiatives the Council is devoting its attention to the contribution that Products, People and the Working Environment make to the Engineering Dimension.

Production and marketing of products

The Council recognizes that in some areas British industry has fallen behind its major international competitors, especially in product design and development and in manufacturing techniques; there is an urgent need therefore to attract more of the best people into engineering. The Council is further convinced that marketing is of vital importance to establish the appropriate attitude to product definition and design. The design of new products and processes and the means to manufacture products and install them competitively must be recognized as an interacting and iterative process.

The Council is determined to secure recognition of the importance of, and current weakness in manufacturing technology and to seek jointly with industry and academia the means to improve the position.

People

The Council seeks to achieve a proper balance between engineering and other related activities in an enterprise and to promote a better understanding by management of the place of the engineer. In turn the Council will use its influence to ensure that engineers have a wider appreciation of the business aspects of the enterprise and are trained and equipped to manage.

The educational phase of an engineer's development calls for greater injection and integration of relevant practical experience into courses. This in turn requires a more positive response from industry to provide more industrial training places. Success in design, development and manufacture requires engineers with expertise in more than one discipline. The initial training and expertise of engineers should include exposure to the concepts of good business practice including finance and marketing. There is less enthusiasm for the treatment of finance and marketing as independent disciplines during undergraduate education. Practising engineers will be encouraged to gain a greater appreciation of the role and importance of finance and marketing functions. The Council expects that engineers will prepare themselves to become leaders and managers of industry.

The working environment

The Council accepts the need to change fundamentally the attitudes and initiatives towards engineers throughout industry. To meet the needs of industry, the Council will interact with and consult relevant organizations including (a) The Fellowship of Engineering, (b) the Professional Engineering Institutions, (c) companies in industry, financial institutions and trade associations, (d) Government Departments, (e) educational establishments and research organizations, and other bodies such as the National Economic Development Office (NEDO), the Manpower Services Commission (MSC) and the Engineeering Industry Training Board (EITB). The Council is enquiring directly from industry the emergent knowledge and skills it requires of engineers and technicians and, in the course of doing so, identifying present bottle-necks and taking account of existing and anticipated developments in technology over the next decade. The approach to this enquiry will be through companies quoted in the *Financial Times* share listing where engineering is a relevant consideration and at the same time to seek the views and co-operation of the Engineering Employers' Federation (EEF) and the Confederation of British Industry (CBI).

The Council recognizes the contribution that the financial institutions concerned with investment in industry are making, and will encourage them to give a higher priority to questions about engineering. The aim is to make both the financial institutions and companies, particularly those in manufacturing industry, more aware that engineering resource is a major criterion in assessing a company.

The Council, having been given the responsibility of creating its own register of Engineers, one of the main aims of the Council is to secure a much better understanding in industry of the value of employing Registered Engineers, Technician Engineers and Engineering Technicians. This will take time but it is an essential long term objective.

Education and training

The Council is convinced of the importance of attracting more able men and women into the profession in order that they may play their part in the greater success of British industry. Their education and training ranges from the teaching of mathematics, science and technology in the schools to the technological courses offered by universities, polytechnics and technical colleges to training in industry and later up-dating of engineers throughout their careers.

It is the Council's intention to promote a higher standard of technological literacy within the education system and to engender a better understanding of the contribution that engineering makes to the life and prosperity of the nation. The Council is determined to encourage the development and teaching of mathematics, science and technology in schools in a way which is relevant to the needs of society, industry and in the engineering profession. It is important that the education must not be narrow. The country needs engineers who are literate, articulate and widely educated.

Starting from recommendations of CONCEET, the Council is formulating policies in regard to the development of the secondary school curriculum and examination system and will use its influence in this area. The Council is concerned that greater recognition should be given to courses in schools which adopt a project approach to learning without sacrificing the intellectual content of basic mathematics and science based subjects.

The Council will seek to influence those responsible for offering careers advice in schools and will examine what is being done to investigate young people's attitudes to careers in engineering and will encourage further research into this subject. In seeking to achieve this the Council recognizes the closer integration which must be achieved between the curriculum and careers education. In line with the Finniston recommendations the Council is keen that more girls should be persuaded to take up a career in engineering and will seek ways of assisting those who desire to enter the profession.

The Council recognizes the contribution from engineers whose education and training lead to specialization at an early age. However it recognizes that in comparison with our international competitors there should be more broadly based courses in engineering.

The Council is convinced of the need to increase the liaison between industrial companies and universities, polytechnics and technical colleges. It expects to see more engineers in industry teaching in academic establishments and more senior academics spending time in industry and consultancy work. The Council will also take steps to encourage the recruitment of industrialists with senior management experience into engineering faculties, especially at professorial level.

The Council is concerned at the reduction of available training places in industry and is appreciative of the need to integrate training with university and polytechnic courses.

The Council recognizes the accelerating pace of technological change and the effect this is having upon the engineering industry. To ensure that industry remains competitive, it is essential to provide continuing education throughout an engineer's working life, both in the technological and wider business senses. while much of the responsibility for this task falls on industry itself, there is a significant contribution from higher education establishments, the professional institutions and the Open University.

The Council intends to give special consideration to the education and training of Technician Engineers and Engineering Technicians in recognition of the valuable contribution they make to industrial performance. There is already considerable concern that there is a shortage of technicians in some parts of industry.

Professional institutions

The Engineering Council's Charter states specifically that the Council shall establish and maintain a register for the purpose of registering by stages professional engineers, technician engineers and engineering technicians, and shall from time to time nominate Chartered Engineering Institutions and other bodies corporate or unincorporate to identify persons meeting the standards and criteria for education, training and experience determined by the Council.

The Council has already made it clear that it wishes to work with and through those nominated institutions in the accreditation of courses and the setting of standards required for qualification. The Council sees a major role for the Professional Institutions in this area. In time the Council will expect to represent the UK Engineering Profession on international organizations.

CEI examinations

In addition to taking over the registration of the profession, the Council will wish to establish an examination process equivalent to the present CEI system, through which candidates without an accredited degree may progreess to Chartered status.

Nomination of institutions

The Council will work through nominated institutions in matters concerning accreditation of courses, training programmes and experience leading to registration of individuals. Nomination standards will be set and published by the Council and institutions will be assessed prior to acceptance as nominated institutions. The Council does not intend to set any arbitrary limit to the number of institutions which can be nominated.

The Council membership

The Charter of the Engineering Council states that for the period of three years, the first Chairman and up to 24 members will be appointed by the Secretary of State for Industry. Thereafter the Chairmen and members will be selected by the Council from a list. It is envisaged that when a steady state is reached, each member will be appointed for a three year period with approximately eight new appointments or reappointments per annum. The bodies which will be asked to put forward names for the list will be:

1. Nominated Chartered Engineering Institutions
2. Organizations of employers
3. Education establishments.

In making the selection, the Charter specifies that the Chairman and at least two-thirds of the other members shall be Chartered Engineers and that at least one half of the members have experience as employers or as managers of practising engineers and of engineering technicians.

The Register

The Register of the Council will be computer based and will have separate categories for Chartered Engineers, Technician Engineers and Engineering Technicians: each category will identify the three stages of career development which are set down in the Charter. It will be capable of assimilating the present Engineers' Registration Board data, but will hold greater information including addresses for those in each category.

Engineering assembly

The Engineering Council is giving consideration to the possibility of an engineering assembly which would meet periodically to debate matters of interest and concern to the profession, and to make recommendations to the Engineering Council. Membership of this assembly would be on the basis of elected representation.

Funding of the Engineering Council

It is the intention of the Council that the Secretariat will be small and of high quality staff and that it will work through, and with other appropriate organizations. The costs will be limited to the overheads associated with a Secretariat limited on present assessments to 25–30 people. For the first three years it is being funded by a grant-in-aid from the government. Thereafter it will look to the Professional Institutions, government and possibly industry for its funding on the basis that each sector has a responsibility to assist the Council in its objective of raising the performance of engineering and engineers for the nation's benefit. It would not expect to receive more than half its funding from any one of the three sources.

Members of The Engineering Council
1983–1984

Sir Kenneth Corfield	FEng; Chairman and Chief Executive, Standard Telephones & Cables plc.
Professor Gordon Beveridge	BSc, ARCST, PhD, FEng, FIChemE, FRSE; Head of Department of Chemical & Process Engineering, University of Strathclyde.
Viscount Caldecote	DSC, MA, FEng, FIMechE, FIEE, MRINA; Chairman, Investors in Industry Group plc; President, Fellowship of Engineering.
Professor Bernard Crossland	CBE, MSc, PhD, DSc, MRIA, FRS, FEng, FIMechE, FIProdE, FWeldI, MASME; Special Research Chair, Department of Mechanical & Industrial Engineering, The Queen's University, Belfast.
Geoffrey Drain[1]	CBE, JP, BA, LLB; lately General Secretary, National & Local Government Officers' Association.
Professor Derek Embrey	CEng, FIEE, FIMechE, FIERE, MIGasE; Group Technical Director, AB Electronic Products Group plc; Visiting Industrial Professor, Loughborough University.
John Fairclough	BSc(Tech), ScD, CEng, FBCS, FIEE; Director, Manufacturing and Development, IBM United Kingdom Ltd; Chairman, IBM United Kingdom Laboratories Ltd.
Christopher Farrow[2]	Assistant Director, Bank of England.
Sir Alistair Frame[3]	MA, BSc, FEng, FIMechE, FIChemE; Deputy Chairman, The Rio Tinto-Zinc Corporation; Director, The Plessey Company plc; Director, Vickers plc; Director, Toronto Dominion Bank Ltd; Director, Britoil plc.
Professor Alec Gambling	DSc, FRS, FEng, FIEE, Hon. FIERE; British Telecom Professor of Optical Communication, University of Southampton.

---

[1] Relinquished appointment on 31 December 1983.
[2] Joined Council on 1 January 1984.
[3] Relinquished appointment on 31 December 1983.

Geoffrey Hall	BSc, FEng, SFInstE, FRSC; Director, Brighton Polytechnic; Member, Science & Engineering Research Council
Eric Hammond[4]	OBE; General Secretary (Elect) Electrical, Electronic, Telecommunications & Plumbing Union.
Malcolm Harker	BSc; Managing Director, Harker & Sons (Engineers) Ltd.
Professor Sir Alan Harris[5]	CBE, BSc(Eng), FEng, FICE, FIStructE, MConsE; Consultant, Harris & Sutherland Consulting Engineers.
Michael Harrison	CBE, MA, FBIM; Chief Education Officer, City of Sheffield; Vice President, Standing Conference on Schools, Science & Technology.
Ronald Hooker	FEng, FIProdE, CBIM; Chairman, Henry Sykes Ltd; Chairman, Dubilier plc; Deputy Chairman, UKO Int plc; Director, Hambros Industrial Management Ltd; Industrial Advisor to Hambros Bank; Member of Management Board, Engineering Employers' Federation.
Dr John Horlock[6]	MA, PhD, ScD, FRS, FEng, FIMechE, FRAeS, FASME; Vice-Chancellor, Open University; Director BL Technology Ltd; Director British Engine Insurance Ltd.
Dr John Illston[7]	CEng, FICE; Director, The Hatfield Polytechnic.
Joanna Kennedy[8]	MA, CEng, MICE, ACIArb; Senior Engineer, Ove Arup & Partners.
Hugh Lang[9]	CBE, BSc, ARCST, CEng, FIProdE, FIMC, CBIM; Chairman P-E International Ltd.
John Lyons	BA, FRSA; General Secretary, Engineers' & Managers' Association & Electrical Power Engineers' Association; Member, General Council, TUC.
Robert Malpas	CBE, BSc, DTech, FEng, FIChemE, MIMechE, FIMH; Managing Director, The British Petroleum Company plc; Chairman BP Chemicals International.

---

[4] Joined Council on 1 January 1984.
[5] Relinquished appointment on 31 December 1983.
[6] Relinquished appointment on 31 December 1983.
[7] Joined Council on 1 January 1984.
[8] Joined Council on 1 January 1984.
[9] Joined Council on 1 January 1984.

Peter Martin	CBE, CEng, FIMechE, FInstE, FCIBS, AMRAeS, MConsE; Consultant, The Oscar Faber Partnership, Consulting Engineers.
Detta O'Cathain	OBE, BA; Director & General Manager Milk Marketing, Milk Marketing Board.
Hamish Orr-Ewing[10]	Chairman, Rank Xerox Ltd.
David Plastow[11]	Managing Director and Chief Executive, Vickers plc; Director, Guest Keen & Nettlefold plc.
Baroness Platt of Writtle	CBE, DL, MA, CEng, MRAeS; Chairman, Equal Opportunities Commission.
Ralph Quartano[12]	MA, CEng, MIChemE; Chief Executive, PosTel Investment Management Ltd; Member of Board, Britoil.
Derek Roberts	CBE, FRS, FEng; Technical Director, The General Electric Company plc.
James Stevenson	BSc, ARCST, CEng, FICE, FIHT; Deputy Managing Director, Balfour Beatty Ltd.
John Waters	TEng, FSCET; Laboratory Manager, Structures Laboratory, Wimpey Laboratories Ltd.

---

[10] Joined Council on 1 January 1984.
[11] Relinquished appointment on 31 December 1983.
[12] Relinquished appointment on 31 December 1983.

International Comparisons of Engineering
NIESR's review February 1989

Source: *Hansard* 18 November 1988

Mr Anthony Coombs: To ask the Secretary of State for Education & Science how many people achieved a recognized engineering qualification at degree or post-degree level in Britain in 1987; and what the comparable figures were for France and West Germany.

Mr Jackson: The latest readily available information is for 1983 and is given in the table below, together with qualification rates. Higher education below degree level is included because the assignment of courses between the degree and sub-degree categories tends to vary from country to country.

Home students successfully completing higher education programmes in engineering, trade, craft and industry in 1983:

	France[1]	*Prais*★	West Germany[1,2]	*Prais*★	United Kingdom[3]	*Prais*★
Qualifiers/thousands						
Below degree level	17.3	*35.0*	14.0	*44.0*	20.5	*29.0*
First degree	11.5	*15.0*	17.7	*21.0*	14.4	*14.0*
First degree and below	28.8	*50.0*	31.7	*65.0*	35.0	*43.0*
Postgraduate	2.4	*6.3*	0.8	*5.0*	2.3	*2.7*
First degree and postgraduate	13.9	*21.3*	18.6	*26.0*	16.8	*16.7*
Total higher education	31.2	*56.3*	32.5	*70.0*	37.3	*45.7*
Qualification rates[4]/percentages						
Below degree level	2.0		1.5		2.3	
First degree	1.4		1.8		1.6	
First degree and below	3.4		3.3		3.9	
Postgraduate	0.3		0.1		0.3	
First degree and postgraduate	1.6		1.9		1.9	
Total higher education	3.7		3.4		4.2	

[1]May include a small number of students from abroad completing programmes in trade, craft and industry.
[2]Some below degree level data estimated.
[3]Includes estimates for professional qualifications at public sector institutions. Excludes private sector institutions.
[4]To aid comparison, the qualification rate used is the percentage of successful completions relative to a derived single year group. The latter is calculated by taking the total population for the ages providing at least 70 per

cent of the qualifiers and dividing by the number of ages involved. For the United Kingdom this is the population of ages 21 to 24 divided by 4. OECD recommend this procedure.

*These figures were taken from Professor S J Prais's paper on 'Qualified Manpower in Engineering' on behalf of the National Institute of Economic & Social Research and appeared in the National Institute Economic Review in February 1989.

Transcript of interview on the
Today Programme
Thursday 3 December 1987

BBC RADIO FOUR

TODAY

DECEMBER 3, 1987 07.44am

PRESENTER:

Britain is producing more engineers per head of the population than France, Germany and the United States and it isn't as far behind Japan as has previously been said, says the government, quoting UNESCO figures.

It's not true says the CBI, the Engineering Employers Federation and the Engineering Council. So our education correspondent Wendy Jones asked Dr Kenneth Miller, who is director general of the Engineering Council, whether he was saying that the UNESCO figures are simply wrong.

DR KENNETH MILLER:

I believe they are wrong, because everything in our judgement suggests they're wrong. And the reasons are partly explained in the qualifications at the end of the report, that each country can interpret the guidelines on classification as it sees fit, and therefore all these Unesco figures are utterly variable from one country to another.

They should have had the advice of other people as to whether the figures they were using were comparing like with like. We believe that the Japanese figures quoted in this report are grossly under-stated.

WENDY JONES:

What about the other countries, that's so much for Japan, what about Germany and France and America, are those figures accurate do you think?

DR KENNETH MILLER:

We do not know, because we have not yet had the detailed work done and that must clearly now be done, but it must be done in this very thorough way, of looking at the national statistics, and not just taking figures that have filtered through UNESCO with a series of other uncertain definitions being imposed on them.

WENDY JONES:

Overall then, this report is suggesting that for producing engineers the United Kingdom may not be as far behind Japan as was previously thought, and is in fact slightly better than France, and Germany and the United States. You disbelieve that?

DR KENNETH MILLER:

We think that is completely and utterly misleading. They admit themselves their numerical foundation is not sound, and it goes right against our broad judgements and all the messages we get from industry. All industry is telling us that there is a crying shortage of engineers and technicians at every level, and I have been discussing this both with John Banham of the CBI and Jim McFarlane of the Engineering Employers Federation, and they both take exactly the same view as I do.

WENDY JONES:

Why should the Government put out a report though saying this sort of thing, because Kenneth Baker and other Government Ministers have frequently talked about the need to produce more engineers and technologists? Why should there be a Government report now saying that we're doing better than we thought?

DR KENNETH MILLER:

Well, you're quite right. The Government are and have been saying, making all what I would consider the correct noises.

This is a report, which I believe has emanated as it says from the statisticians; it's very much an officials' report, and I think there are other forces at work there, of which you really have to ask them why they have done this.

WENDY JONES:

You say it's an officials' report, but presumably it has been approved by Government Ministers.

DR KENNETH MILLER:

They have managed to get one Government Minister – I don't know which one – to approve it. But you know, these things do happen.

WENDY JONES:

So you're saying this has virtually gone through on a nod and a wink? Is that what you're suggesting?

DR KENNETH MILLER:

Well there's a very good TV programme called 'Yes Minister'. And the more I see of the workings of Whitehall, the more convinced I am that 'Yes Minister' is alive and kicking. As a manager in industry, if something of this nature crossed my desk for publication, and one had so many qualifications about the soundness of it, I would have thrown it back to square one and said start again.

WENDY JONES:

Do you think this is going to be something of an embarrassment to the Government?

DR KENNETH MILLER:

Well it could be an embarrassment, if they feel they have to back it up at Ministerial level. But the real danger, I think, is that won't happen. It'll be sort of quietly put aside and then it will be quietly used as back-up information with a supposed authenticity on which to build Government policy and Government decisions for making money available for different parts of higher education.

And that I think is the risk, and that is why we believe we have got to come out loud and clear and say that we do not believe the figures in this report.

PRESENTER:

Dr Kenneth Miller. Well no government Minister was available to discuss that report this morning, but spokesmen at both the Department of Education and the Department of Employment defended the report, stressing its limitations are recognized and that it will be followed by a further study.

END

Letter to Prime Minister of 13 March 1989 and PM's reply of 3 April 1989

Oxshott (0372) 842093

4 Montrose Gardens
Oxshott
Leatherhead
Surrey
KT22 0UU

<u>Strictly confidential</u>

13th March 1989

The Rt. Hon. Margaret Thatcher MP FRS
Prime Minister
10 Downing Street
Whitehall
London

Dear Prime Minister

<u>Education and Training</u>

As an industrialist who has spent the last six years helping to establish The Engineering Council, I am writing to express my grave concern , which I believe you may share, of weakness in a key area - the attitude and behaviour of the senior officials in the Department of Education and Science.

I appreciate that you and your colleagues have directed the funding for the Technical and Vocational Education Initiative through the Manpower Services Commission, while the new Schools' Enterprise and Education Initiative is funded by the Department of Trade and Industry, and the Enterprise in Higher Education by the Training Agency.

The new Education Reform Act has set the scene - the political and conceptual thinking has been done. What is now required is a real commitment for executive action. I believe success could be frustrated by the debilitating effect of the attitudes of the senior DES officials. I instance two examples.

The first is the experience of Baroness Cox and Dr John Marks when senior DES officials misrepresented to ministers the statistical facts behind the comparison Cox and Marks had carried out between the Comprehensive and Selective School Systems. This culminated in Sir Keith Joseph making an unprecedented statement to the House of Commons in November 1983 vindicating the Cox and Marks research. It is disturbing that the official (Mr N W Stuart) responsible for briefing the Minister, has since been promoted from Under Secretary to Deputy Secretary.

The second case concerns The Engineering Council, and the persistent attempts over the last three and a half years, by the most senior officials in the DES to show that the UK is producing as many Engineers as the USA, France and Western Germany, and almost as many as Japan. The officials chose to use highly questionable UNESCO statistics. Despite strong protests from The Engineering Council on the misleading message which would be sent through Higher Education the figures were published in an article in the Employment Gazette in December 1987. Subsequent reports from The Engineering Council in May 1988, and Professor Prais of the National Institute of Economic and Social Research in February 1989, have thoroughly discredited these UNESCO figures, and confirmed that the UK lags seriously behind our international competitors in the output of Engineers and Technicians. Even so, Mr Robert Jackson in an answer to a Parliamentary question, quoted the UNESCO figures for France and Western Germany as recently as last November, when the officials were aware of Professor Prais' work. A fuller description of the International comparisons is given in Annexe I.

These two examples show a grave misuse of statistics which reflects badly on the management of this part of the Civil Service. It suggests either serious incompetence on the part of the statisticians, or a deliberate misrepresentation of the information by senior officials in an attempt to frustrate any policy development repugnant to departmental doctrine. Baroness Cox and I can substantiate our experiences with a wealth of documentary evidence.

In making this severe criticism of the DES officials I must add that this is in marked contrast to the high opinion I formed of the officials in both the Department of Trade and Industry and the Manpower Services Commission with whom I have worked equally closely over the last six years. My purpose in writing is to put two suggestions to you, which could help to overcome this problem.

The first suggestion is for the Department of Employment to take over the education element from the DES. This would effectively put education and training to-gether, and allow the Education Reform Act to be applied in a positive manner. The successful accomplishment of this Act will also require a well motivated teaching force. My second suggestion is that the Teaching Profession could be revitalised by the Government giving positive support to the setting up a "General Teaching Council". I am influenced by my Engineering Council experience in making this suggestion. I attach a more detailed case for these two suggestions in Annexe II.

I urge you Prime Minister to give this your consideration, and hopefully your personal support.

Yours sincerely

Kenneth Miller

Dr Kenneth Miller CBE FEng.

206

ANNEXE I

INTERNATIONAL COMPARISONS OF ENGINEERING MANPOWER.

The Department of Education and Science has conducted a long campaign in an attempt, based on highly questionable UNESCO statistics, to prove that the UK is producing as many Engineers as the USA, France and Western Germany, and almost as many as Japan. They have persisted in these attempts, despite the volume of contradictory external statistical evidence, and the known real shortage of Engineers and Technicians in the UK.

When in June 1985, Sir David Hancock first raised this with Sir Francis Tombs (then Chairman of The Engineering Council) and myself (then Director General) we both dismissed it as being completely contrary to our own industrial experience, and the messages we were receiving from industry.

The DES officials raised these UNESCO figures again in the summer of 1986 at the start of the work of the Steering Group set up under the chairmanship of the Director General of The Engineering Council to examine the shortage of Production Engineers. With the help of the DTI officials it was dismissed from the discussions as irrelevant to the work of the Steering Group.

Unknown to The Engineering Council, an Interdepartmental Working Group of statisticians from DES, DTI, MSC, DEmp and the Scottish Office was set up on "International Comparisons of Higher Education in Engineering". In their interim report of June 1987 they qualified the UNESCO figures by saying "each country interprets the guidelines in its own way and there is considerable doubt about the comparability of the qualifications recorded". In August 1987 The Engineering Council was told of the intention to publish this interim report.

Despite the reservations of the government statisticians and a strong protest from The Engineering Council on the misleading message which would be sent through Higher Education, the DES were instrumental in having this interim report published in the Employment Gazette in December 1987. In the accompanying press release the qualifications and interim nature of the report were omitted. The Engineering Council simultaneously published a strongly worded statement pointing out the misleading nature of the publication. Both the Confereration of British Industry and the Engineering Employers' Federation also came out with strong statements supporting The Engineering Council. Next day the press and radio castigated the article, and no Minister was available to comment. The concern of The Engineering Council was that a wave of complacency would sweep through the Higher Education System, as these erroneous figures became accepted as the perceived wisdom.

This concern was well founded, because in the February 1988 issue of the MSC Skills Bulletin the UNESCO figures were repeated, and the interim nature of the report omitted. The Engineering Council carried out its

207

own detailed study comparing the UK with Japan, and their consultant used the original Japanese records. This demonstrated that the UNESCO figures had omitted a key group of Engineers from the Japanese Special Training Schools (Senshus). The results published by The Engineering Council in May 1988 showed that Japan produces many more Engineers per million population than the UK.

One would have expected that to have been the end of the matter, but not so. Although the UNESCO figures for Japan were clearly discredited, the same source was used by officials to prepare the answer to a Parliamentary Question on the German and French comparisons, given by Mr Robert Jackson in a written answer (Hansard November 18 1988). By this time Professor Sigbert Prais of the National Institute of Economic and Social Research was carrying out a full study from craftsmen to professional engineers for all the countries covered by the UNESCO figures, but going back to the actual figures of each country.
Professor Prais' paper was already in draft by October, and to my certain knowledge was being circulated for comment to interested parties including the officials at the DES. Professor Prais' paper "Qualified Manpower in Engineering" was published on 28th February 1989 and showed, as we all expected, that the UK is lagging seriously behind France and Western Germany as well as Japan. This totally contradicts the answer given to the Parliamentary Question last November.

Despite Professor Prais' discussions with the DES statisticians it would appear that Mr Robert Jackson is still being briefed on the basis that the UNESCO figures could be correct, because in his reply to Mr Andrew Smith (Hansard 28 February 1989), he says "There is a controversy about the international comparisons to which the hon. Gentleman refers. He will have studied the report in the Department of Employment Gazette on that point." I understand that Professor Prais is now taking this up with Mr Robert Jackson.

It is hard to explain why the officials persisted for so long with this misinformation, but it may be significant that on two occasions in March 1984 and March 1987 the Chairman and Director General of The Engineering Council persuaded the Secretary of State for Education and Science to increase the number places for Engineering in Higher Education. On both occasions International comparisons were part of the background, and it was clear to them that they had persuaded the Minister against the advice of his officials.

Kenneth Miller

Dr Kenneth Miller CBE FEng.   13th March 1989.

1. EDUCATION AND TRAINING DEPARTMENT.

In Britain we have a long tradition of keeping education separate from training. Education is seen as a pure intellectual pursuit, while training carries connotations of manual work and is altogether inferior. This may be said to be a gross exaggeration, but Correlli Barnett in a recent article in the Sunday Telegraph attacked the academics who maintain the tyranny of high-mindedness.

The report of the Manpower Services Commission and the National Economic Development Council on "Competence and Competition" in 1984 made the point that Germany, Japan and USA all speak about Vocational Education and Training, and all three countries see education and work competence as a key to their economic success. This same report showed clearly that the UK has lagged seriously behind these main competitor countries across the whole field of vocational education and training.

The fact that only 32% of our children remain in full-time education to the age of 18, compared with 70% in France, 85-90% in USA and Western Germany and 96% in Japan is itself a damning indictment of the education of our academically middle to lower group of children. The need to improve the vocational education and training of the bulk of the 16 - 19 year olds has never been greater.

I believe the Government has appreciated the shortcomings of the current administrative machinery to direct the education system to meet the national needs in this technological age. The Technical and Vocational Education Initiative was funded through the Manpower Services Commission, while the new Schools' Enterprise and Education Initiative is funded through the Department of Trade and Industry, and the Enterprise in Higher Education by the Training Agency.

It is vital now to raise the vocational education standards of the whole population if we are to compete in world markets. It is not just the young passing though the initial education system, but the colossal task of raising the competence of much of the present working population.

It is suggested therefore that the Department of Employment should take over the education element of the Department of Education and Science. This would emphasise the life long commitment to training following school based education. The new department could be renamed the Department of Education and Training.

The question then arises as to what to do about the Science element of the DES. I would suggest that serious consideration should be given to funding the five Research Councils through the main user Departments:

Thus   (a)Medical Research Council   to   Department of Health.
        (b)Science and Engineering   to   Department of Trade and
           Research Council.   Industry.

(c)Agriculture and Food	to	Ministry of Agriculture,
Research Council.		Fisheries and Food.
(d)Natural Environment	to	Department of the
Research Council.		Environment.
(e)Economic and Social	to	Home Office.
Research Council.		

The time is also ripe for the transfer of the research element of the dual support system for the Universities from the Universities Funding Council to the Research Councils. The universities will protest but as truly independent Chartered bodies it will be their task with fully costed grants from the Research Councils, to ensure that they have well founded laboratories. It would also help the Polytechnics to have a fair share of the Research funding. The Universities Funding Council and the Polytechnics and Colleges Funding Council would fund the teaching element of their institutions.

2. THE GENERAL TEACHING COUNCIL.

The long term industrial and commercial success of the country will depend on our school system. All the international comparisons show how far we lag behind our competitors. Much is now being done with the new Education Reform Act, but it will come to naught if we fail to motivate the teachers. The Educational bodies are coming together and have produced a Discussion document "Towards The General Teaching Council". They appreciate that a Professional body has a primary responsibility to the public and must under no circumstances take on the role of a Trade Union. It is good management practice on behalf of society for the leaders of the Teaching Profession to be responsible for the appropriate standard of entry. Each of us, as a professional person, has a vested interest to see that the standards of our own profession are maintained.

I am convinced from my Engineering Council experience that the moment is right for the government to put its weight behind the setting up of a "General Teaching Council for England and Wales". I suspect the mandarins in the DES will stall on this proposal as they would lose power and influence. The establishment of this body could lead to the effective privatisation of parts of the H M Inspectorate.

Kenneth Millar

Dr Kenneth Miller CBE FEng.   13th March 1989.

210

1O DOWNING STREET

LONDON SW1A 2AA

THE PRIME MINISTER

3 April 1989

Dear Mr. Miller,

Thank you very much for your letter of 13 March about education and training. Your comments were as ever refreshing and stimulating to read and so obviously spring from the great care and concern you have for the engineering profession which showed during all your time at the Engineering Council.

Yours sincerely

Margaret Thatcher

Dr. Kenneth Miller, C. B. E.

Letter to Lord Tombs of Brailes on Federal Systems

Dated 25 September 1994 and his reply dated 9 October 1994

25th September 1994

Lord Tombs of Brailes
Honington Lodge
Honington
Shipston-upon-Stour
Warwickshire CV36 5AA.

Dear Frank

I imagine that you have been observing the machination of our successors on
The Engineering Council as I have, and I expect you are not surprised that
they are now coming round to the view that a federal system for the
engineering profession is inevitable. One might almost say, they should have
concentrated more on making The Engineering Council more effective!

I wondered if you had come across an excellent book by Professor Charles
Handy entitled "The Empty Raincoat". I can thoroughly reccommend it.
Charles Handy makes out a strong case that although not easy to operate,
federal systems have much to commend them, and he argues that in a complex
world we have no real alternative. He goes on to explain the key concepts in
federalism of twin citizenship and subsidiarity. His thesis matches my
experience over the last decade with two different federal systems; the
engineering profession and more recently The Standing Conference on Schools'
Science & Technology (SCSST) with the 50 Science and Technology Regional
Organisations (SATROs).

Arising from this I have a written "Some Thoughts on Federal Systems", which
I did in the first instance in order to write and compliment Charles on what I
believe is a piece of first class fundamental thinking. I thought you might like
to see my comments, if only to encourage you to read Charles Handy's book. I
believe that you will find his work extremely relevant to the future of the
engineering profession.

I should add I have had an interesting response to my comments from Charles
Handy saying he found my description of my federal experiences fascinating
and illuminating.

Best wishes,

Yours sincerely

Kenneth

Dr Kenneth Miller.

213

**Honington Lodge
Honington
Shipston-on-Stour
CV36 5AA**

Tel: (0608) 661437

9 October 1994

Dr Kenneth Miller.
4, Montrose Gardens,
Oxshott.
LEATHERHEAD.
KT22 0UU.

Dear Kenneth,

Thank you for your letter of 25th September and for the copy of your interesting note on federal systems.

You and I are at one on this. I had little sympathy with Monty's solution on the grounds that it would be unacceptab;e to the engineering institutions and would anyway result in the loss of much that was good.

Latterly I tried, unsuccessfully, to dissuade John Fairclough from pursuing a similar path. The necessary weight has to be put, and has increasingly been put, behind a federal solution - unglamorous though that may seem. The success of the Engineering Council owes much to your efforts to bring that about and we must now look for a renewal of those efforts.

Yours sincerely,

Frank

Index